what works in online trading

what works in online trading

edited by
MARK ETZKORN

John Wiley & Sons, Inc.
New York • Chichester • Weinheim • Brisbane • Singapore • Toronto

ISBN 0-471-37288-9

Printed in the United States of America.

10 9 8 7 6 5 4 3 2 1

contents

section three
risk control and
money management

section four
traders on trading

about the contributors

Dewey Burchett is president and senior editor of StockLogix.Com (www.stocklogix.com), located in Shreveport, Louisiana. He is a registered investment advisor and writes daily market commentary that includes both technical and fundamental analysis geared toward the active trader/investor. Prior to launching StockLogix.Com (formerly Online Daytraders.com) in March 1999, Burchett managed trading accounts for individuals and trained traders at a day-trading brokerage.

Gibbons Burke is editor of MarketHistory.com. His email address is editor@markethistory.com.

Mark Etzkorn is editor-in-chief of *Active Trader* magazine and www.ActiveTradermag.com. He has worked in the markets for 15 years as a financial editor, writer, analyst, and trader. He has authored or edited seven books on the markets and trading, including *Trading with Oscillators: Pinpointing Market Extremes* (1999, John Wiley), and has written extensively on market analysis and trading systems. His work has been translated into four languages and distributed on five continents. He is former senior editor of *Futures* magazine and former member of the Chicago Mercantile Exchange.

Robert Krausz is president of the Fibonacci Trader Corporation (www.fibonaccitrader.com) and president of Wizard On Wall Street, Inc. (www.the-wow.com), publisher of a home-study course for traders. He has been a private trader and trading coach for more than 20 years. His work in the area was featured in Jack Schwager's *New Market Wizards*. He is also author of the book *A W.D. Gann Treasure Discovered*. In addition, Krausz is a master hypnotist, British Council of Hypnotist Examiners (MH, BCHE).

M. Rogan LaBier is a former Nasdaq market maker, sales-trader, registered principal of Terra Nova Trading and head trader at MB Trading.

Currently he is CEO of Rocket Trading (www.rockettrading.com), a company catering to high-end "hyper-active" day traders. He is also author of *The Tools of the Trade,* the best-selling e-book about trade execution. *The Nasdaq Trader's Toolkit,* published by John Wiley & Sons, is the updated hardcover version of this book.

Dave Landry is a commodity trading advisor and president of Sentive Trading. He writes nightly columns on stocks, options, and futures for TradingMarkets.com (www.tradingmarkets.com) and is the author of the book *Dave Landry on Swing Trading: A Momentum-Based Approach to Capturing Explosive Short-Term Market Moves.*

Chuck LeBeau and **Terence Tan, PhD.** LeBeau is coauthor (with David W. Lucas) of *Computer Analysis of the Futures Market* and founder of the Systems Trading Club (traderclub.com), an organization providing members with educational material and guidance relating to the design and testing of computerized trading systems. He has more than 30 years of trading experience and has been a consultant to major financial institutions including the Bank of China in Beijing and the Abu Dhabi Investment Authority in the United Arab Emirates.

Tan has been trading and developing computer-based trading systems for the financial markets since 1993. He is a programming consultant specializing in the evaluation, development, and implementation of proprietary trading systems. Clients include LeBeau's System Traders Club and Nelson Freeburg's Formula Research.

The two are currently writing a book about exit strategies and have created a Web site for short-term stock traders, www.streakingstocks.com.

Teresa Lo worked in the stock-brokerage business for more than a decade prior to her retirement from the industry in 1998. She is a technical trader and uses simple, classic techniques to analyze the market. She holds a BA in Economics and Psychology from the University of British Columbia. Lo is cofounder and conscience of Intelligent Speculator, www.intelligentspeculator.com, an original, noncommercial Web site focusing on technical trading, risk, and money management. It features extensive resources for those who would like to improve their trading performance.

Steve Moore, Jerry Toepke, and **Nick Colley.** Moore is the founder and president of Moore Research Center Inc. (MRCI, www.rci.com). As a pioneer in performing computerized analysis of futures price movement, Moore has provided research for the CME, CBOT, and KCBT, as well as publications for private traders since the early 1990s. He began his trading career in the early 1970s in the highly seasonal timber industry.

Colley is the research director of MRCI. He has more than 24 years of total programming experience. He has spent 12 years writing software to perform statistical analyses of futures and stock price movement. For the past five years, Colley has been designing and maintaining MRCI's Web site.

Toepke has more than 22 years of experience as a futures broker, trader, and analyst. He is responsible for selecting the MRCI trading strategies, and writes a weekly Spread Commentary and a weekly MRCI Online Update, available both on the Web and by e-mail to subscribers.

Jeff Ponczak became Associate Editor of *Active Trader* magazine after 10 years in the newspaper business as an editor and reporter. As Associate Editor, Ponczak focuses on the news side of the trading industry, including topics such as decimalization, market fragmentation, and online brokers. He also writes feature stories for *Active Trader* on trading approaches and market trends.

Henry O. (Hank) Pruden, PhD, is professor of business and executive director of the Institute for Technical Market Analysis, Golden Gate University, San Francisco. He is also the editor of the Market Technicians Association Journal (www.mta.org). He can be reached at www. hankpruden.com.

Mark Seleznov is a general securities principal and managing partner of Trend Trader, a NASD, SIPC broker-dealer firm in Scottsdale, Arizona. A professional trader for more than 25 years, he was a market maker on the Philadelphia Stock Exchange, a retail registered representative and a futures trader. He is a recognized expert in equity day trading and conducts stock day-trading seminars. In addition to his TV appearances and regular newspaper and magazine contributions, Seleznov is a featured analyst three times a day on KFNN 1410 AM radio in Phoenix.

Gary Smith is a full-time, home-based trader and author of *How I Trade for a Living.* Smith, who has not had a losing year (and only a few losing months) since 1985, has turned a $2,200 trading account into nearly $1 million and a career. He has been profiled extensively in the financial press and is a frequent speaker at trading seminars.

Thomas Stridsman is senior editor of *Active Trader* magazine, and the author of *Trading Systems That Work.* At *Active Trader,* he specializes in articles on technical analysis, trading systems, and money management. Before moving to Chicago in 1997 to work as a writer and editor for *Futures* magazine, he operated a Web-based trading advisory service for Swedish traders. During this time, he also was a regular writer and analyst for several Swedish financial daily and monthly publications, and the chair of the Swedish Technical Analysis Federation. He holds a degree in economics with emphasis on statistics and social psychology.

Steve Wendlandt has more than 15 years of trading experience in the stock, futures, and options markets. He is currently the chairman of Sequoia Capital Management Inc., a money management firm focused primarily on sector rotation. Formerly, he was a Commodity Trading Advisor specializing in mechanical systems trading. Wendlandt primarily focuses on researching and trading U.S. equities and options.

Jerry Wood is a Chicago-based trader and freelance writer. He was an options market maker on the floor of the Chicago Board Options Exchange from 1985 to 1997, trading both S&P 100 Index (OEX) options and individual equity options for his own account. He actively trades stocks, options, and futures.

preface

To get an accurate sense of what it takes to trade for a living, it helps to have input from many sources and as diverse a range of opinions as possible. There is no single, correct way to trade, although there are certain principles—risk control, capital management, and discipline, to name a few—that all successful trading and investing approaches share. How those principles are implemented is a different story.

There are almost as many types of traders as there are markets to trade; a truth borne out by the diverse contributions to this book. A sage bit of trading advice is to find a trading style or strategy that fits you— an approach that you understand and feel comfortable with. If nothing else, this will enable you to stick with the approach even when your trading isn't going as well as you had hoped. It's tough to maintain the necessary discipline for trading if you don't really grasp how your strategy works or how it will behave in different situations. Familiarity, in this respect, breeds content.

We all have limits to how much stress we can take, how much risk we can accept, and how much time we can commit. For these reasons and others, some people find they're destined to be position traders; others discover they're more comfortable as long-term investors; for others still, things will click in the world of active day trading. The trading strategies and concepts presented here span stock, options, and futures markets, with time frames ranging from a few minutes to a few weeks. To provide as broad a perspective as possible, we have compiled material from a wide range of subjects and disciplines: Level II day trading, swing trading, position trading, longer term seasonal analysis that provides the context for various trading approaches, interviews with practicing traders, and a healthy dose of the most important issues, risk control and money management. We also have extensive information for beginners, focusing on the direct-access/online trading model that is transforming the industry. You need to know how the new trading technology works— and doesn't work—before you can use it in your trading.

While much has been made of the revolutionary aspect of the *online trading paradigm,* the reality is that the basic principles of successful trading have remained constant, no matter what mode traders use to actually place their trades or what time frame they operate in. It's interesting to see how two traders, with diametrically opposed opinions on trading strategy, both make good livings in the market. They might not be able to agree on what to trade, let alone how to trade it, but the bottom line inevitably comes out: Both traders will focus on limiting risk, selecting markets or instruments that fit their respective approaches, and ensuring that their strategies are based on observable price patterns and market principles.

While this book is more or less dedicated to a relatively new branch of trading, you'll find that it is grounded in the principles that have always distinguished profitable trading: simplicity, risk control, money management, and discipline. Merging these principles with today's online technology should be the goal of any trader interested in short-term online trading.

acknowledgments

For a project like this, to which so many people have contributed, it is difficult to give proper credit to all involved. First, thanks must go to all the traders, analysts, and writers who have contributed to *Active Trader* magazine over the past year, especially those who appear in these pages, and who helped us establish our publication in the industry. Second, thanks to the readers and advertisers of *Active Trader,* who have made the magazine the success it is.

Special thanks also to the entire staff of *Active Trader* magazine, and especially Bob Dorman, Phil Dorman, Jeff Ponczak, Thomas Stridsman, Amy Brader, and Laura Coyle, whose hard work made the magazine and this book possible. Thanks to all the data and software vendors who allowed their graphics to appear throughout this book.

Finally, everyone at John Wiley & Sons, especially Pamela van Giessen and David Biello, deserve credit for their patience with this project, and for their contributions in improving it and putting it together.

MARK ETZKORN

Chicago, Illinois
January 2001

section one

trading basics

Many people rush into trading before they're ready, like 16-year-olds with freshly minted driver's licenses who can't wait to get behind the wheel. But like the novice driver whose first trip is down the Autobahn, beginning traders who enter the markets prematurely are headed for a crack-up. There is a great deal to learn before you make your first trade, and this knowledge goes well beyond mastering the basics of trading strategy, the first priority of most traders.

Trading is a process—one that demands understanding of a number of disciplines: strategy, probability, rules and regulations, and last but not least, technology. You can have the best trading strategy in the world, but if you don't know how to implement it—both in terms of how you enter a particular order and of having the necessary hardware, software, and communications technology to do so—you are wasting your time. Similarly, trying to use sophisticated trading approaches without understanding basic market principles will lead to confusion and error.

In this section, we'll look at some *trading basics*—issues traders must understand before they even think about buying and selling. These topics range from trade order types and what to consider when you open a trading account, to basic technical analysis, an overview of how markets function and the new electronic trading technology, and the realities of short selling and trading on margin.

Many traders pay scant attention to these topics, instead being obsessed, at the beginning of their careers, with different entry and exit techniques. But patience has its virtues. Traders who take the time to build a strong foundation for their trading will reap rewards in the long run.

chapter 1

a fool and his money

Mark Etzkorn

How do I pick a broker?

When can I sell short?

Should I position trade or day trade?

If you've never traded and these are the questions you're asking yourself, you'd better take a step back.

The market has a knack for regularly making fools of even the best-prepared and conscientious traders and investors; it will utterly humiliate (or worse) the unwary, lazy, or foolhardy.

That leads to a question almost never asked—one that gets lost amid the excitement over a stampeding bull market and point-and-click order-entry technology—but is nevertheless the most important thing would-be traders should ask themselves: Should I trade?

That very few people ask themselves this question before putting money at risk, at least partially explains the low success rate of new traders.

If you were an engineer and wanted to start your own business in a completely new field—say, open a restaurant—you probably wouldn't do it on a whim. You certainly wouldn't quit your job, dump your life savings into your new business, and, without knowing the first thing about what you were doing, expect to make an easy killing. If you were smart, you'd probably:

- Spend a great deal of time researching your new field, consult with professionals in the business, and even try to gain some hands-on experience.

- Put together a plan outlining the goals of your business and establishing steps to accomplish them.
- Make sure the business is adequately capitalized, using the most conservative possible estimates.
- Start slowly, put in the time and effort required of any entrepreneur attempting to launch a new business, expect your business to go through rough times initially, and prepare yourself psychologically and financially to survive this incubation period.
- Make sure the business is adequately capitalized. (Yes, that's twice.)

Sounds fairly reasonable, right? But this is precisely what many, maybe even a majority of, new traders don't do.

Why? Maybe people tend to think they know more about trading than they really do. Everyone sees the recaps of the day's market action on the nightly news (or watches round-the-clock financial coverage), gets their quarterly 401(k) reports, or logs on to the Internet to check quotes and graphs and enter orders for their favorite stocks.

It makes it easy to feel like you really have a handle on things, especially when the Greatest Bull Market in History has had a nice habit of bailing people out of bad (i.e., seat-of-the-pants) trades by consistently rebounding—usually sooner rather than later. Anyone can do it, right?

And if you think being a part-time trader means you don't have to put in the same time and effort as a full-time trader, think again. You'll still be competing against full-time traders, and full-time traders tend to be people you'd describe as Type-A personalities only because there isn't a letter that comes before A in the alphabet.

Trading is *never* a hobby. It probably requires more work than most other businesses and often carries the unique risk (if you trade on margin) of losing more than you initially invested. But, for those who approach the profession soberly and with reasonable expectations, the rewards are there.

so you want to be a millionaire

There are certain realities to trading. They don't have anything to do with wanting to trade or having the right or privilege to trade, but rather with being able to determine whether you're likely to benefit from trading. After all, the goal is to make money. If circumstances exist that make this a less-than-likely prospect, perhaps the best trading decision you can make is not to trade.

The simple truth is that trading is not for everyone. Just as some people are not cut out to be engineers, lawyers, teachers, or NBA point guards, some people would do themselves huge favors in the financial and mental-health departments by not trading. One study estimated there are fewer full-time professional traders in the United States than professional athletes—a sobering thought. (Maybe that point guard dream isn't so unrealistic after all.)

Trading for a living is not easy, and it's not something that can be mastered overnight. It's a business, and to succeed in it you should expect to invest the same kind of time and equity (both real and sweat) you would to launch any other business. You shouldn't trade because you think it's an easier or faster way to make money than opening a restaurant. You should trade because you think it's a *better* way to make money than opening a restaurant. Plus, there should be a reason you think that way, one that has nothing to do with luck or wishful thinking.

Sufficient time (both for learning the profession and practicing it), persistence, a love for the business, and yes, some aptitude are a few oft-quoted characteristics of successful traders. These certainly are key components to tackling the markets (or any other business, for that matter), but they are rendered moot by something far more academic. Money.

money changes everything

The number one reason, by far, most new traders fail is the same reason most new businesses of any kind fail: lack of capital. You can talk about discipline and strategies all you want, but the greatest trading approach in the world won't do you any good if you don't have the money to trade it.

Determining how much you need to trade is more complicated than simply meeting your brokerage's minimum account balance requirement. It's the end result of the interaction of your age, net worth, outside financial responsibilities, risk tolerance, and the specific trading plan you intend to follow.

Pressured traders are never good traders, and if you have too little money, or your trading equity represents too big a portion of your total worth, you will be apt to make poor (read: emotional) trading decisions. Or, you simply will not be able to weather the natural volatility that accompanies many trades before they become profitable.

A little common sense goes a long way here. Putting half your net worth in a trading account is one kind of proposition for a single 29-year-old with no debt and another entirely for a 49-year-old with a mortgage who also must put two kids through college in the next few years. Similarly, someone in or approaching retirement would be wise not to risk a substantial portion of his or her wealth in short-term speculation. A "risk slope" (Figure 1.1) shows the inverse relationship between how much money (in terms of percentage of income or net worth), relative to age, a person should probably devote to short-term trading.

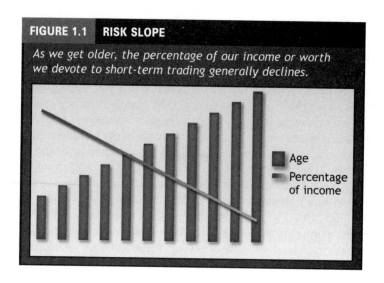

FIGURE 1.1   RISK SLOPE

*As we get older, the percentage of our income or worth
we devote to short-term trading generally declines.*

■ Age
■ Percentage
of income

The downward slope of the money line is based on a few assumptions. First, young people generally have fewer financial obligations and are thus freer to speculate with more of their money; they have more time, and years of future income, to bounce back from any setback. As people get older, they tend to assume greater financial burdens (mortgages, children), so the percentage they can risk probably will be limited—you don't want the kids' education cut short because you risked the college fund on a "hot" IPO that went cold. Finally, as people approach retirement, preservation of capital should become the key goal. Speculating with a large percentage of the funds you need to take you through the rest of your life, when you will have less time and ability to replace them, is hardly prudent.

Keep in mind, though, that because people tend to earn more as they get older, the absolute dollar amount they can devote to trading can increase, even if it is a smaller percentage of their total capital. The 49-year-old with the two college-bound children may have more money with which to trade, even if he's only risking 10 percent of his investment capital compared with 40 percent for the 29-year-old. An "equity arc" (Figure 1.2) shows how the line from "risk slope" might look when adjusted for income and a 5-percent annual increase in earning power over someone's working lifetime.

Every trader's situation is unique. The object is to trade with as much money as possible while minimizing the impact, psychologically and financially, on the rest of your life. Nervous money tends to become someone else's money.

When you start talking about putting specific dollar amounts on what it takes to trade, another layer of considerations unfolds. First, no

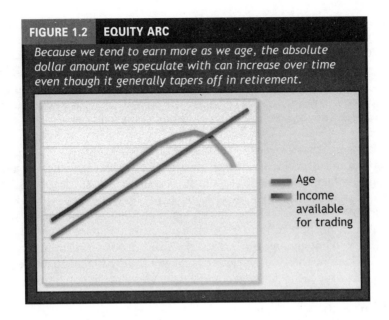

FIGURE 1.2 EQUITY ARC

Because we tend to earn more as we age, the absolute dollar amount we speculate with can increase over time even though it generally tapers off in retirement.

Age
Income available for trading

fixed amount of money gains your entry into the trading club. All brokerages have certain financial requirements customers must meet—minimum account equity, net worth, annual income. Some are more stringent than others, and they may limit the kind of trading you can do depending on how much you have in your account. But for the most part, these requirements are designed to protect the solvency of the company, not the individual trader (although they may also function in this respect).

A typical online discount broker may let you open an account with as little as $2,000, but such brokers are generally used by more traditional investors and less by active traders. If you're an active, short-term trader (and especially if you're day trading), a quick survey of several direct-access brokerages tells a different story: $35,000 to $50,000 is a typical account minimum, and some would prefer you to have $100,000. (Sometimes you can open an account with less, but again, you may have restrictions put on the kind of trading you can engage in.) A decade-old study of future trading accounts found the odds of success jumped dramatically with accounts $50,000 and larger. Things haven't gotten any cheaper since.

Still, you should not measure your suitability for trading by whether you meet a brokerage's requirement, but by whether you can stand up to a much more stringent measuring stick: How much money it will take to successfully trade a particular strategy.

How can you determine this? Research. Testing. Real trading results from someone who has used a strategy or approach you're interested in.

Several software packages allow you to program trading ideas and test them over years of historical price data. Say you test a strategy you're interested in and discover that over the past 10 years, this approach has been down as much as $15,000 on several different occasions, even though it was profitable over the long haul. Common sense would tell you that you need at least $15,000 to trade this system successfully. If you had less, the expected loss would knock you out of the game, sooner or later.

But wait, there's more. Professional traders will quickly tell you the maximum potential suggested by such historical testing will almost certainly be larger in real-life trading. The biggest loss is always in the future, the old saying goes. Accordingly, professional traders will typically double (or more) the maximum loss estimate of a historical test to determine what their potential loss in real trading is likely to be and plan accordingly. That means our strategy would probably produce at least a $30,000 loss in the real world. What if you had $20,000 to trade with? Should you trade the strategy and hope you didn't run into a losing streak until you had had enough winning trades to bump your account equity above the $30,000 mark?

You could, and this is exactly what many traders—losing traders—try to do. (That dirty word, hope.) The professional, however, would take one of three tacks: refrain from trading the strategy, wait until he or she has adequate capital to trade the strategy safely, or determine if trading fewer shares (or some other adjustment) will reduce the strategy's risk to the point that a $20,000 account is sufficient.

This is a simplification, but it at least gives an idea of the kind of due diligence necessary to give your trading career a positive start. The great thing about today's technology is that it gives you more direct and immediate access to the market and the ability to take charge of your own trading and investing than ever before. But, as in all areas of life, this freedom comes with a great deal of personal responsibility.

It's no coincidence that many top traders claim to focus more on limiting risk than reaping profits. Take care of the risk, and the profits will take care of themselves. No one can be careful for you when it comes to trading—you have to do it yourself.

preparation

After money, the new trader's best ally is time, both on a daily basis and in terms of committing to a potentially lengthy apprenticeship.

You can go to any number of trading seminars and listen to someone tell you that, no matter what, you have to "pay your tuition" in the market (i.e., you'll lose $5,000 or $10,000, or $20,000, or more) before you begin making money. Just as you would have to spend money to learn to become a lawyer or doctor, this line of reasoning goes, so must you pay to learn to trade.

Maybe so. Losses are part of the game, and one of the distinguishing characteristics of successful traders is that they are able to accept losing trades (relatively) unemotionally and move on. But, there is no rule that states you must kiss away a sizable chunk of money because of impetuousness or impatience.

There are other ways to pay your trading tuition: You can give yourself time to learn about both the market and the process of trading, and even more time to research, design, and test trading strategies. You may still lose money out of the gate (not necessarily a bad thing, since overconfidence has claimed more than its fair share of traders), but your tuition bill might be a little smaller than it would have been had you dived into the market headfirst.

For many years, a bit of sage advice from conscientious traders was to "paper trade"; instead of placing real trades, keep track of the performance of trades you would have made to see how your strategy might fare (without risking actual dollars). It's a sound (if not foolproof) concept, and one made easier today with various kinds of software and online trading aids to help with the process.

There is simply no excuse for blundering into the market unprepared. The ease with which potential traders can access price data, financial research, analytical software, and sophisticated trading simulators leaves no reason for foolhardiness. Give yourself time to learn—study, research, and practice. Time is on your side. The market will still be there 10 weeks, 10 months, or 10 years down the line. There's always a psychological shift when your paycheck is finally on the line, and no amount of paper trading or simulated trading can totally prepare you for it. However, being as thorough as possible before you risk real money can make the adjustment much easier.

When you start trading, start small, far below what you've determined to be your normal risk level. Doing so will allow you (even more so than simulated or paper trading) to master the actual process of trading without putting undo stress on your psyche—or wallet—when you make the switch to real money.

full circle

Building on our original proposition—that trading is a business like any other—it's possible to give an idea of where a trader should be when he or she is finally ready to place a trade.

It's all about having a plan, be it a rigid system or a set of general rules you modify depending on circumstances. Such a plan should determine:

- How, when, and why to enter a trade (which implies there are times you don't take a trade).
- How, when, and why to take a profit on that trade.
- How much capital to commit to a trade and how to control losses on that trade (stops orders, etc.).

The "why" part of the equation cannot be downplayed. If you don't understand why you're doing something, you won't be able to do it under adverse circumstances. When things aren't going well, you'll second-guess yourself—a major hazard considering executing a plan is half the trading battle. You must understand your approach and base it on sound market principles to be able to trade it effectively.

Neither the hows nor whys can be based on casual observations or gut feelings. They must be based on logical market behavior and confirmed by extensive research. You must prove to your own satisfaction that your basic trading idea is sound and your plan for executing it is practical.

If you're not willing to do what it takes to get to this level, you probably shouldn't be in any rush to trade. Just as many people only understand the stove is hot when they burn their fingers on it, many people will ignore the advice outlined on these pages. Then again, they'll be the ones giving you their money.

should i or shouldn't i?

For those with the proper capital, patience, persistence, time, and a certain proclivity, trading can be a viable way to make money independently, either on a full- or part-time basis. But it's not for everyone, and it's much better for certain people to devote their income to longer term, less risky investment options if the odds of trading success are not in their favor.

A successful trader once said, "Trading is not an IQ contest." This may offer comfort to some and dishearten others who had hoped that what they thought was superior gray matter would be the key to their success. But if trading isn't about matching wits with others in the marketplace, what is it about?

Maybe it's fair to say trading requires a specific kind of intelligence that recognizes the realities of the business and is dedicated to approaching it professionally. With that in mind, the coming chapters will give you insight into how professionals approach their trades, control risk, and manage the challenges of the markets.

After all, to the professionals go the spoils.

chapter 2

the mechanics of trading

order up

Mark Etzkorn

Getting in the markets starts with your trade order, but there's (a little) more to it than merely clicking the "Buy" or "Sell" button. Trade orders come in all shapes and sizes: orders to get you in a trade, orders to get you out of a losing trade, and orders that are only executed at particular times. It's important to know the different methods at your disposal and understand the advantages and disadvantages of each. Before explaining different order types, though, let's put some basic definitions on the table.

At any given time in a stock, option, currency, or future, there is a lowest price at which sellers are willing to sell (the offer or ask) and a highest price at which buyers are willing to buy (the bid). The difference between the two is called the *spread* or the *bid-ask spread*.

Figure 2.1 shows a hypothetical stock with a current bid of 87 and an offer of 87⅛. The highest price buyers are currently willing to pay for the stock is 87; sellers will only let it go for 87⅛. The current bid-ask spread is ⅛.

The number of shares currently being bid and offered (the *size*) is also shown. In this example, 500 shares are bid at 87 and 1,500 are

FIGURE 2.1	THE BID-ASK SPREAD			
Stock	Bid	Ask	Bid Size	Ask Size
XYZ	87	87⅛	5	15

offered at 87⅛ (stocks are quoted in *round lots* of 100 shares, so 5 and 15 correlate to 500 and 1,500).

If you were willing to pay 87⅛ for 1,500 shares, you would enter your buy order and *lift* (or *take out*) the offer; if you wanted to sell the 500 shares bid for at 87, you would enter your order and *hit* the bid.

Now that you have a little basic language under your belt, it's time to delve into the various types of trade orders.

giving orders

Not only do different order types work in different ways, they often have different price tags attached to them. In addition, while most brokerages accept the same basic menu of order types, they reserve the right *not* to accept certain kinds, either because of the potential difficulties of executing them or because some orders can expose them to unwanted risk.

Always check with your brokerage to make sure you know what kinds of orders they accept and which have extra commission fees attached to them.

Figure 2.2 is an example of an online order-entry interface. Entering a particular type of trade order is typically a matter of clicking a few buttons and typing in a ticker symbol and price. (Remember, though, you never know when you'll have to call your broker and do things the old-fashioned way.)

The major order types are market orders, limit orders, stop orders, good-till-canceled orders, day orders, fill-or-kill orders, all-or-none

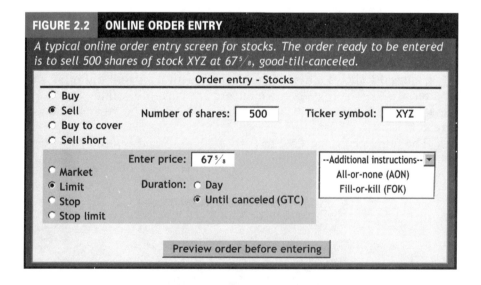

FIGURE 2.2 ONLINE ORDER ENTRY

A typical online order entry screen for stocks. The order ready to be entered is to sell 500 shares of stock XYZ at 67⅝, good-till-canceled.

Order entry - Stocks

○ Buy
◉ Sell
○ Buy to cover
○ Sell short

Number of shares: 500   Ticker symbol: XYZ

Enter price: 67⅝

○ Market
◉ Limit   Duration: ○ Day
○ Stop   ◉ Until canceled (GTC)
○ Stop limit

--Additional instructions-- ▾
All-or-none (AON)
Fill-or-kill (FOK)

Preview order before entering

orders, market-on-close orders, and market-if-touched orders (that's a lot of orders, and there are even more out there). Here they are:

- *Market order.* An order to be executed immediately at the best price currently available.

Usually, a buy market order will be filled at or near the current ask price and a sell market order will be filled at or near the current bid price. If you called a broker on the phone, you would enter a market order by saying: "Buy 100 shares of Veritas (VRTS) *at the market.*"

The advantage of market orders is that a fill of some sort is guaranteed (barring suspended trading or other market disruptions). If you really need to get in or out of the market immediately and are not concerned about the price, market orders do the trick.

On the down side, market orders give you no control over the price at which your trade will be executed. In fast, volatile markets, this can result in a fill far away from where the market was when you entered the order.

But market orders have one advantage over all other types of orders: They are usually the cheapest to place because they place the least demand on a brokerage.

- *Limit order.* An order to buy or sell at a specific price, as in "Buy 100 Oracle (ORCL) at 90" or "Buy 100 ORCL at 90 *limit.*"

If you know you want to buy or sell at a particular level, use a limit order. The advantage is you can never be filled at a price worse than the one you specify (and you can sometimes get a better fill, but don't count on it). The catch is that you might not get filled at all. Limit orders generally cost more than market orders.

- *Stop order.* An order to buy or sell if a specified price (the stop price) is reached or passed. There are two specific types of stop orders: stop-loss and stop-limit.

A stop-loss order is a buy order above or a sell order below the current market price. It is designed to cap losses on a trade. For example, if you were long Geron (GERN) at 50 and wanted to risk no more than a point on your trade, you would enter a *sell stop* at 49: "Sell 100 GERN at 49, stop."

A stop order becomes a market order as soon as a trade occurs at that price, so there is no guarantee you will be filled precisely at your desired stop level. If you are trading a volatile or illiquid stock, your odds of getting an exact fill decrease.

The stop-limit order is designed to address this problem. It stipulates a worst price at which a stop order can get filled. The GERN stop order previously described could be transformed into a stop-limit order as follows: "Sell 100 GERN at 49, stop, 48 *limit.*"

This order guarantees that your stop (which becomes a market order once its price is touched) can be filled no lower than 48. This might sound great, but the catch is the order might not get filled (or only partially filled) if the market is dropping quickly. In that case, the order, or the remainder of the order, will stay in the market as a standard limit order (in this example, at 48). If the stock keeps tanking, you're stuck in a losing trade.

You also can use stop orders to enter trades (confirm with your broker regarding particular markets). For example, if you believe a move above 50 in Dell (DELL) is a sign of a monster rally, you could enter a buy-stop order ("Buy 100 DELL at 50, *stop*") to get into the market as this move gets underway.

- *Day order.* An order that is good for one day only—it will automatically be canceled at the end of the day's trading session.
- *Good-till-canceled (GTC).* An order that remains active until you or your brokerage cancels it (or, in the case of options and futures, until expiration). Also called an open order.

If you didn't get filled today and you know you want to buy at the same price tomorrow (or the day after), use a GTC order. Most brokers, however, set a limit on how long a GTC order remains active (usually between 30 to 60 days), so it's important to check with them. If they have no expiration date, it's up to you to cancel it, if necessary, to avoid unwanted fills.

- *Market on close (MOC).* Executed as a market order as close to the end of the trading day as possible. Many trading strategies revolve around the closing price and are structured around entering and exiting trades on the close. Also, pure day traders use MOC orders to make sure they liquidate all positions before the day ends.
- *Market on open (MOO).* Same as the MOC order, except that it is executed when the market opens.
- *Fill-or-kill (FOK).* An order that must be filled immediately or not at all. It is typically used to capitalize on short-lived market opportunities.
- *All-or-none (AON).* An order that must be filled in its entirety or not at all. If you're bidding on 500 shares and only 250 are available to buy, your AON order would not be filled.

- *Market-if-touched (MIT).* A limit order that becomes a market order when a trade occurs at the limit price. For example, if you have an order to sell 100 shares of Human Genome Sciences (HGSI) at 140 "market-if-touched," your order would become a market sell order as soon as the first print occurs at 140 on the ticker. You could get filled exactly at your price, at a better price or at a worse price.

- *Contingency orders.* A generic term to describe orders that are dependent on certain market conditions being satisfied. For example, you may want to buy a particular stock if it reaches a certain price level or if its sector index establishes a new high and the S&P 500, Dow, and Nasdaq indexes are all up on the day. Or, you may want an order executed when another order is filled or canceled.

Your broker may or may not accept such orders. Online discount brokers do not enable you to enter such trades, although some higher-level direct-access firms are beginning to offer such capabilities. For the most part, you will only be able to use contingency orders with a full-service broker with whom you have a close relationship (in other words, you have a lot of money in your account).

The type of order you should use depends on your particular trading situation. For the most part, the vast majority of trading can be done with market, limit, and stop-loss orders. Keep in mind that the more exotic the order type, the less likely your broker will execute it (or the more it will charge you for doing so).

These quick definitions should make things less confusing and give you a little more confidence when you're ready to start trading.

five things to think about before opening your trading account

Jeff Ponczak and Mark Etzkorn

In theory, the trading journey begins with a small, simple step: You send a broker some money; the broker allows you to trade stocks.

But in reality, you should only take this step when you're ready to actually trade. And a good deal of research and preparation is necessary to get to that point.

When you're ready, you have a few choices to make. If you've never had a trading account before, the choices can be confusing. Dozens of online brokers are vying for your trading dollar. Where you open an account will depend on both your level of experience and your trading style.

The markets are full of surprises, so you hardly need additional ones when establishing a trading account. Here's a quick look at the process of opening an account for short-term, online trading (assuming you're going to trade from home rather than at a trading office) and questions you should consider beforehand.

1. *What kind of trading am I going to do?* Short-term traders have different needs than long-term investors; day traders have different needs than swing and position traders.

Brokers have traditionally divided into two basic categories: full-service (the most expensive) and discount (less expensive). Full-service brokers are the firms such as Merrill Lynch that offer extensive trading advice and support, as well as access to a wide range of related financial services. Discount brokers, almost all of whom have some kind of on-line presence (standard Web-based brokers such as Charles Schwab, E*Trade, Ameritrade, etc.), offer less in the way of services in return for a cheaper commission. However, as competition has stiffened among these firms, the range of services they offer has expanded. (There are also firms known as "deep discount" brokers that offer the lowest commissions in return for bare bones support and trading options.)

Most short-term traders, whose trades last anywhere from a few minutes to several days, trade online. For them, there are really two broker types to consider: the previously mentioned standard Web-based online brokers or the "direct-access" brokers such as CyBerCorp and Tradescape.

Your particular trading style will influence the kind of broker you use, which in turn will determine your costs. If you're going to trade on an extremely short-term basis—say, with an average trade length of a few minutes or less—a direct-access broker is necessary because you need immediate execution and confirmation of trades.

When you place an order through a standard (Web-based) online discount broker, you are basically just sending them an e-mail. After receiving your request, someone at the other end will send the order to a market maker, who will then execute your order. The entire process may not take more than 30 to 45 seconds, but that is a lifetime to a very short-term trader.

With a direct-access broker, you trade through software programs that route your trade orders directly into the market. For intraday traders trying to buy on the bid and sell on the offer ("making the spread"), direct access is essential.

Direct-access brokers are generally more expensive than traditional online brokers. If you're trading longer term, where making the bid-ask spread and getting immediate fills are not critical to your bottom line, a traditional online broker may be a cheaper alternative.

It's a good idea to have more than one trading account in place (see Question 5) in case of communications breakdowns and other technical problems that are an unavoidable part of online trading. For example, a trader who uses a direct-access broker may have a Web-based broker as a backup.

2. *How do I open/fund my account and how much money do I put in it?* In most cases, you can either apply for an account online or you can have an application form sent to you. The firm's Web site is always the place to start for information. After you're approved, there are several ways to fund your account, including bank check, personal check, or wire transfer. If you have an account at a "bricks-and-mortar" broker, your online broker will be able to transfer your account. There is a small fee for this, but it's worth it because of the phone calls and paperwork it will save you.

First, you need to be aware of the different minimum requirements for various brokers. Most standard discount brokers require $1,000 or $2,000 to open an account; some brokers will even allow qualified account holders to trade with no initial balance, as long as payment is received within three days. Traditional full-service brokers generally require a much higher minimum account balance, sometimes as much as $25,000, and many direct-access brokers also often have steeper minimum requirements (although there is a trend toward lower account balances for direct-access brokers). For more on account minimums, see Question 4.

How much you put in your account, though, shouldn't be based so much on what a particular broker sets as an account minimum, but rather on what your research has indicated you'll need to trade your approach. There's no point in opening an account until you're ready to trade, and to be ready to trade you should have done extensive study, paper trading, and/or computer testing of your trading strategy. This will indicate how much you'll have to risk to trade your approach successfully.

For example, if you had an approach that lost $20,000 during its worst losing period in the past (its maximum "drawdown"), common sense would dictate you should have at least that much in your account to be able to survive such a setback. In reality, though, future drawdowns are likely to be bigger than those shown in historical testing, which is why prudent traders double (and sometimes triple) the maximum historical drawdown to estimate how much money they'll need to trade a particular approach safely.

Be conservative. Proper capitalization is the first necessity of successful trading. Every trader and trading strategy has its losing streaks. You have to have enough money to weather adversity to be able to profit in the long run.

3. *Features and services: Should I go with the cheapest commissions?* A big concern for many traders is commissions, which vary greatly from broker to broker. Discount brokers earned their name by charging $15, $12, $8—even $5—per trade (for market orders; limit orders are usually more expensive). For the most part, you'll pay more to trade with direct-access brokers (somewhere between $15–$40, although these prices are dropping) and even more to trade with a full-service broker.

Because several brokers may meet your criteria, choosing one may be difficult. To truly find out which one is best for you, remember the cliché, "the difference is in the detail."

For example, consider how different brokers allow you to add additional funds to your account. All will accept checks, but it can take up to a week before the amount of the check is added to your account. Some brokers, though, allow automatic withdrawal from your savings or checking account. You specify an account and a date each month, and the money will automatically transfer into your brokerage account.

Also, think about what you're interested in besides buying and selling stock. Are you intrigued by IPOs? Do you want to open an IRA, or possibly buy a mutual fund? Do you want to trade options? Can you reach your broker by phone to place orders and get information (and is the phone number toll-free)? Different brokers provide different services and it's important to find a firm that best suits your trading needs.

Other points to consider:

- Will you earn interest on your account balance (usually only possible if you have a large account)?
- Can you trade after hours? Which Electronic Communications Networks (ECNs) do you have access to?
- Are there rebates or a sliding commission scale if you're a more active trader?
- Can you trade both listed and Nasdaq stocks? What are the limitations, if any, in placing stop orders on Nasdaq stocks and in using other nonstandard order types (fill-or-kill, market on close, etc.)?
- Is the firm's software/trade-entry interface understandable and easy to use?
- Are the research and analysis features adequate for your needs (i.e., are there real-time quotes, Level II access, etc.)?
- Is your account insured?

Several Web sites rank various standard online brokers (including www.gomez.com and www.smartmoney.com) but very few offer information on direct-access brokers. One that does is Don Johnson's Online Investment Services (www.sonic.net/donaldj).

4. *Will I use margin?* If you're trading on margin (meaning you're borrowing money from your broker to increase your buying power; see "Trading on Margin" on page 18), federal law requires a minimum balance of $2,000; a much higher amount is necessary at some online brokers (especially the direct-access variety, which can sometimes demand $25,000 or more for a margin account). Also, if you plan on selling short, you have to do it out of a margin account. Similarly, most day-trading accounts are margin accounts by default.

However, trading on margin is not a necessity and is generally not advisable for true beginners. Margin should only be used after you reach a certain level of trading competence.

5. *Do I have backups in place?* If you're thinking about opening a trading account, you should be thinking about opening two.

Today's communication technology is a wonderful thing, but it's not fail-safe by any stretch of the imagination. Traders should have a backup in place for every link in their trade entry chain: their computer and software, their Internet connection, and their broker. Communication disruptions and outages are a cost of doing business. How big a cost they are depends on how prepared you are. For starters, you have to make sure you have a computer system that meets your broker's technical specifications (more of an issue for using the software of direct-access brokers). And again, make sure you know how to place an order by phone and whether there is a higher commission for doing so.

take care of the little things

Certain troubles, such as the aforementioned Web outage, are unavoidable. However, a representative from a leading discount broker told us most complaints and/or problems can easily be prevented.

When you open an account, you'll be given a password. You'll need it to log in and access your account. Write down this password and keep it in a safe place (i.e., a place only you have access to). This advice might sound juvenile, but customer service departments get calls every day from people who have lost their passwords. You can avoid such situations with some planning.

You'll get plenty of documentation before (and after) you open an account. Read everything carefully (twice if you must) and ask questions before you begin trading. Also, make sure you have a perfect understanding of how to place an order online, and what happens after you click the "buy" or "sell" button. Don't be like the trader who, unsure whether his order for 100 shares of Dell went through, clicked "buy" five times and wound up with 500 shares. Many brokers allow you to practice trading on demo systems before you trade for real; take advantage of these opportunities.

It's also important to note that any disputes you may have with the brokerage will almost certainly be settled in arbitration, not in a court of law. Arbitrators use a different set of guidelines in making their decision; what might seem like a clear-cut situation to a judge won't necessarily appear that way to an arbitrator.

Remember: When you open an account and begin trading, it's your hard-earned money at stake. If you don't do your homework, it's like throwing that money away.

trading on margin

Mark Etzkorn

Trading, at every level, is a balancing act between risk and reward. Accept the risk of trading more volatile markets for the potentially higher returns? Use a tight stop to minimize losses but run the risk of getting taken out of a trade prematurely? The choices are endless.

One of the most fundamental risk-reward decisions you must make is whether to use *leverage:* Do you pay for a trade in a stock, futures contract, or other instrument in full or on *margin,* that is, by putting up part of the money for a trade and borrowing the rest from your broker?

Trading on margin amounts to putting a "down payment" on your trade. The standard margin for stock trades is 50 percent, which means if you want to buy 100 shares of a stock trading at $50, you can do so with $2,500 in your trading account (rather than the full $5,000). Your broker lends you the other $2,500 necessary to buy the stock.

Margin trading is a basic issue many novice traders don't understand and take for granted. All they know is that they can buy $5,000 of stock with the $2,500 and it seems like a good deal. Given the remarkable run of the stock market in the recent past, it's not surprising that many stock traders don't think twice about the downside of using leverage. But it's not an issue to take lightly.

There are advantages to using margin (especially for short-term traders), but very real risks. Case in point: events like the April 2000 Nasdaq sell-off (see Figure 2.3), which brought the issue home to traders who finally felt the sting that comes with trading on margin in a market that decides to go down—dramatically—rather than up.

Margin may seem like a free ride when the market's going your way, but when it's not, the ride can get rough, as many traders found out this spring. Find out about the rewards and risks of this aspect of trading and whether it's a tool you should use.

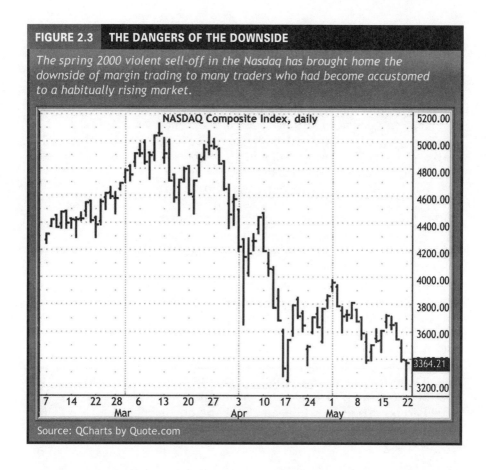

FIGURE 2.3   THE DANGERS OF THE DOWNSIDE

The spring 2000 violent sell-off in the Nasdaq has brought home the downside of margin trading to many traders who had become accustomed to a habitually rising market.

Source: QCharts by Quote.com

the trading fulcrum

Leverage is simply a generic term to describe the ability to buy more of a stock (or futures contract or currency, etc.) than you could with just the cash in your trading account. When you trade on margin, you're using leverage, a practice that varies from market to market, and in different market conditions. A brief review of the use of leverage in the stock and futures markets will effectively illustrate its most important aspects for new traders.

stock margin

As mentioned previously, trading on margin means putting up part of the money for a trade and borrowing the balance of the trade amount from your broker. A number of rules govern margin trades.

First and foremost, to trade stocks on margin, you must open a *margin account* (as opposed to the standard cash account in which you have to pay for all trades in full). The typical minimum balance required for a margin account is $2,000. Certain firms (like direct-access brokerages used by many active traders) may require much more money to open a margin account.

As mentioned, the typical margin rate for long stock trades is 50 percent ("2-to-1" margin), meaning you need 50 percent of the total cost of a trade in your account, and your broker lends you the rest (and, of course, charges you interest). For example, if you wanted to buy 100 shares of a stock trading at 60, you'd only need $3,000 in your account instead of the full $6,000 to make the purchase.

Why do this? Because your gains will be doubled, on a percentage basis, if the trade goes your way. Say the stock rallies 10 points to 70. The dollar value of the gain is $1,000, which is what it would be regardless of whether you bought it on margin. But a $1,000 profit represents a 33.3 percent gain on a $3,000 margin account while it's only a 16.7 percent gain on a $6,000 cash account.

What's the catch? Easy—the exact opposite occurs if the stock moves against you. Your losses are doubled if you're trading on margin. If the stock dropped 10 points to 50, you've lost 33.3 percent if you're trading on margin, while you've lost only 16.7 percent if you've paid in full.

Big deal, you say? Well, it can become a big deal very quickly, if the sell-off continues. If the stock falls 30 points (and if you think that's not possible, you haven't watched the Nasdaq market closely enough), your $3,000 account is gone, while you'd only be down 50 percent of a $6,000 account—small consolation, to be sure, but at least you'd still be alive and kicking.

futures margin

Nowhere are the advantages, and very real dangers, of margin more on display than in the futures markets. The 50 percent margin rate available to stock traders is nothing compared to the leverage available in futures—the precise reason many traders are attracted to this market.

While margined stock positions require a 50 percent down payment, futures positions (long or short) can be established with as little money down as 2 to 3 percent of a particular contract's value. Margin rates (sometimes referred to as *performance bond* in futures) vary from contract to contract and are adjusted by the exchanges on which they trade according to the level of volatility in the market, among other factors.

For example, in January 2001 you could have traded one S&P futures contract with $23,438 in your account. If that sounds like a lot, keep in mind that, trading at 1,470, one S&P contract has a nominal cash value of $367,500, which comes out to a margin rate of 6.4 percent.

This kind of leverage means that profits and losses are exaggerated to an even greater extent if you trade using the minimum margin requirement (which you don't have to do—see the concluding section). If you bought one June S&P at 1,470 and the market rallied to 1,490, you could pocket $5,000 ($250 per point times 20 points), or a 21.3 percent return on the $23,438 minimum margin. By comparison, this gain would amount to only a 1.3 percent profit if you had paid in full for the contract.

The catch is the same as it is in stock trading: If the market goes against you, you can lose more than your initial stake, and given the very high leverage available in futures, traders who do not adequately limit risk on trades can watch their account equity evaporate quickly.

the two words you don't want to hear: margin call

Technically, there are two kinds of margin: initial and maintenance. Initial margin is what you must have in your account to execute a margin trade: 50 percent for stocks and variable for futures contracts.

Maintenance margin is the equity you must keep in your account to maintain your position. For stocks, it is 25 percent of the current value of the position. Your equity is your stock's current market value minus your margin debt. For example, if the $60 stock you bought on margin for $3,000 dropped 28 points to $32, the position's current value would be $3,200. But you borrowed $3,000 on margin, so your current equity is only $200—less than 25 percent of the stock's current value ($3,200 × .25 = $800).

A margin (or "maintenance") call occurs when a margin trade goes against you and your brokerage demands that you deposit more money in your trading account to cover your losses and bring your account equity back above the maintenance margin level. If you don't, they have the *right* (yes, the right; read your margin account agreement) to liquidate your trade (i.e., sell off your losing position) to prevent further losses.

Here's another important point: Brokerages have discretion in setting margin rates and issuing margin calls. The 50 percent initial margin and 25 maintenance margin rates are industry minimums established by the Federal Reserve Board. Brokerages can, and do, establish more stringent requirements based on overall market conditions and the performance of particular stocks. Highly volatile stocks (like Internet stocks), for example, may be margined at a higher rate than more conservative blue-chip names.

Because the broker is, in effect, lending you money in a margin trade, he or she is participating in the risk of your trade, which is *not* why people get into the brokerage business. As a general rule, brokers have minimal tolerance for such losses. Traders have three business days, in most situations, to deposit the necessary funds to meet a margin call.

day trading and margin

Trades are margined after each trading session: Open trades are "marked to market" (valued according to the day's closing price) each night, and margin calls are issued when position's dip below the broker's maintenance margin level.

Day traders avoid such margin concerns by closing all positions by day's end. If a day trader ends the day *flat,* margin simply equals the net trading loss at day's end.

Day traders do not have carte blanche. The 50 percent minimum margin for all stock trades applies to day trading as well. (Technically, futures traders can sometimes trade contracts on an intraday basis with less than the minimum margin requirement, depending on their relationship with their broker.) Firms monitor positions and have the discretion to halt a trader's actions, liquidate trades that exceed a trader's proscribed trading limits, or immediately demand the deposit of additional funds in the trading account.

Intraday lending practices for day traders have come under close scrutiny in recent months, with some day-trading firms being accused of giving traders extensive intraday credit lines (increasing their margin buying power to multiples of more than 100 to 1).

Proposals are being discussed to increase the minimum account size for day trading margin accounts to $25,000 (from the current $2,000 for all margin accounts) but officially increasing the intraday buying power of a day-trading account from the standard 2-to-1 (50 percent) to 4-to-1 (25 percent).

Short-term traders who cap losses quickly on their trades effectively minimize many of the potential risks of margin trading. Low-risk trading strategies would in most instances exit losing positions before they reached the level of triggering margin calls.

margin homework

This is key. There are finer points to trading on margin—how you can use unrealized profits on open margin trades to trade other stocks, and so on—so make sure to read all your broker's literature (tedious though it may be) on margin trading and ask questions until you are thoroughly familiar with their margin policies.

margin is not compulsory!

A commonly overlooked, but very important, aspect of this issue is that margin is voluntary. No one points a gun at your head and forces you to trade on margin. It can offer increased flexibility and the opportunity for greater returns, but these benefits will never materialize if you do not keep the downside in mind and practice strict risk control. As noted in Chapter 8, trader John Saleeby states that he did not use margin at all for more than the first year he traded professionally.

For longer term traders and investors, trading on margin is a questionable practice. If you're in it for the long haul, you take the bad with the good, weathering sizable losses on the way to a (hopefully) large payoff. If you buy long-term investments on margin, you run the risk your broker will liquidate a position (if the market goes against you and you are issued a margin call) that you would have stuck with had you paid for it in full.

Nevertheless, margin is a highly useful tool for the experienced and risk-conscious short-term trader. Beginners probably are better off avoiding margin and only making trades when they have the cash to do it, but traders who use strategies with well-defined stop-loss, exit, and position-sizing rules can use margin to their advantage, increasing their percentage returns.

If you decide you want to trade on margin, do yourself a favor and read the fine print of your account agreement (or, gulp, call your broker on the phone) and familiarize yourself with your firm's margin policies. When will you be issued a margin call? How long do you have to get the funds into your account and what methods can you use to do so?

Good traders tend to worry about risk first and let the reward side of the equation take care of itself. When it comes to using leverage, the prudent course of action for novice traders is when in doubt, don't.

a walk on the short side

Jeff Ponczak and Mark Etzkorn

Good traders are flexible traders: They admit when they're wrong, get out of losing trades quickly, and move on to the next trade.

Ironically, traders who only operate from the long side of the market—even if they're well diversified and cut their losses quickly—are denying themselves one of the most readily available means to add flexibility, enhanced profit potential, and risk management to their trading: short selling. To futures traders, selling short is just the flip side of buying. But many stock traders are conditioned to think exclusively in terms of the long side of the market.

Selling stocks short has unique rules and risks, but is often the victim of a great deal of misunderstanding and even superstition among traders. Short selling is an important skill for traders, and one that will become more so in the event of an extended downtrend or bear market. Certainly, anyone who trades actively cannot afford to rule out the potential offered by declining markets.

By exercising proper risk control, short sellers can turn downtrends into opportunities rather than liabilities. Doing so effectively is a matter of understanding the mechanics of selling short and knowing which situations are best for short-side approaches.

the short side of the street

When considering the short side of the market, remember that traders are not investors. Traders seek to exploit short-term price swings and trends while investors hope to capitalize on long-term price trends and economic cycles, which in the stock market has translated into the traditional buy-and-hold approach.

But at any given time (within reason), a stock may be as likely to move down as it is to move up. Short selling is simply the process of selling high (first) and buying low (second) to take advantage of a potential price decline.

From a broad, strategic perspective, selling stocks short is simply a matter of inverting the principles that would normally trigger a long trade. Instead of identifying points where you think a stock is likely to move to the upside, and buying, you identify points where you think a stock is likely to drop, and sell. If the market goes your way, you buy back your position at a profit.

Well, it's not quite that simple. Short selling is a much more common practice in the futures markets because of their nature as hedging instruments. One of the primary economic functions of futures is to protect against price drops in a financial instrument or commodity. If you were long a portfolio of S&P stocks, the Japanese yen, corn, or crude oil and you wanted to guard against a downside move in your respective market, you would sell (go short) the appropriate futures contract.

From an execution standpoint, there are no restrictions on short-selling futures as there are with stocks (to be explained later); futures traders can, and generally do, sell and buy with equal ease.

Two major elements make shorting stocks a more complicated proposition than shorting futures: The first are Securities and Exchange Commission (SEC) rules dictating when and how short trades can be executed. Simply, you can only sell stocks short in certain conditions.

The second is the longer term upside bias of the stock market and the inherent differences between uptrends and downtrends. Bull moves tend to be longer and more gradual, and bear moves tend to be shorter and sharper.

The combination of these factors, as well as the established buy-and-hold bias of the long-term investment community, has given many traders an almost exclusively "buy first, sell (much) later" mentality when it comes to trading stocks.

In a sense, this is appropriate (or at least it has been for the past several years). It's true that you shouldn't try to fight the market. When the major trend is up, you want to trade with it, not against it.

But in another sense, this mind-set limits a trader's options. After all, there are situations when short selling is appropriate. Understanding the mechanics of short selling and the realities of down moves versus up moves will put you in a position to know when and how to effectively trade the short side of the market.

Short selling becomes an even more important trading skill in extended downtrends or bear markets, when "not fighting the market" is a matter of capitalizing on a prevailing downside bias. Bears may be endangered, but they're not extinct. No trend or market cycle lasts forever; when a bear market occurs, many traders who have profited handsomely in the current bull environment will be unable to make money.

Seasoned traders understand that knowing how to operate on the short side of the market adds flexibility and diversification and, when done properly, should not be significantly riskier than trading from the long side.

a short history

While many people find the idea of selling something they don't own a completely unnatural concept, short selling has been around since the earliest organized securities markets formed in the Netherlands in the early 1600s.

Short selling has been widely practiced in the United States since the early twentieth century, when market legends such as Jesse Livermore and Bernard Baruch made fortunes shorting stocks. The practice eventually assumed a dark reputation as organized groups of shorters known as "bear raiders" would band together and repeatedly sell short in an attempt to deflate stocks and buy them back at a discount.

Unrestricted short selling allowed well-financed market manipulators to bully stocks down (often using pliant journalists to help spread rumors), triggering artificial sell-offs that victimized investors who did not have the financial wherewithal to survive such drops. The investors panicked, sold off their positions and the raiders swooped back in and bought back the stock at dirt-cheap prices.

Bear raiders were often blamed for the stock market crash of 1929, although investigations by the New York Stock Exchange in the years following the crash found no evidence that was the case. (However, short-side manipulation of stocks by high-powered market operators undoubtedly took place.) Nonetheless, these investigations sparked the foundation of all current securities laws and regulation: the Securities

Act of 1933, the Securities Exchange Act of 1934, and the Securities Exchange Commission (SEC), which was formed in 1934. (Ironically, the first chairman of the SEC was Joe Kennedy, who was widely rumored to be a bear raider during his tenure on Wall Street.)

From the postcrash SEC came the rules regulating short selling that are still in effect today. It's crucial to understand them before attempting to short. The three big rules to keep in mind are (1) you have to short on an *uptick,* (2) you have to short from a margin account, and (3) the stock has to be "available to borrow."

the "(up)tick" rule

The most important restriction on short-selling stocks is the one that requires short sales to be executed when the market is moving up, if only temporarily.

The Securities Exchange Act authorized the SEC to regulate short sales, which they define as any sale of a security that the seller does not own, or any sale consummated by the delivery of a security borrowed by, or for, the account of the seller. SEC Rule 10a-1, also known as the "tick rule," was established in 1938. Under the tick rule, short sales on listed (NYSE and AMEX) stocks are only allowed if the last price of a stock is higher (on an uptick) than the previous price (or equal to the previous price, if the price before the previous price was an uptick—the "zero-plus" tick rule).

Basically, to allow a short sale, the most recent trade price has to be higher than the previous trade price. The purpose of this rule is to force short sellers to execute their trades when the market is rising (indicating there is at least some buying interest in the stock). For example, if the last three trades in a stock were $29^{15}/_{16}$, 30, $29^{15}/_{16}$, a short sale would not be allowed because the last trade was at a lower price (a downtick) than the previous trade. If the next trade occurs at 30 (an uptick), however, you could sell short at 30.

The zero-plus tick rule works as follows: If the last trade was at the same price as the previous one, but the previous one was an uptick from the trade before that, a short sale is allowed. In our example, if another trade at 30 followed the first trade at 30, you could still sell short at 30, even though this most recent price was not higher than the previous price.

Nasdaq stocks were originally (the exchange began trading in 1971) not subject to the tick rule. (And, after the 1987 market crash, short sellers again had the finger pointed at them. As was the case in 1929, though, investigation found no correlation between the crash and the abuse of short sales.) Still, in 1994 the Nasdaq passed its own tick rule, which is slightly different from Rule 10a-1; it's based on the current bid rather than the last trade. You can sell on an uptick of $^{1}/_{16}$ above the current bid. For starters, the price to consider for the uptick is the bid price, which is not necessarily the trade price. A short sale can be made on an uptick of the bid, or on a downtick if that downtick is $\frac{1}{16}$ above the current bid. (If the spread on a Nasdaq stock is $\frac{1}{32}$, the stock can be shorted at or above the offer.)

The Nasdaq Level II screen generally indicates up bids and down bids with up or down arrows, respectively. This makes it easy to know when you can sell short: While the up arrow is showing next to the bid price, you can execute a short trade. Figures 2.4 and 2.5 compare situations in which short selling is legal and when it is not.

If the most recent trades on a Nasdaq stock were $29\frac{15}{16}$, 30, $29\frac{15}{16}$, you could sell short at the second print at $29\frac{15}{16}$ (even though it's a downtick) if the current *bid* is $29\frac{7}{8}$. Essentially, the Nasdaq rules allow a short sale at a price that would, when executed, represent an uptick, even if that price level is not currently an uptick. It sounds complex, but it's really not. The goal is simply to require short sellers to trade into up moves so they don't exacerbate down moves. (Our thanks to Mark Seleznov, Futures Trader LLC, for his insight on the intricacies of the SEC's and NASD's short selling rules.)

selling what you don't own

Many novice traders are confused by short selling simply because they don't understand how you can sell what you don't own.

Actually, you can't. The second hurdle (after the uptick rule) the short seller must jump is *borrowing* stock to sell. When you go short, you

FIGURE 2.4   SHORT SALE: GREEN LIGHT

The up arrow (next to the bid price) on the Nasdaq Level II screen indicates short sales can be made at the bid price at this time.

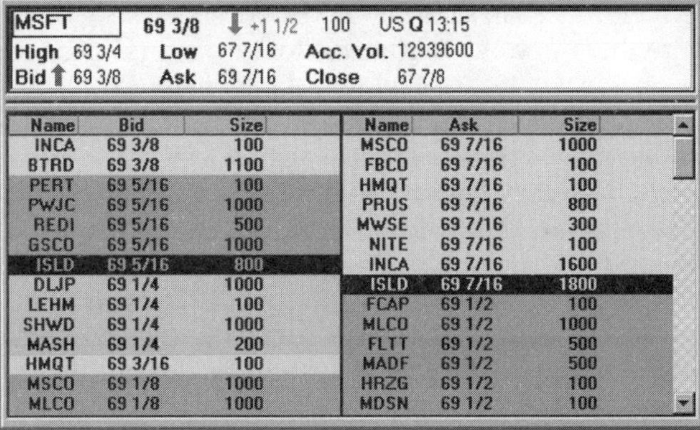

MSFT	69 3/8	↓ +1 1/2	100	US Q 13:15
High 69 3/4	Low 67 7/16	Acc. Vol. 12939600		
Bid ↑ 69 3/8	Ask 69 7/16	Close 67 7/8		

Name	Bid	Size	Name	Ask	Size
INCA	69 3/8	100	MSCO	69 7/16	1000
BTRD	69 3/8	1100	FBCO	69 7/16	100
PERT	69 5/16	100	HMQT	69 7/16	100
PWJC	69 5/16	1000	PRUS	69 7/16	800
REDI	69 5/16	500	MWSE	69 7/16	300
GSCO	69 5/16	1000	NITE	69 7/16	100
ISLD	69 5/16	800	INCA	69 7/16	1600
DLJP	69 1/4	1000	ISLD	69 7/16	1800
LEHM	69 1/4	100	FCAP	69 1/2	100
SHWD	69 1/4	1000	MLCO	69 1/2	1000
MASH	69 1/4	200	FLTT	69 1/2	500
HMQT	69 3/16	100	MADF	69 1/2	500
MSCO	69 1/8	1000	HRZG	69 1/2	100
MLCO	69 1/8	1000	MDSN	69 1/2	100

Source: RealTick® by Townsend Analytics, Ltd.

FIGURE 2.5   SHORT SALE: RED LIGHT

The down arrow (next to the bid price) indicates short sales cannot currently be made at the bid price.

MSFT	69 7/16 ↑ +1 9/16 100	US Q 13:13
High 69 3/4	Low 67 7/16	Acc. Vol. 12922100
Bid ↓ 69 3/8	Ask 69 7/16	Close 67 7/8

Name	Bid	Size	Name	Ask	Size
GSCO	69 3/8	1000	MSCO	69 7/16	1000
ARCA	69 3/8	2800	FBCO	69 7/16	100
ISLD	69 3/8	1000	HMQT	69 7/16	100
PERT	69 5/16	100	PRUS	69 7/16	800
PWJC	69 5/16	1000	MWSE	69 7/16	300
REDI	69 5/16	500	INCA	69 7/16	1600
INCA	69 5/16	3000	ISLD	69 7/16	1800
DLJP	69 1/4	1000	FCAP	69 1/2	100
LEHM	69 1/4	100	MLCO	69 1/2	1000
SHWD	69 1/4	1000	FLTT	69 1/2	500
HMQT	69 3/16	100	MADF	69 1/2	500
MSCO	69 1/8	1000	HRZG	69 1/2	100
MLCO	69 1/8	1000	NITE	69 1/2	100
NITE	69 1/8	100	MDSN	69 1/2	100

Source: RealTick® by Townsend Analytics, Ltd.

are really borrowing the stock from your broker (who *borrows* it from another trading account at the firm or another broker); the process is transparent to you. You are then able to sell the stock in the open market and the proceeds from the sale go into your account. If the stock goes down, you can buy back the stock at a lower price, *paying back* your broker and pocketing your profit.

If you sell short 100 shares of a stock trading at $50, your account is credited $5,000. If the stock drops to $45, you can buy back the position for $4,500 and pocket a $500 profit, minus commissions and fees.

Before a broker can lend you stock to short sell, he or she must first make sure that the stock is available for borrowing. In many cases, that will not be an issue. But in highly volatile markets (especially when the market is in a nosedive), brokerages produce *hard-to-borrow* lists, which typically contain stocks traders are most eager to short. A stock on the list may not be available for shorting. Brokerages typically produce lists you can consult each day to know which stocks can and cannot be shorted.

One way to tell if a stock might be difficult to borrow is to check its short interest, which is the number of shares that have been sold short but not yet repurchased. If a stock's short interest comprises, say, 25 percent or more of the float, the stock might be difficult to borrow. However, because of the level of arbitrage in the market today, short interest is not the straightforward barometer it once was. Short positions might be hedged with options or other positions, making what might seem like high short interest less significant.

Also, keep in mind that your broker can demand you buy back the shares at any time. This might happen if a stock, especially a stock with a large short interest, suddenly experiences a large run-up in price. If a broker is having difficulty locating stock for all the new buyers who have entered the market, he or she may require you to buy back your short position regardless of the price of the stock, or the price you bought it at. Moreover, if your broker cannot contact you, he or she has the right to buy back your stock, without your permission, at whatever price the stock is trading. A broker buyback almost always occurs during times of volatile price increases and it is never good news for the short seller.

margin

The final requirement for executing a short sale is that it must be done from a margin account (a *short margin* account). Contact your broker regarding opening and maintaining a margin account (as mentioned earlier in the chapter). Initial margin for a short account works the same as it does for a long account; whatever you have in your cash account, you can borrow the same amount for trading.

Because all short sales must be done on margin, your account will be subject to margin interest. However, brokers generally don't charge interest on day trades, short or long. Another note on interest: Usually, any cash a trader has in a brokerage account can be placed in an interest-bearing money-market fund. Most brokerages will not pay interest on funds deposited from a short sale; however, preferred customers (i.e., ones with a large account balance) can sometimes negotiate an interest rate with their brokers.

Understanding the tick rules, stock availability requirements, and margin concerns unique to short trading takes care of the mechanics of executing a short trade. The more important issues are understanding the risks and knowing how to capitalize on short-selling opportunities.

risky business?

If you buy a stock, your maximum risk is your original investment (unless you're buying on margin), even if the company goes bankrupt and the stock goes down to zero.

Theoretically, however, the risk on a short trade is unlimited because there's no limit to how high a stock can go, and short sellers can lose many times their initial stake.

This assumes no risk control is being used to cap losses on a short trade (which should never be the case). Short-selling stocks does have specific risks, but for short-term traders who control risk on all their trades through diligent use of stop-loss orders, these should not be significantly greater than for long trades.

One point to consider: While a high number of short sellers can contribute to a stock's decline, they can also, inadvertently, be responsible for a violent price rise—the *short squeeze*. If a stock, especially a hard-to-borrow stock with high short interest and a low float, rallies sharply, short sellers will scramble to buy back their stock and cut their losses, pushing the stock even higher.

smart short selling

As discussed earlier, short selling, in the broadest sense, simply involves inverting the principles of a long trade. For example, a simple short-term trading approach is to look for a correction or pause within an established uptrend and buy when the stock moves back in the direction of the trend. A viable short-side approach would simply be to look for a correction or pause within an established downtrend and sell short when the stock makes a downside thrust.

There are several of ways to measure such corrections or pullbacks: a retracement of a certain percentage, or a move back to a moving average or down trendline. The object is to define a downtrending market and look for upside corrections within it that represent selling opportunities.

Figure 2.6 shows a downtrend in Motorola (defined by a downward 10-day/30-day moving average crossover) and two subsequent pullbacks to the shorter term moving average that offered short-selling opportunities. This simplified example illustrates technical signals on which a short trade could be based. The basic principles here are to look for short-selling opportunities in downtrending environments (trading with the trend) and to enter at low-risk entry points.

Short traders must also take into account the overall market environment and the characteristics of specific kinds of price behavior. While some traders argue there's no difference between trading the short and long sides of the stock market, research indicates otherwise. There are, in fact, distinctions between uptrends and downtrends in stocks that traders must consider when applying short-selling strategies. Since 1900, bull markets in the Dow Jones Industrial Average (defined by a 30 percent increase after 50 days or a 13 percent rise after 155 days) have lasted an average of just more than two years. Bear markets, though, lasted about 14 months on average.

A simple test to determine the best combination of moving-average length (to define the dominant trend, up or down) and trade length (on randomly timed trades taken in the direction of the trend) revealed that the best combination for long trades was to use a 260-day moving average to define an uptrend and to hold a position for 18 days. By contrast, the best combination for short trades was a 100-day moving average and a trade length of two days.

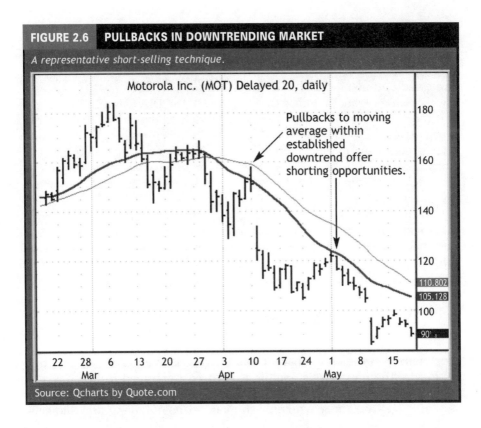

FIGURE 2.6   PULLBACKS IN DOWNTRENDING MARKET

A representative short-selling technique.

Motorola Inc. (MOT) Delayed 20, daily

Pullbacks to moving average within established downtrend offer shorting opportunities.

Source: Qcharts by Quote.com

The longer term differences between uptrends and downtrends in the stock market may be of less concern to short-term traders, but they should still be taken into account when designing short-selling strategies. Simply attempting to invert the rules of a long-side system is a naïve approach.

Keep in mind that the characteristics described in the preceding paragraphs are representative of a bull bias in the stock market. During an extended downtrend or bear market, the defining characteristics of up moves in a bull market (i.e., they develop more slowly and last longer) are more likely to be the hallmarks of down moves.

As with any strategy, strict risk control and money management are absolutely necessary. The risks of short squeezes in popularly shorted stocks make well-defined stop-loss levels and exit criteria critical for short-term traders.

more ways to play

Besides individual stocks, you can use other trading instruments to capitalize on the short side of the market, most notably index shares, futures, and options.

For stock traders, index shares (the QQQs, DIAs, and SPYs) represent the smallest adjustment in trading style and execution. They're exchange-traded stocks that closely mirror the performance of the major indexes and some market sectors. Designed as an alternative to mutual funds, they trade like stocks, giving traders an easy way to trade an entire index or sector—free of the short-selling restrictions and borrowing availability issues of standard stocks.

Futures and options also allow traders to short indexes and individual stocks without worrying about uptick restrictions. However, traders must take into account the expiration dates and margin considerations unique to these instruments. Congress recently passed a law allowing single-stock futures, although trading of these instruments is still several months away.

in short

Short selling in the stock market has unique risks and restrictions, but it's hardly the mysterious gamble it is often portrayed to be. Markets go up and markets go down; traders who can profit in both situations have an edge over those who only think in terms of buying first and selling later.

Applying effective risk-conscious short-selling techniques under the appropriate circumstances actually decreases your overall risk by allowing you to profit in downtrending market phases (as well as by playing markets against each other—going long one market and short the other in an intermarket spread). Although short selling is sometimes treated like market witchcraft, professional traders know that shorting the market is an effective, and sometimes necessary, trading tool.

what are the odds?

Thomas Stridsman

Whether you're a systematic, rule-based trader 100 percent of the time or prefer to use discretion; whether you're new to the game or a seasoned pro, it is paramount to know the odds you're up against every time you put on a trade.

For the rule-based trader, this is easy enough. All you need to do is to *back-test* your trading strategy, using one of several software packages that allow you to simulate trades on historical price data. Back-testing, if done properly, will give you the results of a particular trading system, thus providing a barometer for how much you might make (or lose) in the future.

But if your trading is more discretionary, figuring out your odds can become more complex. First, you need an actual track record of trades, preferably profitable ones.

Also, keep in mind that discretionary traders still generally follow specific guidelines—they are just not as rigid as systematic traders. This means that as a discretionary trader you still should be able to do the same types of calculations as mechanical traders, except that you cannot work with fictitious trades—you must rely on your own track record and your ability to trade consistently in the future.

Finally, you also need to be careful to consider only previous trades consistent with your current style of trading. If you change your trading style, you cannot use any prior trades to determine your future odds of success.

knowing your average

Once you have a significant number of actual or hypothetical trades, you can begin to determine how likely it is for an individual trade to end up as a winner, or how much you can expect to make per trade in the future. Among statisticians, "significant" usually means more than 21 samples, but the number can vary greatly depending on whom you ask. Some say more than 30, others say at least 100 or even several thousand. In the medical field (e.g., when testing a new drug) nearly 1,000 samples are required to deem the resulting conclusions reliable; there is no reason to treat your money any less seriously.

To calculate your average trade value, simply divide the net dollar profit (loss) of all your trades by the number of trades: If you have five trades that produce profits (losses) of 1.5, −1, −.75, 2, −.5, your average profit per trade will be .25 (1.25/5).

The greater the (positive) number, the better. However, depending on what market you're trading (or if you trade several different markets), you're sometimes better off looking at the net percentage value rather than the net dollar value, especially if the markets you're trading are prone to trend. In such situations, the size of the dollar-based moves will contract and expand with the dollar value of the market (increasing as the market rises and decreasing as it falls), while the percentage-based moves will stay approximately the same. The same holds true for all other types of profit or loss calculations, such as the value of your average winner and loser, and largest loser or maximum drawdown. For simplicity's sake, we'll stay with the dollar-based calculations for now.

In the preceding example, another way to reach the same conclusion is to:

1. Calculate the likelihood of each trade being a winner or loser.
2. Multiply these respective probabilities by the average winning and losing trade values.
3. Add the results.

In this case, there are two winning trades and three losing trades. The likelihood of a winning trade is 40 percent (2 out of 5), while the likelihood of a losing trade is 60 percent (3 out of 5). The average winning trade in our sample is 1.75 (3.5/2) and the average loser is –0.75 (–2.25/3). Multiplying the probabilities of winning and losing trades by the respective average winning and losing trades, and adding these values together gives up a result of 0.25 [(0.4 × 1.75) + (0.6 × –.75)], which can be referred to as the *mathematical expectation* of the trading strategy.

Knowing how to perform calculations like these also enables you to estimate how many trades it should take to get you out of the red when you're in a period of losses (or a *drawdown*). For example, if you know your strategy will lose three out of five times for a total loss of 2.25, there might be instances where you will lose six trades in a row for a total loss of 4.50 (e.g., you lose three trades at the back end of one five-trade sequence, then immediately lose three trades at the front of the next sequence).

With an expected average profit of .25 it will take you, on average, 18 winning trades to get back to even (4.5/0.25). Suppose each trade lasts for an average of three days. If you're always in the market, it will take 54 trading days before you will see a new equity high in your trading account (whether this information will help you sleep better at night is for you to decide).

factoring profits

Another way to get a feel for the probabilities of your trading approach is to calculate the *profit factor,* which is simply the total profit divided by the absolute value of the total loss. Using the same numbers as earlier, the profit factor for this strategy comes out to 1.56 (3.5/2.25), which means you can expect to make $1.56 for every dollar you lose.

When back-testing and building a mechanical trading strategy, a certain degree of *curve fitting* will always be involved. This means that, with the benefit of hindsight, the trading strategy or model will be fitted to the data. As a result, the strategy is unlikely to perform as well when applied to future unseen data. For this reason, most strategy developers and system vendors suggest you should not trade a system with a historically back-tested profit factor of less than 2 (some even say 3). A trading system rarely performs as well in real trading as it does in historical testing.

However, while it may seem important to trade a system with a high profit factor, recommending a system with a profit factor of 3 is ridiculous. A profit factor of 3 means that you will make $3 for every dollar you lose. Suppose you have a system with a 50/50 chance to produce a winner; suppose further that you are willing to risk $1 per trade. If you begin with $2, make one losing trade and one winning trade, you end up with a total of $4, equal to a 100 percent return on initial equity. Ask yourself how likely it is that you will be able to double your capital every other trade, on average, in a consistent manner. Perhaps you've done it once and thought you've found the holy grail, only to burn yourself severely the next time you try the same strategy; or, at least, after a few more trades, realized that a once-in-a-lifetime result had occurred. In fact, the reason some system vendors advocate such high historical profit factors is probably that they don't know how to build a robust and reliable trading strategy in the first place.

That may seem like a harsh statement, but consider this: The higher the historical profit factor, the more curve-fit the system is; the more curve-fit the system, the less likely it will work in the future, in real trading.

In fact, when it comes to mechanical trading strategies, you probably will be better off looking for a profit factor as low as possible, as long as it stays above one and is high enough to make up for slippage and commission. At least you will know the degree of curve-fitting is very low and, therefore, the system is more likely to produce profitable results in the future, if only marginally so. Similarly, a trading strategy that performs in a consistent manner over a wide variety of markets is more reliable than one that does not.

adding it up

A system's value is not necessarily directly related to how high or low its average trade value is. Ideally, the average trade value should be as high as possible, but the overall profitability also depends on how often the system signals a trade. The more often you get to trade a profitable system, even if it's only marginally so, the sooner you get to use your profits to increase your stake.

And, the more you can trade, the more you will make, especially if the profit factor suggests that the system is equally likely to perform as well in the future as it did in the past.

chapter 3

online technology and the new trading landscape

the direct connection

Gibbons Burke

The surge in popularity of online trading indicates the Internet has hit a sweet spot in the financial markets. The Web has given the everyday trader access to information and execution capabilities formerly the preserve of traditional brokerage houses.

Previously, the brokerages not only held the keys to the gate that led to the exchanges, they also served to distribute the information needed to make trading decisions—in a way, acting as a filter between the trader and the markets.

The Internet has unleashed a revolution in online investing. Thousands of Web sites now offer investment advice and trading. Analysts who formerly sold their work to the brokerages now communicate directly to the trading public via the Web. In trade execution, a similar revolution is taking place. The function of the conventional brokers is being whittled down to that of an account custodian and identity-verification service. They are still the gatekeepers to the exchange doors because they essentially and collectively own the exchanges. It will probably be some time before this franchise is completely broken.

But not all online brokers are created equal. Different kinds offer different levels of connectivity to the market and, depending on your trading style, one may offer obvious execution and cost advantages over another. Online broker services can be broken into three categories:

1. *Traditional broker.* These are the full-service firms with established lines of business who are trying to offer new online

services without cannibalizing the interests and commissions of their sales force.

2. *Web-based online brokers.* These firms offer services through Web-based order-entry systems. Often, their trades are handled by firms such as Knight Trading Group, and Spear, Leeds and Kellogg—market-making firms who pay these brokers for "order flow." (Or, they may take the opposite side of customer orders themselves, profiting from the spread.) Along with firms such as E*Trade and Ameritrade, discount brokerages such as Schwab and Fidelity, which were quick to adapt their traditional models to the online revolution, lead this category in terms of accounts and trading volume.

3. *Direct-access brokers.* These brokers enable customers to enter orders directly in a software application designed for the task, rather than through a Web page.

There are good arguments for all three types of brokerage services. Each has its pros and cons. There are even good arguments for having accounts at all three, to diversify your risk and provide backup execution capabilities, and provide greater access to a wider range of financial instruments. Most direct-access brokers, for example, don't offer checking on your brokerage account, or access to mutual funds, futures, IPOs, or other vehicles for investment. A well-rounded financial plan should include a variety of instruments to augment the income based on trading.

direct versus web

Most online brokerages provide their services using forms displayed on Web pages. Direct-access brokers differ in two major ways: First, a direct-access broker provides software that enables you to place orders over the Internet without using a Web browser. Second, the direct-access broker lets you control where that order will be sent. Let's look first at why a software application is better than a Web page for entering trades. These are the typical steps to placing an order with a Web-based online brokerage, in this case Fidelity (see Figure 3.1):

1. Connect your computer to the Internet.
2. Launch your browser. (Sometimes steps 1 and 2 are combined into one.)
3. Point your browser at your broker's Web page.
4. Log onto your broker's Web site.
5. Choose the account you want to trade in.

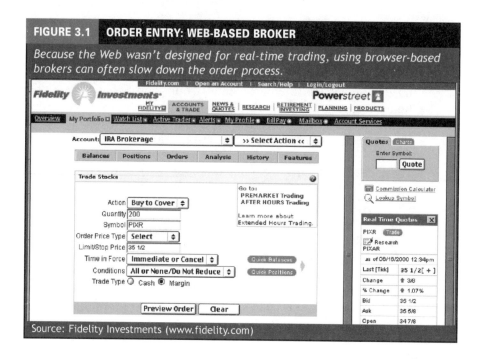

FIGURE 3.1   ORDER ENTRY: WEB-BASED BROKER

Because the Web wasn't designed for real-time trading, using browser-based brokers can often slow down the order process.

Source: Fidelity Investments (www.fidelity.com)

6. Select an action—"Trade Stocks"—which pulls up an order screen.

7. Select the order type—"Buy," "Buy to Cover," "Sell"—from a pull-down menu.

8. Type the quantity of shares to transact.

9. Type the ticker symbol.

10. Type the limit or stop price.

11. If you want a special order (good-til-canceled, fill or kill, immediate or cancel, on the close, on the open) select that from a pull-down menu. Otherwise, the default choice is for an order that is good till the end of the normal trading day.

12. If you want more special conditions to apply (all or none, do not reduce, or both) select that option from another pull-down menu.

13. Choose whether the trade will be done with cash or margin monies.

14. After all that, click the "Preview Order" button.

15. Wait for the Web server to get the order, process it back, and then show exactly what you just spent five minutes typing. If there are any problems with your order—if you have forgotten,

for example, to specify whether this was a buy or sell—you will get an error message on the preview page. You then have to go back and fix the mistake on the order page.

16. When you finally get a preview you like, send the order in.

17. Wait for the Web server to give you a confirmation of the order.

18. When the order is confirmed, go to the Orders page to see if you received a fill. If you didn't, keep pressing the Update button to see if the situation changes.

Just getting an order in can take five minutes or so—not a situation you want to be in when the market is breaking out to the upside. If you are using limit orders, you may need to cancel the order to enter another one at a higher price. And, you can't see the latest prices on these pages. This also must be done by going to another Web page and waiting for it to load.

Contrast this with the order process used by a representative direct-access broker, in this case using CyberCorp's CyberX application (Figure 3.2):

1. Connect your computer to the Internet.

2. Launch CyberX.

3. Type your account password and hit "Enter."

4. Type the symbol you are interested in.

5. Enter the number of shares. You can preset a default number of shares, and the application will usually remember your last settings.

6. Click the "Buy" (or other applicable order) button.

7. A dialog appears asking you to confirm your order. If you click "Yes," the order is sent. (This confirmation dialog can be turned off, if you are confident in your abilities.)

8. Check the message window for a confirmation message. Your open order will now appear in the Orders window.

9. When the order is filled (which can be in a matter of seconds), another message will scroll across telling you that you were executed. You don't have to keep pressing an update button.

When an order is filled, the position is moved from the Orders screen to the Open screen. When you close the trade, the order is moved to the Exec(uted) area. Net profit and loss on all open positions are tracked in real-time as the market updates. Your buying power is updated immediately as well, a significant advantage over brokers who don't give you an updated account balance until after the close of the day, or sometimes not until the next morning.

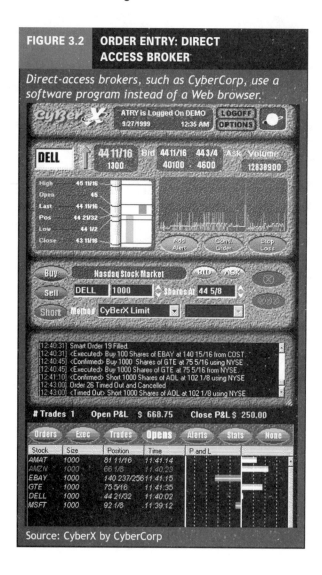

FIGURE 3.2   ORDER ENTRY: DIRECT
ACCESS BROKER

Direct-access brokers, such as CyberCorp, use a
software program instead of a Web browser.

Source: CyberX by CyberCorp

Clearly, this is a much more streamlined process. What makes this possible is that the direct-access program was written to do one thing and do it well—let you enter orders into their system with lightning speed and keep abreast of your account positions in real time.

The Web-based interface is clunky and awkward because the Web wasn't designed for real-time traders in the financial markets. It was designed to share academic research in nuclear particle physics. A Web browser is a universal information display machine; in trying to be all things to all users, it doesn't do a very good job in some particular cases—like trading—that require extreme speed and interactivity. The same thing applies to getting price quotes and other market information. Web pages are not well-suited to delivering streaming information. The "push" technology that began when the Web first started was a flop for financial data. By the time the page loaded, the prices displayed were yesterday's news.

The Java programming environment was supposed to solve these problems by providing a more dynamic box within the browser window. There are a few somewhat capable Java "applets" that can handle real-time quotes, but they aren't problem-free. Java still suffers from the fact that it is a virtual computer running within your real computer. To make things happen, programming instructions written in Java must be translated on the fly to the language spoken by your computer. "On the fly," though, is perhaps the wrong phrase; it should be "on the crawl," because Java applets are slow compared to native applications that are designed to run on your computer. Another problem with Java applets is that they have to be downloaded every time you want to use them. Java still has a lot of potential to deliver more dynamic Web-based interfaces, but it is not yet a mature technology.

Part of the larger problem in the online brokerage arena is perception. Because most people experience the Internet via the Web (and experience all that the Web does very well) the perception is that the Internet *is* the Web. They don't realize the Internet is just a bunch of computers connected to each other, and that you can use something besides a Web browser to send and receive information over the Internet. For example, when a direct-access broker's software connects to its servers, you don't even have to have your Web browser running. It is dialing up the server directly without using the Web at all. The communications between the software and the server can be relatively small compared to a Web page, which can contain elements that are quite large and can take a long time to fully load on your computer.

With a direct-access broker, the "page" you are looking at is already known by the application. All it needs is the numbers to fill in where appropriate. This makes fewer demands on your Internet bandwidth, and means that a direct-access broker with an application doing the display work can deliver its services more efficiently to more customers without the traffic bottlenecks that sometimes bedevil Web-based brokers.

paper route

The second major advantage the direct-access brokers provide is the flexibility of being able to manage how your order is handled and by whom. For example, most direct-access software lets you route Nasdaq orders to the Nasdaq SelectNet and SOES systems, both of which let you specify the market maker to which the order will be sent. It also allows you to route the order directly to a number of Electronic Communication

Networks (ECNs) such as Island, Instinet, Attain, Archipelago, REDI-Book, MarketXT, and Bloomberg. Or, you can use a couple of auto-routing mechanisms that check each of these markets and execute your order wherever the volume of shares at the price you specify can be found.

The RealTick III software (www.realtick.com) by Townsend Analytics also is a favorite of day-trading brokerages because it offers many different trade-routing options. Several direct-access brokers are based on the use of private-label versions of this software.

This flexibility of direct-access technology eliminates what can be particularly costly and mostly hidden in the world of Web-based online brokers: middlemen. Many brokers either take the opposite side of customer orders (profiting from the spread) or route them to third-party market makers who actually execute them. The originating broker (who is working for you) gets paid for each order they send to the executing broker. The executing broker makes this money back (and then some) by fielding your order against other orders coming in from customers.

This payment for order flow makes it possible for some online brokers to offer extremely low commissions, because they will make it back in the end. Choosing a broker because they have the lowest commissions can sometimes be a case of being penny wise but pound foolish, as the saying goes. To its credit, Datek Online (www.datek.com) will refund to the customer any payment it receives for order flow. The company is one of the best Web-based online brokers for the very active trader. Datek Online owns the Island ECN, which is the most active ECN other than the institutional gorilla Instinet.

Direct-access brokers do not receive much attention from Web sites purporting to find the best online brokers. Gomez.com is one site that has a lot of clout when it comes to rating online brokerages, but they are complete Web snobs. In rating the brokers for suitability in the "Hyperactive Day Trader" category, Gomez.com didn't even mention the availability of streaming quotes or direct-access capabilities. For an extensive list and plenty of reviews of several day-trading brokers who offer direct access, check out www.sonic.net/donaldj/day.html.

Is direct-access technology the right thing for everyone? If you are the sort of position trader who puts his or her stops in and doesn't even watch the markets during the day, direct access won't offer you much. Also, although direct-access brokers are dropping their commission rates, they are still, on average, more expensive than Web-based discount brokers; and, some require larger minimum account balances than standard online brokers.

But if you consider yourself an active trader—and certainly if you are considering the kind of trading where every tick counts—direct access is the way to go. It is like driving your own car rather than taking the bus: You get there quicker, do a lot less waiting around, and have far more control over your route.

digital revolution: the electronic communications networks (ECNs)

Jeff Ponczak

Until relatively recently, trading was completely dominated by open outcry exchanges such as the New York Stock Exchange (NYSE) and the various Chicago and New York commodity exchanges. Traders gathered on the massive trading floors of these institutions and bought and sold stock face to face. However, modern electronic communications have forever altered that paradigm—to the point that it is in danger of being permanently supplanted by the online/electronic model.

In 1971, the National Association of Securities Dealers Automated Quotations (Nasdaq) was granted exchange status. Previously, it had been known as the *over-the-counter* (OTC) market, where unlisted stocks (NYSE stocks were referred to as *listed* issues) were traded by brokers using an electronic quote posting mechanism that is now known the world over as the "Level II" display. It was not a true electronic exchange—Nasdaq traders were able to disseminate information over their network, but trades were not actually cleared with it—but it was still an important step toward creating the online stock market that is still evolving to this day.

An even more recent—and potentially more significant—example of the power of electronic trading has been the ascendancy of the Eurex. A German, purely electronic futures exchange (formerly known as the Deutsche Terminborse), the Eurex is now the largest futures exchange in the world, surpassing the once unassailable, open-outcry Chicago Board of Trade (CBOT) and Chicago Mercantile Exchange (CME).

In the stock market, the digital revolution is epitomized by the various Electronic Communications Networks (ECNs) that handle as much as 30 percent of the trading of Nasdaq stocks on a given day.

what is an ECN?

An ECN matches bids and offers in stocks (originally only Nasdaq stocks, although NYSE issues are being traded in increasing numbers), kind of like an electronic singles bar for stocks. There are no brokers or middlemen of any kind. If you want to buy a stock, you enter your bid. If you want to sell a stock, you enter your offer. If there is a match for your order, your trade will be filled instantly. If not, it will be entered into the ECNs *order book,* a list of all the outstanding bids and offers.

The original ECN was Instinet (started in 1969), which was an order-matching system for institutional traders who needed or wanted an alternative to exchange trading (they could place bids and offers anonymously, and thus attempt to hide their intentions from the market).

Rules and practices for the different ECNs vary, but in most cases, the highest unmatched bid and lowest unmatched offer in an ECN's order book will be entered into the Level II quote display.

ECNs have played a key role in the increased interest in pre- and post-market trading. Most ECNs are trading before the 9:30 A.M. EST opening bell, and do not stop until well after the 4 P.M. EST close. Their availability has led to increased volume and liquidity in the before- and after-hours market and has made it easier to trade during those time periods.

In the fall of 1996, after the Securities and Exchange Commission (SEC) found that Nasdaq market markers bypassed customer orders in an attempt to increase profits, the SEC allowed for the creation of "alternative trading systems" that would "disseminate market maker orders to third parties and permit such orders to be executed through the system." Thus, the retail ECN was born in January of 1997. Currently, the two most widely used ECNs for retail customers are Island and Archipelago, although there are a total of 10 (including Instinet).

Retail traders do not use ECNs as they would use brokers (i.e., you can't set up an account with Island if you want to trade stocks through Island). Rather, certain brokers have arrangements with ECNs that allow their customers' orders to be routed via an ECN. Many direct-access brokers have access to all ECNs, and the more traditional online brokers use ECNs for their pre- and postmarket trades.

The ECNs are not exchanges, although many of them have applied to the SEC for exchange status, and the Archipelago ECN has partnered with the Pacific Stock Exchange to acquire de facto exchange status. Rather, ECNs are quasi-exchanges that function as electronic order entry mechanisms. The "integration" of the ECNs into the Nasdaq Level II quote montage is a primary reason for the advent of electronic day trading: Traders were able to—with a click of their mouse—get (nearly) immediate fills and trade confirmations.

We'll say more about the operation of ECNs and their role in electronic trading later in this chapter.

is 24-hour trading really on the horizon?

Although it is still years off (for regulatory reasons as much as, if not more than, technological ones), the future of trading seems irrevocably headed toward an all-electronic, multimarket, global marketplace.

While U.S. market hours have already been expanded through ECN trading, these hours are likely to expand in the future. Similarly, as trading in foreign markets becomes more widely available, a 24-hour, global market may be accessible through the average retail trader's desktop. They may be able to trade domestic and foreign stocks—as well as currencies, bonds, and futures contracts—through a single electronic trading interface that gives them access to markets and exchanges around the globe and around the clock. Some of these interfaces already exist, but they are for institutional trading firms and come with hefty price tags.

islands and archipelagos: navigating the ECNs

M. Rogan LaBier

There are many trade execution routes available to the Level II trader, and they all work differently. It is not enough to simply know these routes exist; you must know exactly how they work to be able to trade effectively.

We'll explore the ins and outs of ECNs, the computer networks that offer trading of Nasdaq (and now, New York Stock Exchange) stocks, how they work (and don't work) depending on circumstances.

First, we will briefly explain the Nasdaq's two order execution systems, SelectNet and Small Order Execution System (SOES). Depending on trading conditions, SelectNet and SOES have their own advantages and disadvantages as trade execution systems. While the following explanations will be brief, a rudimentary understanding of these systems will help to understand the way ECNs work.

SelectNet and SOES

Unlike the NYSE, the Nasdaq does not have a trading floor where traders buy and sell stocks face to face. On the Nasdaq, trades are executed over a network of roughly half a million computers, through which market participants can post bids and offers. SelectNet and SOES are trade execution systems run by Nasdaq.

SelectNet can "broadcast" orders to a wide field of market participants or "preference" (route) orders to particular market participants. SelectNet even can be used to negotiate a better price than a market maker has advertised.

But SelectNet's biggest use is to preference orders at the market makers' shown price and size. Market participants are required to keep firm quotes in Nasdaq small-cap and large-cap stocks—they must honor the bids and offers they show, both the number of shares and the price.

Because SelectNet operates like an instant messaging system, bids or offers placed via SelectNet will not show up on the Level II quote display. A SelectNet preference order to an ECN results in an auto-execution at electronic speed, as long as another trade has not already occurred at this price with this market participant.

But a SelectNet preference to a market maker works differently from a preference order to an ECN, because, among other reasons, market makers are allowed 30 seconds to respond to a SelectNet preference order at their shown price/size. A market maker is liable only for the number of shares shown at the advertised price shown. He may trade more if he chooses, but if he declines to trade more at that price then he must change his bid or offer accordingly. He still has 30 seconds to decide. These aspects of SelectNet are especially important because the active ECNs, like Archipelago, use SelectNet.

SOES works differently. It gives smaller investors and traders immediate fills on up to 1,000 shares of Nasdaq stocks subject to regulations and rules specific to the use of SOES. SOES will automatically execute against a market maker, without his choice. However, it is important to know that SOES will not transact against ECNs.

This is a basic overview of how SelectNet and SOES work. However, the Nasdaq has proposed alterations to SOES and the Level II quote montage (the so-called "SuperSoes" and "SuperMontage" changes) that will impact basic Nasdaq order handling. (For more information on this topic, see "The Nasdaq's Super Plan" in the November 2000 issue of *Active Trader* magazine.)

the execution solution

Superior trade execution is all about identifying the current trading situation and knowing which tool is appropriate for a given job.

Which trade-routing method works best? The answer comes in two parts: understanding the trading situation you are dealing with (Level II interpretation); and knowing exactly how all the execution routes work. Level II is like a map—if you know the routes well, you will know which one will get you to your destination fastest. Nowhere is this more important than if you are a direct-access trader. We will examine the ins and outs of ECNs—what they are, how they work, and how they differ from the other available trade execution routes.

electronic communications networks

ECNs have been around since the 1969, when Instinet, the granddaddy of the modern ECN, began offering institutions a venue to trade stocks in what has become known as the "third market." Until recently, though, this market was largely unavailable to individual traders. Since 1997, however, there has been a proliferation of ECNs that provide access to individual traders.

ECNs essentially function as separate exchanges. However, ECNs also allow individuals and institutions to enter bids and offers directly in the Nasdaq, alongside (and in direct competition with) the major institutions. This ability has radically changed the Nasdaq market: While there were practically no ECNs four years ago, today it is not unusual to see 30 percent of Nasdaq's total daily volume traded through ECNs. This technology also has affected the NYSE, which recently voted to repeal Rule 390 and allow Big Board stocks to trade on ECNs.

ECNs are powerful tools for short-term traders, and their usefulness extends far beyond simply displaying quotes on the Nasdaq Level II screen. Active ECNs, such as Archipelago, NexTrade, and Attain, use sophisticated decision-making algorithms and SelectNet to "work" orders—finding, in real time, the best place to execute a trade, as well as get the best price possible. Plus, individual traders are gaining access to new types of orders that previously were reserved for major institutions with high-priced, sophisticated software.

The best software packages today offer direct access to the various ECNs, but they still let the user decide which route to use for the same reason Formula One race cars come with a stick shift, not automatic transmission: There is no substitute for the speed of the human mind and its ability to synthesize information. Until there is, it is imperative to learn the basics of ECN routes to maximize your profits and minimize your losses. We will focus our discussion on the two most popular (by volume) ECNs for individual traders, Island and Archipelago.

Island

The Island ECN (ISLD) has revolutionized the financial markets. A sizable chunk of the total Nasdaq share volume each day is traded on ISLD.

Island allows individuals and institutions to place limit orders; it does not accept market orders. If there is a matching order, it will execute the trade. If not, the order will post to the ISLD order book, and if the order is the "best" bid or offer currently available, it will also post to the Level II quote display screen. There, anyone may execute against that order, either via SelectNet and the active ECNs that use SelectNet (see "Archipelago"), or directly through ISLD if they have access. The limit order book for ISLD is available for viewing in real-time at www.island.com.

When you post an order to the Level II screen through ISLD, you wait for someone to come along and trade with you. It's just like posting a classified ad in the newspaper. Keep in mind, though, you never know how long this will take; the stock may never trade at your price. However, there is so much liquidity in the ISLD book, it has become a favorite among active traders. Your order, while it may not be seen in the Nasdaq Level II quote display, will often be freely visible in the

ISLD book. This can be very useful in fast market conditions, and a great many traders have come to rely on the ISLD as a major source of liquidity.

However, because of Nasdaq's "minimum size" requirement, you may not see small orders reflected in the Level II quotes. A trade must be at least 100 shares to appear on the Level II quote display. For example, if you have an odd lot, say 23 shares, your order will post to the ISLD limit order book, but not to Level II. As a result, your order may take even longer to execute, since only those who have access to the ISLD book will see it.

If ISLD does happen to be on the bid or offer and you wish to hit the bid or take the offer, ISLD can be fast as white lightning: Your order may fill before your finger even leaves the keypad. Remember, going through the ISLD computer directly can be much faster than using SelectNet to link to Island.

ISLD also offers interesting order capabilities such as subscriber orders and hidden orders (although many brokerages do not accept them). Subscriber orders show up in the ISLD book, but not on the Nasdaq Level II quote display. Hidden orders take this one step further: They do not show up at all. When somebody tries to execute against the ISLD bid or offer they see they may receive price improvement from the hidden order. For example, you might see an ISLD bid of $43\frac{1}{16}$, and enter an order on ISLD to sell at $43\frac{1}{16}$. But you may actually sell the stock at $43\frac{3}{16}$, most likely because of a "hidden" bid at $43\frac{3}{16}$. This doesn't happen too frequently, but it can occur.

The users of these features like the fact that the hidden or subscriber-only orders will not affect the appearance of supply and demand in the Level II quote display. However, keep in mind that these orders are only in the ISLD order book, and therefore cannot be seen or traded against by any participants who do not have access to ISLD. The net effect is that these orders rely on the liquidity in ISLD alone.

Because the small size of most orders would not have a massive effect on the supply-demand balance in the Level II quote display anyway, the hidden feature is not for everyone. However, some people swear by subscriber and hidden orders. One advantage, though, of subscriber and hidden orders is that they will not "lock" or "cross" the market like regular ISLD orders can, because they stay in ISLD and are not entered into the Nasdaq market.

Locking the market occurs when you try to enter a bid that would equal the offer price in the Nasdaq Level II screen. A crossed market occurs when you try to enter an offer lower than the current bid or a bid higher than the current offer. Both locked and crossed markets violate NASD fair practice rules. Usually, an order canceled because it would lock or cross markets is the result of someone trying to use ISLD to hit a non-ISLD bid or take a non-ISLD offer. (Remember, you cannot do that with ISLD—it is passive.) In both cases, Nasdaq would automatically refuse the order.

If you wish to deal only with ISLD, you can match with other orders in the ISLD book. For example, if there is an offer in the ISLD book for 100 shares of a stock at 10 and another offer for 1,000 shares at 10⅛, you could, by placing an ISLD order to buy 1,000 shares at 10⅛, take both the 100 shares at 10 and 900 of the shares at 10⅛.

It is important to contact your broker to see what level of connectivity and functionality it offers. Some offer subscriber and hidden orders, while many do not. Some offer direct links to ISLD, while others do not. Also, some may offer real-time display of the ISLD order book as an integrated part of the software, and some may offer full access to ISLD in the after-hours market. ISLD is open until 8 P.M. EST and has tremendous after-hours liquidity relative to the other ECNs.

active ECNs

The active ECNs all have something in common: They will dynamically work an order, attempting to get better prices. To do this, they use sophisticated algorithms to "read" the inside market and then choose the best way to route a trade. They will take market and limit orders, and several of them offer interesting order-entry capabilities previously unavailable to individuals. The best-known active ECNs are Archipelago, NexTrade, and Attain. Archipelago is easily the largest active ECN in terms of volume.

Archipelago

Archipelago (ARCA) offers the next generation of functionality for ECNs. For limit orders, it functions like ISLD: It checks its order book for a match. If there is no match and the order is the best in the book, it will post the order to the Level II screen.

However, that is where the similarity ends. If the order is priced more favorably than the current inside market, ARCA starts its active operations. Using an algorithm, it checks for who is on the inside bid or offer, dynamically deciding the quickest way to route the order. If ECNs are present, it executes against the ECNs using either direct connections to the other ECNs or SelectNet.

A SelectNet link to an ECN is an auto-execution at electronic speed. When there are several ECNs at the inside quote and ARCA goes out to all of them, large orders can get filled—fast. This is one of ARCA's best features. Use of SelectNet allows ARCA not to cross the market and, additionally, to accept market orders, in which case it simply keeps trying to get the best price until it executes.

Also, if you have the appropriate software package (one such program is made by Townsend Analytics) you can place several other kinds of orders on ARCA, including stop orders on Nasdaq stocks and "reserve" orders that allow you to show one size in the Level II screen and actually transact a different reserve size. (For example, you can show 100 shares and actually trade 10,000.) In short, ARCA accepts limit and market orders, and uses SelectNet to execute. Say, for example, 200 shares of a stock are offered at 25 and 100 more are offered at 25⅛. If you placed an order to buy 300 shares at 25⅛, ARCA will "work" the order for you, going out to each participant and taking stock. It will do this all the way up to your price target, or until your total order is filled.

It tries to get the cheaper stock first and, failing that, will try the next best price, all the way up to your limit, executing against multiple market makers and ECNs until you are filled. And if you have access to the ARCA order book (available at www.tradearca.com) you can see all the individual ARCA orders (chippies) bidding or offering a stock. ARCA's use of SelectNet opens up interesting order entry possibilities, but SelectNet is a double-edged sword. Although a SelectNet link to an ECN gives auto-execution at electronic speed, a SelectNet preference to a market maker does not. In fact, market makers are given, by regulation, 30 seconds to respond to a SelectNet preference. Imagine: A stock you are long is tanking hard; sellers are pouring into the market and there are no ECNs anywhere to be seen. You place an ARCA market sell order and wait . . . and wait.

Because of their 30-second time window, market makers can wait (and wait) while the stock market plummets. What just happened is that ARCA routed the order to a market maker, the market maker took his full 30 seconds to respond and the response was a "decline"—the market maker decided not to take the trade. When ARCA receives notice of the decline it runs through its progressions and starts the whole process over again. It preferences another market maker, who again takes the 30 full seconds he is allowed to and declines, and so on.

Every tool has a particular job it does best. There are situations for which ARCA is an ideal tool, and others for which it is not. The same goes for ISLD. Understanding the different execution routes and which ECN is best for a particular trading "job" will enable you to execute with confidence.

direct access versus online trading

Many traders believe that because they are using an online broker, they are "trading direct"—that is, participating directly in the Nasdaq or NYSE markets. They are not.

Standard online brokerage houses offer you the same execution capabilities available over the phone—a keyboard has merely replaced the telephone interface. While this is extremely convenient, your executions are no more under your control than when you say "buy" or "sell" over the phone.

At some point, a market maker or trader will execute your trade for you, and as you might expect, he must get paid. So your broker may take the other side of your order (and profit from the spread), or even route your order to a market maker for execution and receive payment for order flow.

An often overlooked aspect of the brokerage business is that broker-dealers can profit from their customers orders. For example, say a stock is bid 10 and offered at 10⅛. You want to buy the stock and enter a bid through a traditional discount online broker, receiving your fill seconds later at 10⅛. It's quite possible the broker "took the other side" of the trade, buying it at 10 and selling it to you for 10⅛. His profit (⅛—$125 on a thousand shares) is his fee for doing the trade. Was the low commission price of $10 worth it? Many traders say no and instead trade direct access, which allows them to try to get a better price for themselves.

When you trade "direct," you are able to show your bids and offers directly in the Level II quotes and effectively cut out the middleman (the market maker or trader who would have handled your order had you placed it through a standard online broker). But with this opportunity comes the responsibility of getting a better price for yourself.

the Level II screen

Mark Etzkorn

One of the primary tools of the short-term trader (especially the intraday trader) is the Level II quote screen, which provides a multitiered picture of the supply and demand in Nasdaq stocks.

The stock quote provided on the typical Web site is referred to as the "Level I" quote. It includes the current best (highest) bid and best (lowest) offer (referred to as the *inside quote*), the number of shares bid and offered on the inside quote (the *size*), and the last trade price. The volume and the price gain or loss for the day is often included as well.

Consider the following Level I quote:

Stock	Last Trade	Bid	Ask	Bid Size	Ask Size	Change	Volume
XYZ	50⅛	50	50¼	1000	5000	+1½	500,000

The stock being traded is XYZ; the last trade was at 50⅛; the highest bid is 50; the lowest offer is 50¼; there are 1000 shares being bid for and 5000 shares being offered; the stock is up 1½ points from the previous close; 500,000 shares have traded hands so far this session.

This gives you a snapshot of the current market, but it also is a very limited—and potentially misleading—piece of information. How much does it really tell you about the real supply and demand balance in the stock, and the likely direction and momentum of the stock? At first glance it might seem that selling pressure holds the upper hand because the current offer is five times the size of the current bid, and that at least a short-term down move is imminent. A trader might be tempted to short the stock (or liquidate existing long positions) under such circumstances.

However, what if you knew that there was a bid for 5000 shares at $49\frac{7}{8}$ and another bid for 10,000 shares at $49\frac{13}{16}$, and that there were only 500 shares offered at $50\frac{3}{8}$ and another 1000 offered at $50\frac{7}{16}$? This might change your opinion of the stock's prospects and make you a little less eager to sell.

This additional level of insight is precisely what the Level II quote screen provides: A look at *all* the bids and offers in a Nasdaq stock, not just the inside quote. This gives you a more complete picture of the supply and demand balance in a stock and the actions individual players—market makers, other individual traders—are taking.

bigger picture: the Level II screen

Figure 3.3 is an example of a typical Level II quote screen. The screens can vary from one software company/trading platform to another, but the same information is available across most displays.

The topmost part of the screen summarizes the action in the stock, much in the same way as the Level I display: It shows the stock (GERN), the market it trades on (Nasdaq), whether it's up or down on the day (the upward-pointing arrow, which is green) and by how much ($1\frac{3}{4}$ points), the previous closing price ($21\frac{1}{2}$), the high of the trading session ($23\frac{3}{4}$), the low of the trading session ($21\frac{9}{16}$), the most recent (last) trade ($23\frac{1}{4}$), the day's volume (135,600 shares), and the current time (2:36 P.M., EST).

But it is the lower portion of the Level II screen that is the important part (we'll discuss the middle section shortly). This is where the different bids (the left half of the screen) and offers (the right half) are displayed. Bids and offers include the following information: Which market maker firm or ECN is on the bid or offer (designated by their Market Maker ID—the "Maker" column in this example), the price, the size (number of shares), and the time the bid or offer was last updated. The bid at the top of the left side of the Level II screen is the best (highest) bid, while the offer at the top of the right side of the screen is the best (lowest) offer—the inside quote. Lower-priced bids are listed in descending order below the high bid while higher-priced offers are listed in ascending order below the low offer.

FIGURE 3.3   LEVEL II SCREEN

Symbol:	GERN	▼	⇧	Prev	21 1/2	Hi	23 3/4	Low	21 9/16
Market:	NASDQ		+1 3/4	Last	23 1/4	Vol	135600	Time	14:36:42

Price	De...	Size	Spread	
23 1/4 * 23 3/8	1 * 2	25 * 2	1/8	
23 1/8 * 23 7/16	3 * 1	12 * 10	5/16	
23 1/16 * 23 1/2	1 * 1	1 * 20	7/16	
23 * 23 3/4	2 * 2	2 * 6	3/4	
22 15/16 * 23 7/8	3 * 1	6 * 1	15/16	
22 5/8 * 24	1 * 4	10 * 8	1 3/8	
22 9/16 * 24 1/4	1 * 2	1 * 2	1 11/16	
22 1/2 * 24 3/8	1 * 1	1 * 2	1 7/8	
21 3/4 * 24 1/2	1 * 1	1 * 1	2 3/4	

Maker	Bid	Size	Time		Maker	Ask	Size	Time
NDBC	23 1/4	25	14:37:53		NDBC	23 3/8	1	14:36:44
REDI	23 1/8	10	14:36:41		REDI	23 3/8	1	14:15:25
ARCA	23 1/8	1	14:15:26		ISLD	23 7/16	10	14:13:51
NITE	23 1/8	1	13:07:28		NITE	23 1/2	20	13:20:38
PERT	23 1/16	1	12:23:58		PWJC	23 3/4	5	11:42:47
FAHN	23	1	12:43:30		JPMS	23 3/4	1	10:41:52
MHMY	23	1	12:24:11		FLTT	23 7/8	1	11:47:46
MWSE	22 15/16	4	12:37:27		MASH	24	4	13:26:23
PWJC	22 15/16	1	13:06:15		PERT	24	2	12:19:17
MASH	22 15/16	1	12:10:45		MWSE	24	1	14:19:43
ISLD	22 5/8	10	14:39:04		MHMY	24	1	12:24:09
FLTT	22 9/16	1	14:10:32		FAHN	24 1/4	1	12:43:30
GRUN	22 1/2	1	12:02:27		GRUN	24 1/4	1	11:18:45
JPMS	21 3/4	1	10:41:52		HRZG	24 3/8	2	11:40:43
LTCO	21 9/16	1	09:50:32		MPAC	24 1/2	1	10/30-09:11
AMPM	21 1/2	1	13:59:34		SLKC	24 9/16	1	10/27-15:17
HRZG	21 5/16	2	11:52:51		INCA	24 5/8	2	13:02:02
INCA	21	10	14:32:33		LTCO	24 13/16	1	10:51:22
SLKC	21	2	09:30:53		SWST	24 7/8	1	10/26-11:06
SWST	20	1	10/26-11:06		AMPM	25 1/2	1	13:59:34
MPAC	19 1/2	1	10/30-09:11		JBOC	33	1	10/23-09:20
JBOC	15 1/2	1	10/12-12:48		BRUT	100	1	11:59:52

Source: WindowOnWallStreet.com

One thing that is missing from Figure 3.3 is color. The different levels of bids and offers on the Level II screen are color coded to make them easily distinguishable. (The different colors can be distinguished somewhat in this example by the varying shades of gray.)

For example, all the highest bid (or bids) will be colored the same as the lowest offer (or offers). In Figure 3.3, there is one order (for 2,500 shares—volume is quoted on the screen in *round lots* of 100 shares) at the high bid price of 23¼, which in the colorized version of this screen is highlighted in yellow. Similarly, there are two orders (each for 100 shares) at the low offer price of 23⅜, both also highlighted in yellow. Below the high bid are three bids at 23⅛, all of which are highlighted in green to indicate they comprise the next level of bids in this stock. On the offer side, there is one order for 23⁷⁄₁₆, which also is colored green to identify it as the next best offer level. The screen progresses on each side from price level to price level, from color to color, showing the full range of buy and sell orders in this stock.

In this example, it appears there is more *immediate* buying pressure than selling pressure. Market makers and ECNs are bidding for a total of 3,700 shares at the two highest bid levels, while they are only offering a total of 1,100 shares at the two lowest offer levels. But as will be discussed in the next section, you cannot always take the bids and offers on the Level II screen at face value.

The middle section summarizes (on the left) the different levels of bids and offers in the market, matching the highest bid with the lowest offer, then the next highest bid with the next lowest offer, and so on; on the right is a histogram (which itself is divided in two—offers on the left, bids on the right) that summarizes the depth of the bids and offers at the different color-coded price levels. The longer a particular histogram line, the more shares bid or offered at that level. This histogram also shows there are more shares being bid at the highest price levels than shares being offered at the lowest price levels.

There is also a *Level III* screen, which is the same as the Level II screen except that it is only available to registered Nasdaq market makers and allows them to update the bids and offers on the screen.

making sense of Level II

However, the information on the Level II screen is not as straightforward as it seems. Level II is not a magical tool that unlocks the mysteries of the market. Every trader has access to the same information now—there is no inherent edge. Plus, the unwary can be easily fooled by what they see on Level II.

For example, a market maker with a great deal of stock to buy may post a series of large offers in an effort to scare the market down so he can buy the stock at a lower price. It takes a great deal of time to get a feel for the intricacies of how prices shift and what different bids and offers mean at a given time. A more detailed discussion of trading with the Nasdaq Level II screen is on page 56 (also see Chapter 7).

time and sales

While it is not part of the Level II display per se, the *time and sales* screen is an integral window in most trading screens and platforms. Unlike the Level II screen, which shows open bids and offers, the time and sales screen shows the actual trades that take place at different price levels. Figure 3.4 shows a time and sales screen for Oracle (ORCL).

FIGURE 3.4 TIME AND SALES

WindowOnWallStreet.com Time & ...

ORCL ⬆ 12/28/00

Time	Price	Volume	Change
16:01:04	31 1/16	900	+3/8
16:00:59	31 1/16	800	+3/8
16:00:56	31 1/16	700	+3/8
16:00:56	31 1/16	700	+3/8
16:00:54	31	54400	+5/16
16:00:43	31	100	+5/16
16:00:42	31 1/16	1000	+3/8
16:00:41	31	1000	+5/16
16:00:41	31 1/16	100	+3/8
16:00:41	31	1000	+5/16
16:00:37	31 1/16	800	+3/8
16:00:37	31 1/16	100	+3/8
16:00:37	31 1/16	4700	+3/8
16:00:35	31	6500	+5/16
16:00:35	31	100	+5/16
16:00:35	31 1/16	100	+3/8
16:00:34	31 1/32	900	+11/32
16:00:33	31	2100	+5/16
16:00:32	31	1000	+5/16
16:00:32	31 1/16	100	+3/8
16:00:32	31 1/16	100	+3/8
16:00:31	31 1/16	200	+3/8
16:00:30	31 1/16	600	+3/8
16:00:30	31	1800	+5/16
16:00:30	31	5100	+5/16

The information provided on this time and sales screen is (from left to right): the time of the trade; the price of the trade; the number of shares traded (volume), and the price change on the day (up or down) the trade represents. For example, in the first line, 900 shares traded at 31 1/16, a price that was up 3/8 from the previous close. Above the list of trades, the window displays the stock ticker, whether the most recent trade is up or down (the up arrow) and the date. Like the Level II screen, software programs generally allow you to modify the display to your liking, but the basic information remains the same.

Time and sales is useful because it is the actual record of trading activity. It can give you a better idea of who is doing what on the Level II screen, because you can see where trades are actually taking place as opposed to whatever manipulation might be evidenced in the shifting bids and offers.

Level II quotes: decoding supply and demand

Gibbons Burke

The Nasdaq Level II quote display, which displays the bids and offers of market participants around the globe, is essentially the same system originally switched on in the early 1970s for use by the Nasdaq dealers themselves. Now this information is powering a new revolution in which markets are being made not only by retail trading desks at large brokerage and trading firms but in home offices and day-trading dens around the country. Is the Level II display useful to the active trader? You bet—as long as you realize the type of game being played and know how to avoid being the sucker at the table.

the next level

The Nasdaq provides several different types, or "levels," of price quotes:

- *Level I.* Shows the "inside quote," that is, the highest bid price and size, the lowest ask price and size, and the last trade. Exchange fee for real-time data: $1 per month.
- *Level II.* Shows all bids and asks the size of the quotes and identifies the market participant who is posting that quote. Exchange fee: $50 per month ($10 per month in some instances).
- *Level III.* Same as Level II, with some additional statistics. Adds the ability to post and change bids and offers. To use it, you must be a registered broker-dealer and have special equipment, connection and software.

the Level II screen: components

The Level II screen lists the limit orders of all market participants who want to buy or sell a Nasdaq-listed stock at a given moment in time. The display shows each participant's best bid and best offer and the amount of shares they want to buy or sell. They may have other orders in their individual order books at less favorable prices.

The Level II display is split in two, separating the buyers from the sellers. The most common layout has the buy orders on the left-hand side and the sell orders on the right, as shown in Figure 3.4. The bids and offers are color coded so the best four price levels are easy to distinguish. Although the different colors are not visible in this black-and-white representation of the screen, the best prices are colored yellow, the second-best prices are green, the next-best are aqua and the fourth-best are red. Most vendors use a similar color-coding scheme—it has emerged as a standard convention. For a more detailed discussion of the appearance of the Level II screen, see the "The Level II Screen" section earlier in this chapter.

The Level II display helps you see the dynamics of supply and demand in action. Looking at Figure 3.5, the market shows more inventory or demand on the bid (buy) side than on the ask (sell) side. You can also see how the bidders tend to accumulate near the whole number 125. There is a virtual "wall" of support at this price: Many market makers bidding on many thousands of shares. One could interpret this as perhaps an indication that the short-term path of least resistance would be to the upside. Now that we've reviewed the data that makes up the Level II screen, let's look at the market participants who are supplying it.

FIGURE 3.5 LEVEL II SCREEN: YAHOO (YHOO)

The standard Level II screen is divided between bids (left) and offers (right) with color coding to highlight the four best bid and offer levels.

II   Yahoo! Inc. {Level II}

MMID	Bid	Size	Time	MMID	Ask	Size	Time
INCA	125 1/2-	1,000+	13:49:41	INCA	125 7/8-	1,800+	13:49:41
ISLD	125 1/2	800-	13:49:41	ISLD	125 7/8-	300-	13:49:39
REDI	125 1/2+	500	13:49:34	BTRD	126	1,300+	13:49:28
NITE	125 1/2+	300-	13:49:40	SWST	126-	100	13:49:20
BTRD	125 7/16	400-	13:49:38	SLKC	126	100-	13:48:36
SWST	125 1/8-	100	13:48:59	NITE	126 1/4+	500	13:48:04
PERT	125 1/16+	100	13:49:27	MONT	126 1/4+	100	13:47:44
DEAN	125 1/16+	100-	13:43:09	FBCO	126 5/8	100	13:42:26
SBSH	125	8,100	13:40:31	REDI	127+	2,500+	13:49:23
PRUS	125	7,600+	13:45:50	MASH	127	800+	13:47:55
BRUT	125-	6,800+	13:49:36	LEHM	127-	100	13:45:24
MADF	125-	4,100+	13:49:21	MADF	127 1/8+	100	13:49:21
HRZG	125	3,500+	13:49:22	SBSH	127 3/8	1,000	13:40:27
ARCA	125-	2,200+	13:49:27	FLTT	127 1/2+	100	13:47:00
DLJP	125+	500+	13:45:28	MWSE	127 7/8+	100	13:49:41
FLTT	125+	300+	13:49:18	HRZG	128	1,000	13:43:02
SHWD	125-	200+	13:49:18	SHWD	128-	200+	13:45:09
SHWD	125-	200+	13:46:22	BRUT	129 1/2+	1,200+	13:49:26
MASH	125+	100	13:49:13	COWN	130-	100	13:47:56
COWN	125+	100	13:47:57	SNDV	130 3/16-	100	13:45:23
LEHM	125+	100	13:46:59	TWPT	130 5/8+	100	13:45:42
BEST	125	100-	13:45:22	ATTN	130 15/16	400	13:25:03
SLKC	124 1/16-	100	13:48:32	DLJP	130 15/16	100	13:22:51
MLCO	124	1,000	13:36:50	MLCO	131	500	13:25:37
DBKS	124-	100	13:45:23	FCAP	131	100	13:38:45
MSCO	124-	100	13:45:22	PERT	131	100	13:37:02
PFSI	124	100	13:13:19	JPMS	131	100	13:22:03
GSCO	123 15/16-	1,000	13:48:51	PRUS	131 5/16	100	13:26:40

Source: QCharts by Quote.com

identifying the players

The Nasdaq market is made up of many different types of participants with different motivations, methods, capital and intestinal fortitude. There are four basic types of players on the Nasdaq: market makers, brokers filling customer orders, proprietary traders and Electronic Communications Networks (ECNs). Table 3.1 lists the various kinds of market participants and their functions in the Nasdaq market. Telling the players apart is an important skill required for using the Level II display effectively.

Market makers come in a few varieties, but the most important are the registered market makers who are obliged to provide a bid-ask quote at all times. They have certain rules governing how they can operate and are granted privileges in return for making the market. They watch the market all day long and know their stocks well.

Order-entry firms are present in the market to represent customer orders. These brokers come in to do their customers' business in that stock and disappear when that business is done.

Proprietary traders are participants who are trading their own or their firm's capital in the market. Individual traders and large firm

TABLE 3.1	IDENTIFYING THE LEVEL II PLAYERS	
Market Participant Type	**Function/Behavior**	**Typical Examples**
Market Makers	Registered MMs required to quote bid and ask at certain size; provide liquidity	MLCO, MADF, WARR, GSCO
Order Entry Brokers	Filling customer orders	MLCO, DLJP, DEAN, LEGG
Order Flow Market Makers	Filling customer orders on behalf of a broker; they pay brokers for order flow	NITE, SLKS, HRZG, MASH
Retail ECN	Retail customer orders for online firms	ISLD, BRUT, REDI, ARCA, STRK, MWSE
Institutional ECN	Institutional electronic market for large trade crossing and well-capitalized day traders	INCA, BTRD
Proprietary Traders	Firms trading their own capital for profit	MLCO, GSCO, JPMS, DBKS, FLTT, WARR

proprietary traders are included in this category. Proprietary traders at larger firms—who also participate as brokers, market makers and investment bankers—tend to be well-informed and well-capitalized. This gives them holding power and the ability to muscle the market in the direction they want it to go, or prevent it from going in a direction they don't. They also benefit from information generated from the firm's other activities. For example, Knight-Trimark (NITE) acts as a market maker executing trades for firms who cannot justify running a trading desk of market makers of their own. NITE pays these firms for their order flow and makes a significant portion of its revenue through proprietary trading. Some firms benefit from being able to see the retail order flow and market open imbalances.

ECNs are automatic, computer-based market participants. Each is like a mini-Nasdaq exchange within the exchange, as they have their own "book" of limit orders that are often matched with other orders on the ECN rather than on Nasdaq. (Although there are exceptions, if the best bid or offer at an ECN is not matched internally, it will appear on the Level II quote display.)

Instinet, represented under the "INCA" identifier on the Level II screen, is the oldest ECN (created in 1969), and probably the most important. It is an electronic network set up for institutional traders to do business quickly, efficiently, and anonymously. For example, when the Fidelity Magellan fund wants to accumulate a large amount of stock, they could use INCA to do this with some degree of secrecy rather than using Fidelity's own market makers. For retail traders, the largest, most liquid player is the Island ECN. Table 3.2 lists several ECNs and their Market Participant Identifiers from the Nasdaq site. The Island ECN and Archipelago offer public access (via the Internet) to their order books at no charge.

A market participant's function can overlap several of these categories, especially the major omnibus brokerage firms such as Merrill Lynch (MLCO) which engage in proprietary trading and retail and institutional brokerage, as well as market making. ECN orders can be motivated in a variety of ways as well. It is extremely important to know how the different players operate in the particular stocks you are dealing with.

You can learn the trading personalities of the various market participants by observing them over time and using common sense. The Nasdaq Trader site (www.nasdaqtrader.com) helps by providing reports of the daily and monthly history of trading volume in various stocks. The most useful of these is the Monthly Share Volume report which shows, for a given market participant, which stocks they traded and how their trading activity ranked compared to other market participants for that stock. The site lets you generate this report for an individual stock so you can see, for any given issue, who the largest players were. The report

TABLE 3.2	ECNS: THE SOUL OF THE NEW NASDAQ MACHINE	
Name	**ID**	**Web Address**
Archipelago L.L.C	ARCA	www.tradearca.com
Attain	ATTN	www.attain.com
B-Trade Services L.L.C.	BTRD	www.bloomberg.com
The BRASS Utility	BRUT	www.sungard.com
Instinet Corporation	INCA	www.instinet.com
The Island ECN	ISLD	www.isld.com
MarketXT	MKXT	www.marketxt.com
NexTrade	NTRD	www.nextrade1.com
Spear, Leeds & Kellogg	REDI	www.redi.com
Strike Technologies	STRK	www.strk.com

is issued monthly; data is available for the previous month, two months prior, and year-to-date totals in the standard reports, but historical monthly data is available for the previous 12 months. The Web address is www.nasdaqtrader.com/static/tdhome.stm. Less detailed daily reports are available as well.

interpreting the Level II display

Making sense of the Level II display is like peeling back the layers of an onion: There are many layers and sometimes they will make you cry. The most basic use of the Level II display is to determine the current supply and demand picture for a given stock—the whole onion. You can simply glance at the volume graph or eyeball the market makers and see whether there is more stock for sale than being bid on.

This total is a good raw measure of where the path of least resistance is for the price of the stock. If there is more supply than demand (more shares offered than bid), price is more likely to go down. When price goes down, the discount will attract buyers, and supply and demand will balance out. Your job as a trader using this tool is to assess those moments when supply and demand are out of balance and likely to affect price—to anticipate and profit from those price movements. The whole onion is also useful for longer term investors who have developed a value-based opinion of their stock and are trying to time their entry into the stock.

analyzing the inside market

After looking at the big picture (all the bids and asks up and down the scale), the next thing to focus on is the inside market—the best bid and the best ask, and the number of market makers and shares bid to purchase or offered for sale. This is where the action is and where trades are taking place—where the immediate supply-and-demand bumps and grinds take place.

The price difference (spread) between the best bid and ask is important—this is the most rudimentary measure of the transaction cost of a stock. It shows how much it would cost you to buy a stock (at the higher offer price) and turn around and sell it immediately (at the lower bid price). This is often a good indication of the liquidity of the stock. When a stock is *overlapped*—meaning the bid price is equal to or greater than the best ask price—a great deal of liquidity or trading activity often ensues. Overlapped markets don't usually last for more than a minute at most—it's the equivalent of a clearance sale and usually has the same effect on the available inventory. Mark Friedfertig and George West, in their book *The Electronic Day Trader,* point out that such overlaps are not mistakes, but rather situations in which a market maker either wants to bully a stock higher to be able to sell at a higher price or is simply alerting potential sellers that he has a massive buy order. They also caution that overlaps usually trigger volatile market reactions.

analyzing the players

The next thing to consider is the quality of the bids and offers, or who is on the inside market. Here is where it is helpful to know the players involved and how they operate. It's one thing for INCA to come in with an order for 30,000 shares, but quite another if it is GSCO (Goldman Sachs) or even ISLD.

Some quotes are more trustworthy than others. Certain market makers may not show the entire amount of the stock they have at a particular level. For example, they may show 100 shares offered at a certain price but actually have 5,000 shares to sell there. They don't want to tip their hand. But they will "park" at a level, and the price effectively dead-ends at that price until they have run out of stock to sell. There is no way to know how deep their pocket goes at that price. Sometimes a market maker will "flash" a large order and quickly withdraw it, hoping to shake out weak holders. Also, market makers have a few ways to back away from their quotes if someone actually bites—which makes their quotes a form of false advertising. You can only learn which market makers represent realistically tradable quotes under different circumstances by trial and error; the education can be costly.

The most honest quotes are those submitted by the ECNs—if a limit order shows up from the Island book, for example, it will be honored quickly if someone else hasn't hit it first. There is no time allowance, such as the rules that govern the SOES that give the market maker a limited amount of discretion if someone else gets there first. Also, the Island book tends to update a second or two faster than the Nasdaq display—it gives you a slight early-warning edge that can be critical in certain situations.

The ISLD and other ECN market makers can often be a sign of the activity of the day traders. If all the ECNs are stacked up on the inside bid it's a sign day traders think a stock is going up and, usually, this hot money causes the market to do a quick bump up. INCA is the 800-pound gorilla in these markets. Institutional players use INCA to operate anonymously and often in large size. In a market where the average quote size is 100, 500, or maybe 1,500 shares, it is not uncommon to see INCA step up with a 30,000-share bid. When this happens, the smaller players on the offer scatter (canceling their offers to sell) and a rapid run-up in price often follows. Sometimes a big player who wants to sell 100,000 shares will come in and anonymously bid 30K on INCA, and when the price moves up to their higher offer price they will unload (perhaps using their regular market maker ID) into the short-term rally.

The next layer of the onion to peel away is to look beyond the inside market and find out where the inventory is located away from the bid-ask spread. You can usually see congregations of orders near whole price numbers or technical breakout points such as the high and low of the day so far, yesterday's close or prices at which important news hit earlier in the day. Again, the size of the orders is important, but nearly as important is who is showing a quote.

So far, all the layers of the onion have reflected a static and unchanging current situation. The next step is to watch the change in these various factors over time. There is a great deal of invisible supply and demand in the market; the movement of the inside bid and ask relative to other orders and the changes in the size of orders is key to detecting the subtle shifts in supply and demand that can affect subsequent price movement.

It is useful to think of the action in the Nasdaq system as a big game of high-stakes stud poker, where each market maker sitting around the table has two cards facing up—his bid and offer quotes. The trouble is, there is no way to know how many cards are in the deck, or how many each participant holds—all you see are the two cards up. You have to infer the rest from the type of player they are and how they have historically operated in the market. This can give you the edge you need to determine how to play the game profitably. Remember, these market participants are well-funded professional traders whose sole purpose in life is to make money by trading. The head fakes and sleight of hand that take place can be costly to smaller traders.

It is important to realize that the Level II display, while providing a much more complete picture of the depth of the market than Level I, still does not tell the entire story of the market. In this game of stud poker where the players are showing only two of their cards, there is an unknown quantity of supply and demand in the cards they are not showing. You can see the entire order book for the Island ECN as a good example. Consider that each market maker in turn has their own order book and you can never know what they contain until price movement forces them to reveal their customer's orders. Likewise, these quotes can disappear as price moves away from that level. The only way to know about this is to watch closely, remember and think—something you can't do if you are chasing every "pump-and-dump" stock that comes along.

who should use Level II?

The Level II display is a requirement for most active traders, whether they are day traders or swing traders. One of the most important reasons hasn't been mentioned yet—last trade reports coming out of the Nasdaq can be significantly delayed. The exchange feed system gives priority to quotes (bids and offers) over trade reports.

When things get busy, the Level II display is the true state of where the market is right now. Charts built from the history of trades can be very deceptive and are often several points away from the true level of the market. This delay is especially evident in busy stocks at the open, but can occur any time the market is extremely busy. The Level II display can even be useful to longer term value investors who want to maximize their returns by getting better executions on trades. Mostly, though, the Level II display illuminates shorter term plays and momentary advantages by outlining the ever-changing supply and demand picture. It can be hypnotic and fascinating to watch and to try to understand.

The Level II display is most suited to traders who are content to trade only a small handful of stocks all the time because it takes an investment in time—and sometimes capital—to learn who the players are and how they behave. A particular market maker can behave one way in one stock and completely different in another. This is probably because a given firm will have a market maker that specializes in making the market in a small number of stocks.

If you plan to go against these players the smart thing to do is to avoid situations where their strengths come into play. Long and careful study of the Level II screen is the only way to understand the nuances of the market makers for a particular stock and to learn the rules of the game they play.

chapter 4

making markets and basic analysis

the original day traders: making markets with the *locals*

Mark Etzkorn

The visitor's gallery of the Chicago Mercantile Exchange (CME) offers a birds-eye view of trading in the world's largest and busiest stock index futures contract—the S&P 500. In this trading "pit," brokers and traders buy and sell contracts representing the shares of the benchmark Standard & Poor's stock index, which consists of 500 leading, large-cap U.S. companies.

It is a bewildering sight for the first-time visitor: On a busy day, approximately 500 traders, brokers, and clerks, decked out in brightly colored (and even better, eye-grabbingly ugly) trading jackets, threadbare ties, khaki pants, and Rockport walking shoes or gym shoes, stand elbow-to-elbow in the 1,270 square-foot octagon, waving their arms, wiggling their fingers, jumping, screaming at the top of their lungs, scribbling frantically on small cards and notepads, and when necessary, shoving and pushing to get noticed or make a trade. To the uninitiated, it looks like slightly choreographed chaos, and the first reaction, after the initial bemusement, is something along the lines of, "How does *anyone* know what's going on down there?"

The scene is actually more tame that it was in the late 1980s before a metal railing was installed along the uppermost rim of the trading pit (the *top step*). This was where all the executing brokers stood, and one of the unofficial responsibilities of a brokerage assistant (*arbitrage clerk*) was—when the action heated up and the pushing and shoving became more emphatic—to prevent his or her broker from being thrown bodily out of the pit by other traders.

But while the view from the gallery may have changed slightly, the game remains pretty much the same as it has been for roughly 150 years in the Chicago futures pits, as most traders and brokers will proudly tell you. And while, more than ever, open-outcry trading floors like the CME and New York Stock Exchange are feeling the competitive heat from the electronic marketplace (the all-electronic Eurex futures exchange recently surpassed the perennially dominant CME and Chicago Board of Trade as the world's busiest futures exchange), the game being played in the S&P 500 pit is educational for anyone interested in any kind of short-term trading—including day trading—be it futures or stocks. This is especially true because of the important role the S&P futures play as an indicator of near-term price movement for many short-term traders. It is an up-close-and-personal look at how financial markets functions and bids and offers are made.

welcome to the club

The average American could be forgiven for assuming day trading is an entirely new phenomenon, the offspring of an unprecedented bull stock market boom and ultra-cheap communications technology. Popular media reinforce this perception with super-hyped (and usually superficial) coverage—25-year-old whiz kids making millions in their bedrooms, or middle-aged doctors and lawyers chucking their stethoscopes and briefcases in favor of laptops and online tickers.

But day traders and day trading are as old as organized markets themselves; the only difference is that until very recently, such traders were part of an insular, *professional* club that attracted little media attention and, for the most part, desired it even less. These were the *floor traders,* independent speculators who risked their own money in the trading floors and pits of the stock, option, and futures exchanges.

market rangers

A popular T-shirt slogan in the Chicago financial community in the late 1980s claimed "Danger is No Stranger to an S&P Ranger." The boast neatly summed up the risks of trading the volatile S&P market and the yee-ha, Wild-West spirit of those who chose to do so for a living. Even those who have prospered in the pit (and at that time, the Merc floor boasted more millionaires per square foot than anywhere else in the country) will tell you it's a "tough way to make an easy living." Most of the traders practice a type of trading called *scalping*—darting in and out of the market, capturing a few *ticks* here and there on dozens of trades per day, in an attempt to produce a steady income. In football terms, it's the grind-it-out, three-yards-and-a-cloud-of dust approach to trading.

Most of the traders in the S&P pit have no opinion about the trend of the market on a daily basis, let alone a perspective that extends to weeks or months. They seek to take small profits on many trades, holding positions for a few seconds to a few minutes. Sound familiar?

Floor trading, such as that traditionally practiced on the CME or the New York Stock Exchange (NYSE), may indeed be headed for the dust bin of financial history in the not-too-distant future, but it still provides the clearest picture of how markets function. Whether it is conducted face-to-face or screen-to-screen, trading ultimately boils down to the same process and principles.

the playing field: getting to know the locals

Because of the close relationship between the cash stock market and the S&P 500 futures contract traded at the CME and the popularity of the S&P futures as a speculative market, the following discussion is framed in terms of that market. But, almost without exception, the principles outlined here are applicable to other markets—stocks, other futures, currencies, or bonds. The S&Ps also provide a simplified arena in which to discuss the nature of making markets, the bid-ask spread, and the relationship between professional and retail traders.

The floor trader, or *local,* in the S&P 500 futures pit has a simple role. He or she trades personal or proprietary income for personal gain. While the economic role of the floor traders is often described in terms of providing liquidity to the market (taking opposite sides of the trades entering the pit from institutional and other public traders and investors), the locals are there to make a profit. They do so at your expense—but that's not necessarily an unjust or bad thing.

Locals have no obligation to supply bids or offers (unlike the *market makers* or *specialists* in the Nasdaq and NYSE markets; see the following section), that is, to provide a reasonable bid and offer in the market regardless of circumstances. An S&P trader can stand with his arms folded as the market nose-dives, or the trader can join in on the selling. These traders are truly independent entities who earn their spots on the floor by purchasing an exchange *seat* (membership). The S&P trader's only obligation is to honor any bids or offers he or she makes at a given time: A trader advertising a bid or offer by extending his or her arms and repeatedly calling out how much, and at what price, he or she wishes to buy or sell only has to honor that bid or offer at that moment: The minute the trader drops his or her arms and stops shouting out a bid or offer, or both, that trader is under *no* obligation to buy or sell. End of story.

the in-and-out game

What is the modus operandi of the typical S&P futures scalper? The process is quite simple, and the relevance to day traders and other short-term traders will immediately be apparent. First, the S&P trader seeks to profit on the bid-ask spread. At any given time, dozens of orders enter the S&P pit from all over the world: equity funds seeking to hedge their portfolios, large individual speculators, hedge fund managers, and program traders. These orders are sent into the pit via hand signal or written order from the trading desks that surround the pit (or routed directly to brokers via hand-held terminals). The filling, or executing, brokers who receive these orders then try to find someone to take the opposite side of their trade—either another broker or a local.

Say a filling broker working for a large firm like Merrill Lynch or Morgan Stanley has just received an order to sell 100 March S&P futures at the market, and the current spread is 1285.50 bid—1285.80 offer. (The minimum price fluctuation, or *tick,* in the S&P futures is .10.) The market has been moving sideways for a while, with a slight upside bias: Buyers are tending to nibble at successively higher offers. Trading is somewhat thin, that is, most of the trading is being done by locals. The brokers (who handle the outside customer and institutional orders) are mostly unoccupied right now.

The broker, who is obligated to fill the order at the best price available at that moment, first offers a few contracts (not all of them, because he doesn't want to let the pit know how many he has to sell) at 1285.80, just to see if any buyers are nibbling at the current offer. They're not. In fact, the locals themselves immediately start to *offer* at 1285.70, then at 1285.60—perhaps guessing this broker has a large sell order that could potentially push the market much lower. The bid then drops to 1285.40. The broker, afraid the market will continue to decline, manages to hit the 1285.40 bid, selling his contracts to several locals at that price—the same locals who just moments before were on the offer side.

Their game? Simple. They "ran in front" of the broker's sell order, helping to deflate the market (but running the risk that they might have to actually sell some contracts in the process) before turning around and getting what they *really* wanted: some long positions at a lower price. After the broker's large sell order is filled, it would be natural for the market to spring back up—prodded by locals who are now trying to goose the market higher so they can sell their long positions out at a profit.

Imagine, a minute later, that same broker receives an order (different customer, different agenda) to *buy* 100 contracts at the market. He surveys the pit and sees a few locals (some of the ones he sold to at 1285.40) offering at 1285.60. This time, he decides not to tip his hand at all and immediately buys (takes out) the offer, a total of 70 contracts at that time. But now the locals know he's a buyer, and some immediately raise their offers (and again, others try to run in front of the broker's order by bidding at successively higher prices). The broker is able to buy the remaining 30 contracts for his customer at 1285.90 and at 1286.00.

What has happened in this example? Well, consider things from a local's perspective: Over the course of 90 seconds or so, he or she may have been able to buy, for arguments' sake, five contracts at 1285.40 when the broker was selling, and then turn around and sell these contracts at 1285.60—or possibly as high as 1285.70, 1285.90, or 1286.00. In the most conservative scenario described here, the trader would have pocketed two ticks (1285.60 − 1285.40 = .20) on five contracts. Each tick move (.10) in the S&Ps is worth $25, so the net profit on the trade comes to $25 × 2 (ticks) × 5 (contracts) = $250. Not bad for 90 seconds of hand waving.

Consider an even simpler and more immediate example. Say the market is 1285.50 bid—1285.70 offer. A broker then gets an order to sell 50 at the market. He offers the contracts to the pit at 1285.60, a tick below the existing offer. Many locals drop their bids in the face of this selling pressure. One nearby local who thinks the market is likely to go up in the near future bids 1285.40 for 50 contracts. The broker, eager to fill the order before the market has a chance to drop lower, hits the local's bid. The market is now at 1285.40 bid (other locals are on the bid), 1285.60 offer, with the last trade at 1285.40. A few seconds later, a different broker gets an order to buy 75 contracts at the market. Some locals abandon their offers; others start bidding themselves. The local who bought the 50 contracts at 1285.40 immediately turns around and offers to sell 50 contracts at 1285.70, one tick above the previous lowest offer. The broker hits his offer immediately. In this case, we have a local who, in the span of a few seconds, was able to make three ticks (.30) on 50 contracts, for a profit of $3,750.

Multiply this by many trades over the course of a nearly seven-hour trading session, and it can add up. These are idealized examples, and scalpers will have many other trades they will either *scratch* (buy and sell at the same price) or lose money on. There are dozens, if not hundreds, of other traders competing for the same ticks; it is indeed a hard way to make an easy living. However, because there are hundreds of orders for tens of thousands of contracts coming in from individual traders, institutions, and hedge funds with different agendas and time frames, locals have ample opportunity to bid and offer, that is, make markets—all day. They provide liquidity—an outlet for the trades coming in from all over the world. If you want to buy, and you want to buy now, there's a good chance you'll have to do it at the offer price that the local sets. When you want to sell, the local will set the bid. They assume personal risk for the opportunity to buy at a lower price and sell at a higher price than the general public.

Notice that in the previous examples it appears that the customer orders got the short end of the stick. Well, on a very short-term basis, they may have. But this is one of the reasons off-floor, retail traders have traditionally been at a disadvantage to the professional—they have to pay the bid-ask spread. It is precisely for this reason that retail traders have been better off trading on a longer term basis that renders the bid-ask spread irrelevant. In these examples, the customer orders were executed at fair prices, given the current market. If these were longer term trades, they could be profitable for the customer. So it is, in fact, possible for the professionals to make money in the short term on the spread and for the customers to make money in the long term on the direction of the market. This is the symbiotic relationship that has traditionally been at the heart of trading.

the "market-making" edge

By consistently presenting a lower bid when the public is selling, and a higher offer when the public is buying, the local profits off the bid-ask spread, which is conversely one of the traditional costs of doing business for the nonprofessional trader. They are able to make an unlimited number of trades because their costs are so low: They have no brokerages fees, since they execute their trades themselves; all they have to pay are the minimal exchange and clearing fees.

The other built-in advantages the locals have is knowledge and time. They have direct and immediate access to the order flow coming into the market: They know what the current bid and offer are; they know which firms are working which orders—they can *see* the real market, as much as anyone can. They can act as quickly as their reflexes allow, getting in and out of trades at the speed they can yell "Buy!" or "Sell!"

a special note on stop orders

The locals' knowledge also translates into another edge: The ability to hunt out public stop orders. Floor traders know that stop orders are likely to rest around whole numbers (1285.00, 1286.00, etc.), as well as at obvious technical levels (above or below established trading ranges, or above or below intraday highs or lows). Say the market has repeatedly rallied during the morning to 1280.50 and then retreated. Floor traders might assume that short-side traders have placed their stops just above this level. Because of their low transaction costs, they can engage in search-and-destroy missions, probing this level with small buy orders to try to trigger the resting stops. Because these stop orders will become market orders when their price level is hit, a short but forceful rally may occur as brokers compete to get their buy stop orders filled. Who is likely to take the opposite side of these orders? That's right, the same locals who bid up the market to trigger the stops in the first place. They sell, getting out of whatever long positions they may have established on the way up, and possibly keeping some open short positions in anticipation of a move back down after the buying pressure subsides.

However, it should be noted that locals have no guarantee that they will find stops when they go hunting for them or that the market will follow through enough to make the gambit worthwhile. It is a calculated risk on the part of the locals—with the risk being limited by their low transaction costs and their ability to get out of positions quickly.

To summarize, the S&P pit trader's edge lies in:

- *Opportunity.* They can establish, and profit from, the bid-ask spread.
- *Immediacy.* They're the first to see what's happening and they can act without delay.
- *Low costs.* They have minimal commissions and fees.
- *Knowledge.* They can see order flow and market players—who's doing what (e.g., a large trading house is working a large order, etc.).

To put this in perspective, let's see how these advantages compare to professional and retail stock traders.

specialists and market makers

In the stock market, the parallels to the S&P locals are the NYSE specialists and the Nasdaq market makers. Specialists and market makers are professional traders who trade proprietary money for their own profit (as opposed to brokers who fill customer orders for commission dollars).

However, unlike the local traders in the S&P pit, specialists and market makers have defined roles mandated by the exchanges, which essentially requires them (although the systems on the two exchanges are different) to maintain orderly markets by providing bids when there are no other buyers present and offers when there are no other sellers present. (This discussion will not address the efficiency or reputability with which different specialists and market makers execute their responsibilities, a question debated among traders.)

One of the primary differences between specialists and market makers is that a single specialist controls all the order flow (he holds the *order book*—all trade orders must come through him) in each of the NYSE stocks, while multiple market makers can make bids and offers in the same Nasdaq stock.

The NYSE is an auction market, which means that all trades sent to the exchange are executed on the floor of the exchange via human interaction. The floor itself is set up with 17 *trading posts,* where the trades are actually executed.

The specialist serves as the *auctioneer* in this environment. All bids and asks on a particular stock are directed to the specialist, who places them in his or her computerized order book. The orders are then matched, either from the available inventory or, if necessary, from the specialist's own account. The majority of retail NYSE orders are routed to the specialist via the SuperDot system. The Designated Order Turnaround (DOT) system allows a broker to transmit a customer order directly into a specialist's order book. Without SuperDot, a broker would have to phone someone on the floor of the exchange, who would then take the order and physically walk it over to the appropriate trading post.

SuperDot makes order routing almost instantaneous. Remember, though, that SuperDot merely routes orders to the floor—the execution of the trade is still the responsibility of the specialist. Unless there are extenuating circumstances, SuperDot orders are generally executed within seconds.

The Nasdaq, on the other hand, is an electronic market. There is no trading floor, no common building where all market makers are stationed. Instead, market makers perform their duties from the confines of their companys' offices. They, too, make money by capturing the spread (Nasdaq rules require market makers to create a two-sided market and post prices on both the bid and the offer), although in 1997 the Securities and Exchange Commission found that many market makers were purposely not posting certain customer orders in an effort to keep spreads high. That led to a significant change in the order handling rules.

Like the specialist, the market maker also has an order book. However, while only the specialist has access to an NYSE stock's order book (NYSE price quotes do show the current bid and ask, as well as the size available at that level), the order books for all Nasdaq stocks are available via Level II screens. Anyone with access to Level II can see every posted bid and ask, including the size of the trade and the market maker offering that price. For that reason, many short-term traders deal primarily or exclusively with Nasdaq stocks. For more information on the Level II screen, see Chapter 3.

Nasdaq's counterparts to SuperDot are the SuperSoes and Select-Net systems. The Small Order Execution System (SOES) unlike SuperDot, is a trade execution system (as opposed to an order routing system). SelectNet is Nasdaq's order-routing system. For more information on SelectNet and SOES, see the "Islands and Archipelagos: Navigating the ECNs" on page 45.

Every NYSE stock has one—and only one—specialist, although some specialists handle more than one stock. On the Nasdaq, many stocks will have more than one market maker; the more popular stocks (Dell, Oracle, Microsoft, etc.) may have dozens. And, many market makers deal in several stocks. This goes hand-in-hand with the order books. Because the NYSE books are only viewed by one person, who handles all the executions in that stock, there is no reason for multiple market makers. However, because the Nasdaq books are open and available for viewing by all, it follows that several different parties should be able to execute trades. Thus, numerous Nasdaq stocks have multiple market makers.

Along those same lines, a specialist can halt trading in his or her stock if there is an order imbalance. This might occur when there is significant news on a stock (e.g., the company makes an earnings warning, the company announces a merger or takeover, or a high-level executive resigns) that forces all the market action to one side of the book. Since specialists are obligated to fill all orders, even if it means buying or selling from their own inventory, they are permitted to stop trading (for 15 minutes at the opening bell and longer later in the day) in an effort to catch up.

Market makers are not allowed to halt trading in a particular stock. However, Nasdaq has the ability to stop trading if there is significant market news or rumor. That, though, does *not* include news released by the company itself, such as an earnings warning. If a stock suddenly and violently declines (or, for that matter, rises), there's no mechanism in place to stop it.

In the past few years, the creation of Electronic Communications Networks (ECNs) have allowed traders to avoid market makers (and, to a lesser extent, specialists) and send trades directly into the exchange, to be executed (often instantaneously) against another ECN or market maker posting a bid or offer. Up until early 2000, it was illegal for many NYSE trades to be executed anywhere but on the floor of the exchange. However, that rule was lifted, and an increasing number of NYSE trades are being done through ECNs, bypassing the specialist.

In return for assuming their responsibilities, specialists and market makers enjoy a number of advantages over public traders, similar to many of the advantages of the S&P local. In short, specialists and market makers have a birds-eye view of the order flow in their markets and have traditionally profited in large part from being able to control the bid-ask spread. They know who's trading in what, and at what size, and they get information first. When the public has stock to sell, specialists and market makers buy it from them at a low price; when the pubic wants to buy, these professionals sell to them at a high price. A tick here, a tick there, on thousands of shares a day, day after day—it all adds up.

Consider the typical Nasdaq online trade entered through a Web-based broker as opposed to a direct-access broker. (See "The Direct Connection" page 36 for the difference): You place your order with your broker, who then routes the order to a market maker to fill it. If you're buying, the market maker may sell you the stock out of his or her own inventory, or send it to another market maker to be filled. The market maker who fills the order will profit from the bid-ask spread. (Market makers often actually pay brokers for their order flow because they can make more money on the bid-ask spread than on the *kickback* they pay the broker. This is one of the reasons online discount broker commissions are so low: Brokers don't have to make as much money directly off of the buyer because they get money from the market makers.)

But it's important to note that a market-making firm buying and selling stock for its own profit may also function as a customer-order broker. In such a case, this firm will have knowledge of the order flow coming in from the public—a definite plus when trying to make money trading.

unprecedented access—the new online trader

What is different now is that today's Internet technology, along with certain rule changes regarding how customer orders are executed, and the steady decline of commissions resulting from the introduction of discount brokerages in the 1970s has given individual traders access to some—but not all—of the advantages of the professional trader.

Instead of calling a broker on the phone, getting a quote, and placing an order, traders now have real-time price quotes, charts, news, and order-entry capability at their fingertips. And with the advent of ECNs and direct-access trading technology, retail traders can now enter their orders directly into the market and receive immediate trade executions and confirmations.

Direct-access trading technology allows traders to interact directly with other market participants, without the traditional broker/market maker middleman relationship. Traders with Nasdaq Level II quotes can see much of the same price information as the professionals and can transact directly with the market maker or ECN of their choice for a fill. As a result, individual traders have the ability to try to profit from the bid-ask spread (or decrease its importance) instead of automatically paying it. Again, the low commission costs enable traders to trade for smaller increments on shorter time frames than ever before—just like their professional counterparts. This is the fundamental change in direct online trading.

reality check

It sounds great, but does the current technology *really* put the off-floor day trader on equal footing with the professionals?

Don't believe all the hype. Individual traders have made incredible strides in recent years, but they are still not on equal footing with the big boys. The real pros still have a number of advantages over retail traders, even those individuals who can afford roughly comparable communications and computing technology.

First, professionals have better access to information. They still see order flow first, and institutional firms still get news first (despite SEC mandates passed in the last year to level the playing field in this regard). For example, a large market making firm that trades proprietary money may also fill customer orders. They know what the public is doing and can plan their own trading around it. If they receive an order to sell 500,000 shares, do you think they just might lower their own proprietary bids to get a better price?

Because they often have no (or minimal) brokerage commissions to pay, market makers and specialists operate with much lower overhead costs. Also, large institutional traders can move and sometimes control the market simply by virtue of the massive capital they have at their disposal. When a money manager has hundreds of thousands of shares of a stock to buy, he or she (and the market maker handling the order) will be able to control the market whether individual traders like it or not.

Typical retail short-term traders cannot hope to truly compete head-to-head with these professionals. But by understanding how the system really works, they can find their niche and develop realistic trading ideas and strategies that exploit the natural tendencies of the marketplace, rather than attempt to fight them. Subsequent sections of this book are designed to help traders in this endeavor.

charting the market

Teresa Lo

Price charts are your road map to the markets. You can navigate the twists and turns of price action on any stock with the different kinds of price charts at your disposal.

Not too long ago, traders plotted price charts by hand each day after the market closed, trying to understand market behavior.

Today, with abundant computing power and the widespread use of reasonably priced (or even free) charting applications over the Internet, the wonderful world of technical analysis is available to all. One thing has not changed, however: the need to understand market behavior. Price charts are the basic tools traders use to accomplish this goal.

While all charts represent the same thing—price data—there are many different types offering unique perspectives on a market. Depending on the type of information a trader needs, one style of chart may be more useful than another.

price chart basics

All price charts have one thing in common: They display the price changes of a stock, futures contract, currency, or other instrument over time.

Figure 4.1 shows a basic chart: The vertical (Y) axis shows the price level, and the horizontal (X) axis shows time. With a couple of minor exceptions, all price charts are variations on this theme. In this case, the chart is depicting an uptrend: Prices are rising as time passes.

The two most commonly used price chart types are bar and Japanese candlestick.

bar charts

The bar chart is (arguably) the most popular price chart type. Each vertical price bar represents a period of time such as one day (on a daily chart), one week (on a weekly chart), one hour (on an hourly chart), one minute (on a one-minute chart), and so on. Each bar plots four price points that occurred during the time period it reflects: the open (the first price of the trading period), high, low, and close (the final price of the trading period).

Figure 4.2 shows a price bar for a daily chart. The dash on the left side of the price bar is the open, the dash on the right side of the bar is the close. The bar's high point marks the highest price the market traded at that day; the bar's low represents the lowest price of the day. Some traders prefer to use bars with only three points, ignoring the opening price.

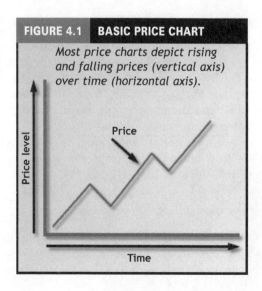

FIGURE 4.1   BASIC PRICE CHART

Most price charts depict rising and falling prices (vertical axis) over time (horizontal axis).

Price

Price level

Time

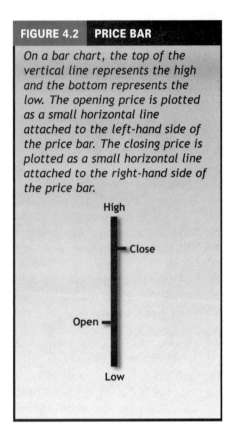

FIGURE 4.2   PRICE BAR

On a bar chart, the top of the vertical line represents the high and the bottom represents the low. The opening price is plotted as a small horizontal line attached to the left-hand side of the price bar. The closing price is plotted as a small horizontal line attached to the right-hand side of the price bar.

The bar would look exactly the same for any other time period— one-minute, weekly, monthly, and so on (see Figure 4.8, which shows 65-minute bars). For a weekly chart, the bar's high would be the highest price of the week, the low would be the lowest price of the week, the open would be the first price of the week (i.e., Monday's opening price, unless there was a holiday), and the close would be the final price of the week (Friday's close, unless there was a holiday).

Figure 4.3 shows a daily bar chart for Qualcomm (QCOM). Volume is often plotted at the bottom of a price chart, as it is in this chart (shown by the vertical lines, or histogram).

line charts

Although it is not as common as the bar chart, the simplest type of chart is the line chart (or *close-only* or *line-on-close* chart). It plots only the closing price of each bar. Figure 4.4 is a line chart of the same price action shown in Figure 4.3.

FIGURE 4.3   DAILY BAR CHART

A daily chart of QCOM, with volume. Each bar represents one day's trading activity; the volume for each session is shown by the histogram at the bottom of the chart.

Source: Omega Research

Some traders believe the closing price of the daily bar is the most significant price of the day because it's the price buyers and sellers arrived at by day's end. These traders prefer to plot only the closing price, producing a series of dots that connect to form the line chart. Incidentally, the line chart is also known as the *stopping chart,* the first type of chart used by the Japanese.

Some traders think the simplified view of the line chart gives a clearer picture of the market by filtering out the intrabar price swings shown on the bar chart, while others believe the high, low, and opening prices are essential to understanding price action.

Japanese candlestick charts

Like bar charts, Japanese candlestick charts use vertical lines to display price action for a particular period. Candlestick charts, however, add another dimension to this information by highlighting certain aspects of price movement.

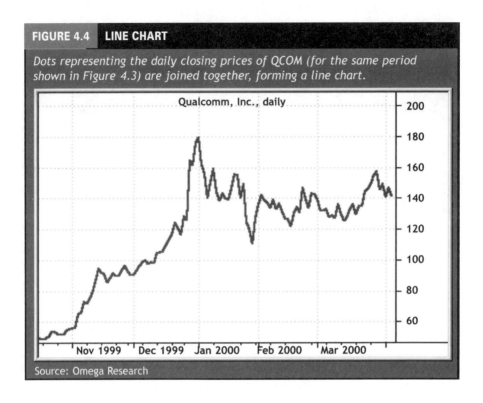

FIGURE 4.4 **LINE CHART**

Dots representing the daily closing prices of QCOM (for the same period shown in Figure 4.3) are joined together, forming a line chart.

Source: Omega Research

Figure 4.5 shows two candlestick bars. The high and low prices of a candlestick are the ends of the vertical line (just like the bar chart), but the open and close are horizontal lines that intersect the vertical line.

These two lines are joined to produce a rectangular area called the real body of the candlestick. If the close of the bar is higher than the open, the real body is hollow, usually white. If the close is lower than the open, the real body is filled, usually black. The portion of the vertical line above the real body is called the upper shadow. The portion of the vertical line below the real body is called the lower shadow.

The color of the candlestick denotes whether the intraday momentum was up (white) or down (black), and groups of candlesticks create unique visual patterns candlestick traders use to interpret price movement. Individual candlesticks are classified and named depending on the amount of space between the open and the close compared with the length of the upper and lower shadows.

Figure 4.6 shows a slightly smaller portion of the time period captured in Figures 4.3 and 4.4, to better distinguish between the bars.

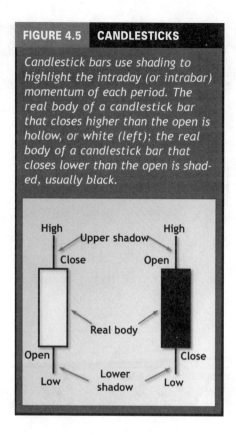

FIGURE 4.5   CANDLESTICKS

Candlestick bars use shading to highlight the intraday (or intrabar) momentum of each period. The real body of a candlestick bar that closes higher than the open is hollow, or white (left); the real body of a candlestick bar that closes lower than the open is shaded, usually black.

point-and-figure charts

The point-and-figure chart is unique in that it removes the time element of the typical price chart. Uptrends are displayed in columns of ascending Xs, and downtrends are displayed in columns of descending Os.

The key to the point-and-figure chart is the box size, which determines how much of a price movement is necessary to add another X or O to a column. If the box size is one point, you add an X to the column of Xs every time the price of a stock rises one point.

You continue to add Xs to this column until the price drops by a specified amount, called the reversal size. The reversal size is often three times the box size, meaning if the box size is one point, a down move of three points is required to start a new column of Os (and vice versa, when the market reverses to the upside).

In a change from Xs to Os, the first O of a new column is plotted next to the second-highest X of the previous column; the first X of a new column starts next to the second-lowest O of the previous column. Also,

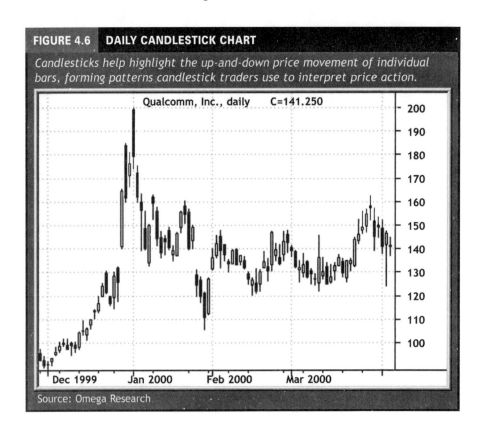

FIGURE 4.6   DAILY CANDLESTICK CHART

Candlesticks help highlight the up-and-down price movement of individual bars, forming patterns candlestick traders use to interpret price action.

Qualcomm, Inc., daily   C=141.250

Source: Omega Research

the reversal size determines the number of Xs or Os to chart when a change occurs (i.e., if the reversal size is three, each new column starts with three Xs or Os).

The box size and reversal amount you choose depend on the absolute level of the stock and the amount of detail you wish to capture. A large box size will filter out smaller price moves. That may be inappropriate for lower-priced stocks that move in relatively small increments. shorter term traders interested in smaller-scale price movement would use smaller box sizes.

Figure 4.7 shows a point-and-figure chart for QCOM covering approximately the same time period as the previous bar and candlestick charts of the stock. Both the box size and reversal amount are three points.

tip for short-term traders

Active traders typically use intraday charts to view price action on smaller time frames. U.S. stocks trade for 390 minutes during the regular

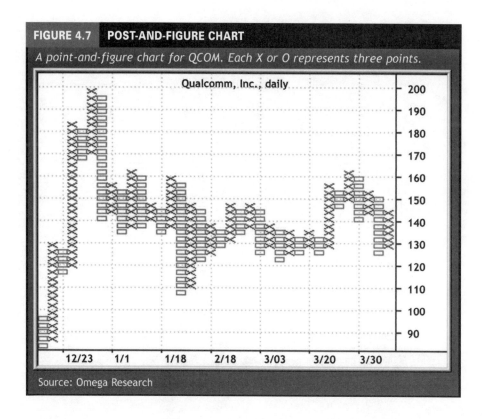

FIGURE 4.7   POST-AND-FIGURE CHART

A point-and-figure chart for QCOM. Each X or O represents three points.

Qualcomm, Inc., daily

Source: Omega Research

day session. To avoid comparing apples to oranges, traders should use time frames that evenly divide the 390-minute session. This guarantees that each intraday price bar represents the same amount of time.

For example, when you use a 60-minute chart, you see seven bars plotted for a single day, but the last bar represents only 30 minutes of data. Changing the chart to a 65-minute time frame will produce six bars, each containing 65 minutes of data, as shown in Figure 4.8.

other chart varieties

While the preceding charts are the most common types, there are several other varieties, including:

- *Swing charts,* usually credited to W.D. Gann, which highlight price swings of a certain magnitude, independent of time (like point-and-figure charts).
- *Tick charts,* which are intraday charts that plot each trade.

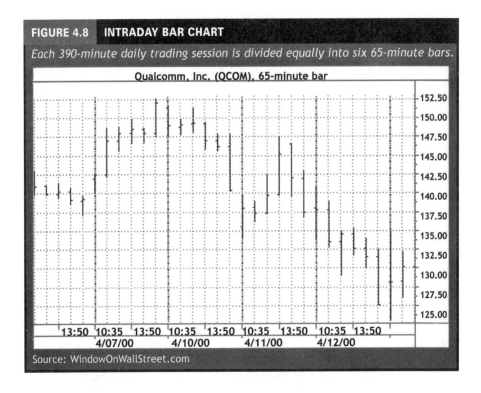

FIGURE 4.8   INTRADAY BAR CHART

Each 390-minute daily trading session is divided equally into six 65-minute bars.

Qualcomm, Inc. (QCOM), 65-minute bar

Source: WindowOnWallStreet.com

- *CBOT Market Profile charts,* originally developed in the mid-1980s by Peter Steidlmeyer, which highlight the times and prices at which the most trading is taking place.

- *Renko, Kagi,* and *three-line break charts,* which are other types of Japanese charts that do not use candlesticks.

As records of market behavior, price charts are useful tools for technical and fundamental traders alike. The different chart types provide different perspectives from which to analyze price action and make trading decisions. Understanding how charts work is the first step toward more in-depth analysis.

support and resistance

Mark Etzkorn

Price is the crucial number that spawns much of the analysis used by traders of all types. And much of that ever-proliferating price analysis is based on the key technical concepts of support and resistance. Following is the groundwork you can use to build your skill in understanding these elements of price behavior.

What do we mean by support and resistance, especially in terms of price? Well, support is a price level that acts as a floor, preventing prices from dropping below that level. Resistance, on the other hand, is a price level that acts as a ceiling, or barrier that prevents prices from rising higher.

Support and resistance levels are a natural outgrowth of the interaction of supply and demand in any market. Increased demand for a stock will cause its price to rise, a so-called uptrend. But when price has risen to a certain level, traders and investors will take profits and short sellers—those who profit from drops in stock price (as discussed in Chapter 2)—will come into the market, creating resistance to further price increases.

The stock price may retreat from and advance to this resistance level many times. Sometimes price will eventually break through the established resistance level and continue to rise to a new one; other times,

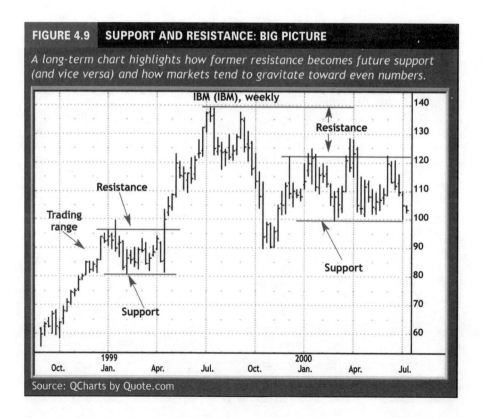

FIGURE 4.9   SUPPORT AND RESISTANCE: BIG PICTURE

A long-term chart highlights how former resistance becomes future support (and vice versa) and how markets tend to gravitate toward even numbers.

Source: QCharts by Quote.com

price will hit the resistance level and then reverse completely. The same holds true for support levels.

Figure 4.9 on page 83 shows various support and resistance levels in IBM (IBM). In early 1999, the stock formed a trading range (a period of sideways or horizontal price movement) with support (the lower boundary of the range) around 80 and resistance (the upper boundary of the range) around 96. In April, IBM's price broke out of this range and rallied to a new high in July, thereby creating a new resistance level the stock challenged (but did not surpass) in September. The stock then declined before establishing another broad trading range with resistance around 122 and support around 100.

An interesting sidenote, that IBM traded above and below 100 for extended periods, highlights the phenomenon of markets tending to consolidate near (or repeatedly test) even numbers, such as $100 and $200 for stocks and 1,000-point increments for stock indexes. The same phenomenon is apparent in Figure 4.13, which shows the price action in Amazon.com (AMZN) from January 1999 through April 2000.

The principles of support and resistance are constant across all time frames. Figure 4.9 is a weekly chart and Figure 4.10 is an hourly

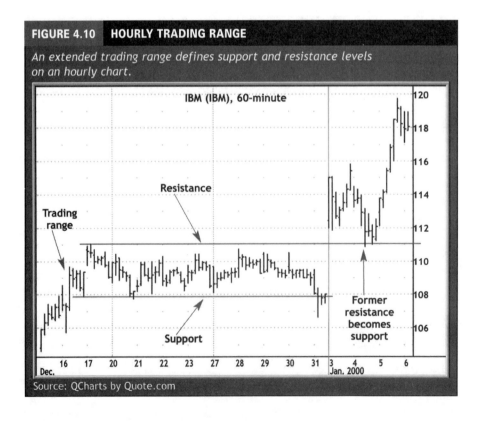

FIGURE 4.10   HOURLY TRADING RANGE

An extended trading range defines support and resistance levels on an hourly chart.

Source: QCharts by Quote.com

chart of IBM. Both highlight extended trading ranges. In each case, when the stock broke through the resistance level of the range, a strong up move ensued. Figure 4.11 shows resistance and support levels appearing on a five-minute chart of the Nasdaq 100 tracking stock (QQQ).

Support and resistance can be used to describe dynamic or diagonal price levels as well, but, using Figures 4.9 through 4.11, we will discuss them in terms of the kinds of horizontal price levels seen in those examples.

key points

Support and resistance should be thought of as general price levels rather than precise prices. If a stock hits a low of 52⅛, rallies slightly, then declines again to 52⅛, then rallies again, a subsequent move down to 52 does not violate the "support level" of 52⅛. In this case, the fact that the stock retraced once to the exact price level it had established before is more of a coincidence than anything else.

As a result, it's necessary to wait for price to break through a support or resistance level by a significant amount, or stay above or below one for a significant amount of time (or both), before that level can be

FIGURE 4.11   INTRADAY SUPPORT AND RESISTANCE

Support and resistance occurs on all time frames. Here, resistance and support levels form on a five-minute chart.

Source: QCharts by Quote.com

considered violated. What constitutes a "significant" move will depend on the market's volatility or how firm the support or resistance level is (in your opinion). If a stock has twice risen a full point above a resistance level and then moved back below the level, a third move, $1\frac{1}{8}$ points above the level, is not necessarily a definitive breakout because this move is of the same magnitude as the previous moves. A new, higher, resistance level may be forming in this case.

One way to define a valid break of a resistance level (or breakout) is to look for a certain number of consecutive closes (i.e., two or three) above or below the level in question.

You can also pinpoint short-term valid breakouts by looking at a longer time frame. If the market for a stock breaks through and closes above a resistance level on a weekly chart, that level can be used as a support level for short-term (daily or intraday) trading. If the market repeatedly fails to break through such resistance, the level's importance is further reinforced.

Another important point is that former resistance levels often become future supports, and vice versa, during a move in either direction.

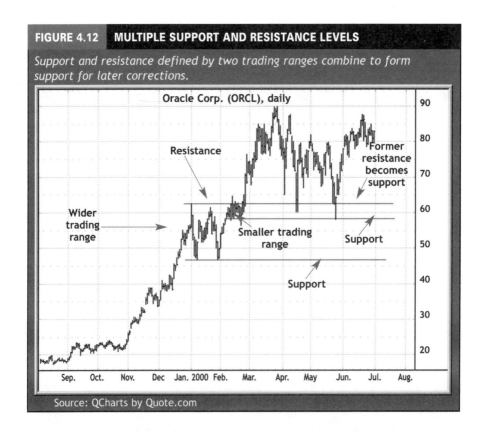

FIGURE 4.12   MULTIPLE SUPPORT AND RESISTANCE LEVELS

Support and resistance defined by two trading ranges combine to form support for later corrections.

Source: QCharts by Quote.com

In Figure 4.10, the resistance defined by the top of the trading range became the support after the stock broke out of the trading range. In Figure 4.12, the top of the wide trading range (resistance) that began in early 2000 later became support when the stock entered an extended sideways period. Also note that the lower boundary (support) of the much narrower trading range that formed in January and February 2000 acted as a more precise support level for the April and May lows.

In addition, significant past highs and lows often become future support and resistance areas. The July 1999 high in Figure 4.9 became a significant resistance level; the stock approached it, but failed to rally past it, in September, and the early 1999 trading range became a support area when the stock declined in the fall. The first two major highs in Figure 4.13 represented two levels of upside resistance in AMZN.

trading with support and resistance

Once a support level is formed, long positions can be established in anticipation of a bounce off support in the future. In Figure 4.9, long positions could have been established as IBM approached the support levels

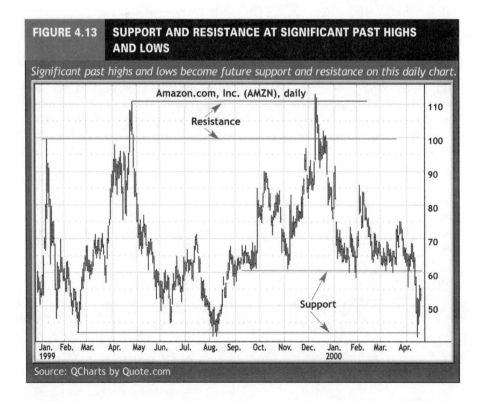

FIGURE 4.13   SUPPORT AND RESISTANCE AT SIGNIFICANT PAST HIGHS AND LOWS

Significant past highs and lows become future support and resistance on this daily chart.

Source: QCharts by Quote.com

of either trading range, in anticipation of the stock rallying off these levels. The same is true of the support level in Figure 4.10. (The same logic holds true for short trades, which are based on profiting from a drop in stock price. In Figure 4.9, such a short trade could have been initiated in September when IBM approached the resistance level defined by the previous high.)

Once established, support and resistance levels also offer clearly defined points for placing stops. When trading tests of support or resistance, stops can be placed on the opposite side of the support or resistance level. If the support or resistance level is penetrated, the reason behind the trade is no longer justified and the position should be liquidated.

Another way to trade support and resistance levels is to buy upside breakouts of resistance and downside breakdowns of support. When a stock price finally pushes above a resistance level or below a support level, it is often doing so because of a significant development that can take price much higher or lower. After such breaks, trends often develop as increasing numbers of traders jump into or out of a stock.

Further, support and resistance levels can be used to determine stop-loss levels. If price falls back below a resistance level by a significant amount after pushing above it (a false breakout), the trade is no longer valid and should be exited. Just be sure to place your stop far enough from the entry price that you don't get stopped out prematurely.

Finally, support and resistance levels can be used to set price targets. For example, if a market has twice rallied to 60 and pulled back to around 40 in the last few months, a trader with a long position might consider taking profits on all (or at least part) of his or her position when the stock approaches 60 again. (Of course, there is no guarantee the stock will not rise further; the resistance level simply offers a logical place at which to take profits.)

bottom line

Identifying support and resistance on different time frames is an essential part of technical analysis and understanding market dynamics. Chart patterns, such as flags, triangles, and pennants, are actually just specific forms of support and resistance.

A final caution: The examples used here illustrate that defining support and resistance levels is unavoidably subjective. Price will frequently climb above resistance or fall below support to one degree or another, or come close but not quite touch them. So remember to think of support and resistance as general price zones rather than specific price levels. New highs and new lows will continually redefine support and resistance as time passes, but in the meantime, you can profit from recognizing support and resistance levels.

diary of a trader

Mark Etzkorn

The life that is unexamined is not worth living—Plato

One of the most effective ways to get your trading off to a positive start is to keep a trading journal or diary—a record of all your trades. It is likely the most concrete step you can take to reach those elusive trading goals you've set for yourself. By instilling discipline and confronting trading mistakes, the practice of analyzing your trades makes you a logical and consistent trader. It's a technique traders of all skill levels and backgrounds should use.

learning from history

Traders come in several flavors: short-term, long-term, technical, fundamental. Compare two successful traders and they have virtually nothing in common other than their profitability. One may exclusively trade tech stocks on an intraday basis, while the other uses a longer term, trend-following approach on futures. One may eschew price charts in favor of the Level II and time and sales screens, while the other lives and dies by patterns on daily charts.

But there is one thing almost all successful traders agree on, regardless of their background or particular style: the benefits of maintaining a trading diary—the why, the when, the result, the lessons learned on each trade made. While today's technology makes it tempting to automatically gravitate toward high-tech analysis tools and techniques, it can be somewhat surprising—and refreshing—to learn that the discipline of maintaining a trading diary can make a greater difference to your bottom line than complex indicators or an Internet connection that is 50 Kbps faster than your last one.

Nowhere is the concept of "those who forget the past are doomed to repeat it" truer than in trading. Most traders, especially early in their careers, tend to make the same mistakes again and again. However, because of the pace and stress of trading, we may not always be able to adequately reflect on what we're doing or why; we're too caught up in the moment to put things in perspective. This is what makes a trading diary so invaluable: It gives you a look inside your logic, motivations, actions, and state of mind, and as a result, it can shed a great deal of light on what you're doing—right and wrong—in the markets.

In his book *The Hedge Fund Edge,* trader Mark Boucher points out that trading problems are more a matter of execution than strategy, and that "few traders and investors who have kept a journal religiously for more than a few years remain market losers." Trader and author Jack

Schwager sounded a similar note in his book *Schwager on Futures: Technical Analysis,* saying the practice ". . . would get the new trader into the habit of approaching speculation in a systematic and disciplined fashion," and "speaking from personal experience, this approach can be instrumental in eradicating frequently repeated mistakes."

tracking your trades

In general, maintaining a journal makes the trader more deliberate and self-aware. Some of the specific benefits include:

- Providing a record of the logic and thought processes behind trades when they are executed.
- Maintaining a record of market events, trading patterns, and other signals that can be analyzed and referenced in the future.
- Showing the stress and emotional challenges of trading and how you handle it.
- Helping ingrain good habits and break bad ones.
- Promoting trading discipline and a planned trading approach.

This kind of record-keeping makes it difficult to live in denial about your trading weaknesses and makes it easier to build on your strengths. A trade might seem like a great idea when you execute it, but when you review it later in your trading diary, away from the emotions of the moment, its flaws may become apparent. Recognizing the mistake and committing it to memory is the first step toward correcting your approach. Similarly, taking inventory of this sort can help you avoid putting on bad trades in the first place. Committing the reasons for a trade to paper before you execute them can sometimes make it clear that the position might not be such a good idea. Over time, patterns in your trading—both good and bad—will emerge.

structuring your diary

There's no single best way to organize a trading diary. Whatever structure you choose should serve the ultimate goal of providing detailed, objective trade records from which you can learn from both your mistakes and successes. In this section, we'll show an excerpt from a sample trading journal. It captures the following information for every trade:

Trade

- Date of trade (time, if applicable).
- Trade entry (market, long/short, price).

- *Type of trade.* Is this a swing trade, a longer term play, a day trade?
- *Reason for trade.* The logic and/or specific strategy used to trigger the trade.
- *Stop.* Where the initial stop-loss is placed.
- *Target.* Price target or exit plan that will be used to get out of the trade.
- *Pluses.* Positive aspects of the trade.
- *Minuses.* Potential problems with the trade.

Result

- *Update (date/time).* A miscellaneous category in which to take note of partial profits, adjusted stops, and so on.
- *Exit.* Price, date (time, if applicable).
- *Reason for exit.* Price target was hit, stop was hit, and so on.
- *Profit/loss.* Dollar (or percentage) gain or loss.
- *Lesson.* What did you learn from this trade? What went right? What went wrong?
- *Trade summary.* Trade entry, exit, and risk information.

A chart is also included to make the trade more tangible and understandable. Another element that can be useful is a brief summary of your emotions or state of mind when placing a trade (nervous, confident, etc.). This can be an invaluable aid for traders who are struggling with stress or generally having difficulty managing their feelings during trades. If you can review a trade and understand why you were feeling particularly nervous when placing it, you can avoid making the same mistake in the future (or perhaps realize your fears were unfounded). The kind of information or level of detail you include is limited only by your time and imagination. You also could compare your eventual exit to the trade's maximum profitability to determine if you're tending to get out of positions too early (or too late, after the market has turned).

Now let's take a look at the trade diary. The following excerpt provides a detailed record of the logic behind the trade, the context in which it occurred, how it turned out, and what lessons were learned.

Trade

Date: 10–11-00
Entry: Short DE @ 33¼
Type of trade: Short-term swing trade

Reason for trade: Stock formed a small rounded top after pulling back to intermediate-term moving average. Because the stock is still in a longer term downtrend, and the overall market has been weak (as it traditionally is in October) a move back to the downside seems likely.

Stop: 36¹⁄₁₆, ⅛ above the most recent swing high

Target: A back to the support level around 30³⁄₁₆ is a viable initial target. Will liquidate partial position at that level and then trail stop to lock in profits and take advantage of potential move below support.

Pluses: Trade is in direction of prevailing longer term downtrend. Broader market is also exhibiting weakness.

Minuses: Low initial reward-risk ratio on trade

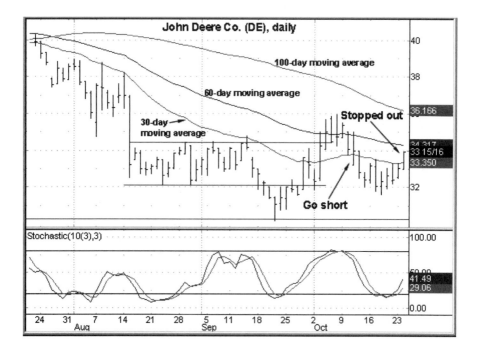

Result

Update (10-23-00, 12:15 P.M.): Eight days after the trade, the market has turned back to the upside after initially following through to the downside (but failing to reach the initial profit target). Because of overall market strength (and the likelihood of at least a temporary bounce given the stock's oversold stochastic), and the lengthening time spent in the trade, the stop is lowered to 33¾, ³⁄₁₆ above the highest high of the previous four days.

Exit: 33¾, 10-24-00

Reason for exit: Stop-loss was hit

Profit/loss: −½ point

Lesson: Given the market's historical tendency to sell off in October and the prevailing downtrend in the stock, the short trade was well-conceived in principle. However, while the initial profit target was logical, it only offered return equal to the initial risk—not the hallmark of a good trade. This alone could have disqualified the trade.

A debate could arise over trade management: While one could argue it was good to adhere strictly to the game plan (not taking profits too early), one could also argue that a reassessment of overall market conditions (i.e., a strengthening broad market) would have led to a decision to get out of the trade with an approximately one-point profit four to five days after entry—the anticipated time horizon of this kind of trade. The market was actually finding support in the area of the former trading range around this time.

Finally, on the plus side, the trade was exited promptly at the established stop level, keeping the loss very small.

Trade Summary

Date	Stock	Entry	Trade Size	Initial Stop	Target	Initial Reward-Risk	Exit	Date	P/L
10-11-00	DE	33¼	200	36⅛	30³⁄₁₆	~1:1	33¾	10-24-00	−½

What does this excerpt from the trade diary tell us? We know when and why we got into this trade. We know what type of trade it is and what our expectations are for it. We know the market conditions in which the trade took place. We know what the risk is on the trade and we know the strong and weak points of the strategy. When the trade is complete, we can then judge the results in the context of this information. Was a losing trade simply a natural occurrence within the framework of our strategy, or did it occur because of some obvious error on our part? Such conclusions are more easily drawn over time, as the entries in the diary increase.

limitations

Obviously, maintaining a trade-by-trade diary can be difficult for more hyperactive scalpers and day traders. In such cases, it can be worthwhile to recap the day's action and analyze your aggregate performance.

Keeping a trade journal is also a helpful exercise for traders who are paper-trading their strategies. Along with system testing, a diary can give you an accurate appraisal of a strategy's potential in the market and what it will be like to trade it. However, how realistic this picture is depends on how honestly and accurately you keep your records. By fudging on stops or losses (such as when the market just *barely* hits your stop-loss and then goes your way) you'll only be short-changing yourself when it comes time to trade.

regular review

Because the markets can be exciting or stressful, we are sometimes not as rational or thorough as we should be when we place our trades. However, in retrospect, it is much easier to see the flaws in our logic, the missteps in execution, and other negative patterns that contribute to trading losses. Reviewing the information in your trading diary will help you be more objective about your trading. Analyzing past trades can sometimes be a painful and humbling experience—it's no fun to relive losses and face up to weaknesses. But doing so is a concrete way to eliminate bad habits and to move your trading in a positive direction.

As Plato might have said, "When it comes to the markets, the strategy that is unexamined is not worth trading."

section two

trading strategies

What makes a good trading strategy? In the abstract, that's an easy question to answer. A good strategy combines entering and exiting positions based on sound logic and observable price patterns with disciplined risk control and effective trade execution.

But there are a number of different roads traders can take to get to this ultimate destination. As the strategies in Chapters 5 through 6 demonstrate, there isn't one particular strategy, system, or concept that guarantees profits. Neither is every trading strategy suited to every trader, nor to every type of market environment. Each market player must develop an approach he or she feels comfortable with and can trade consistently over time. Some traders will discover they are swing traders; others will feel more comfortable with longer term approaches; still others might excel as pure day traders. Examining and analyzing different trading strategies is an excellent way to discover what kind of trader you are and develop techniques you can use throughout your trading career.

But no matter what trading style you adopt, it is important to remember that trading can never take place in a vacuum. You have to keep the big picture in mind. To that end, in addition to the numerous short-term trading strategies detailed in this section, we also cover such topics as trading psychology, longer term market tendencies that provide the framework for short-term trading, and the realities of trade execution that every trader—not just the Level II variety—must understand.

But no matter what time frame these strategies operate on, what they have in common is that they are based on easily observed price patterns and sound market logic. They not only provide you *what* but also explain the *why*.

chapter 5

pattern-based strategies

trading pure price action

Gary Smith

Many traders look at me with a skeptical eye when I tell them how I trade the stock market for a living. That's because I'm totally opposed to perceptual filters like charts, oscillators, waves, cycles, moving averages, and all the other approaches and systems traders typically use to understand price behavior. To add insult to injury, I also believe all the glitzy computer equipment and software so frequently advertised for traders is unnecessary.

For me, less is more. I believe in trading pure price action—market behavior you can see and do not have to measure by traditional (and often lagging) analytical tools. My trading has evolved to the point that if I had to, I could make my trading decisions based solely on half-hourly quotes of the Dow, S&P 500, Nasdaq 100, and Russell 2000 cash indexes.

A year ago, in fact, I had to do just that as I helped a friend move across country. For an entire week, I did not have access to CNBC, the World Wide Web or any of the financial publications I usually rely on for information. I survived solely by making frequent phone calls to get updates on my cash indexes. But my trading did not suffer: I actively traded and made $10,000.

So, you may ask, how profitable has this simplistic trading style been over the years? Starting with a $2,200 account in the spring of 1985, I have methodically parlayed my trading skills and capital in such a way that over the past three years (ending December 1999), I've averaged over $14,000 in monthly trading profits.

Successful trading is about quickness, flexibility, and reacting to market action as it occurs, not after the fact when it can easily be quantified and identified by the analytical horde. That is why over the years I have gravitated toward trading pure price action. This simply translates into being in sync with the rhythm of the market—and that rhythm is its momentum.

key short-term trading patterns

My trading methodology is based on several short-term momentum patterns that keep me attuned to the market's rhythm. These are outlined in this section and followed by real-life trading examples that show how they capture significant price moves.

While these patterns are all short-term techniques, they can sometimes develop into bigger trades. I trade all my momentum and divergence patterns with the expectation they will result in immediate further strength (or weakness) over the next few trading days. If this price strength continues, so much the better:

- *V-bottoms.* V-bottom reversals occur intraday when the Dow has been down the entire trading session (as much as 0.75 percent from its previous close) and then makes a furious comeback, closing either near the unchanged level or, preferably, up for the day. The later in the day the reversal occurs, the more significant it is.

  I instinctively trade V-bottom reversals if the Dow closed down the previous day or if it has been in a recent downtrend. V-bottom reversals that occur after a strong up day or during a period of rising prices are much less important.

- *Late-day surges.* This pattern is closely related to the V-bottom. Late-day price surges normally occur during the last two- to two-and-a-half hours of choppy and nontrending trading days. A late-day price surge should take the Dow to a close of at least 0.5 percent above the prior day's close. Like V-bottom reversals, this pattern is most significant when it comes after a down day or a period of declining prices.

- *Extreme momentum days.* Extreme momentum days are just that—trading days of out-of-the-ordinary price action that has not occurred for the past several months. This type of momentum day is normally followed by a continuation in the direction of the thrust.

- *Weekend patterns.* Some of my more reliable momentum patterns over the years have been Friday-to-Monday patterns.

  Greater-than-average strength on a Friday is often followed by more strength on Monday (or Tuesday, if Monday is a trading holiday). Conversely, extremely weak price action on a Friday typically leads to more weakness on Monday. I buy on the close of any Friday when the Dow and Nasdaq 100 both close up 0.5 percent or more.

A Friday-to-Monday momentum break pattern occurs when extreme strength or weakness Friday does not carry over to Monday. These weekend momentum break patterns are highly significant and indicate short-term trend changes.

- *One-percent selling days.* A 1-percent-true-selling day occurs when, after a period of rising prices (at least 7 to 10 trading days), the cash Dow, S&P, Nasdaq 100, and Russell 2000 indexes all close down 1 percent or more on the same trading day. Such days often are "trend busters"—harbingers of serious price declines.

  I use a little leeway in defining such selling days. For example, if three of the four indexes are sharply lower—say, down 1.5 percent to 2 percent or more—but one index is down only 0.75 percent to 1 percent, I would still interpret that as a true-selling day. Any index down less than 0.75 percent invalidates the true-selling day because it indicates buying interest in at least one segment of the market (in an otherwise extremely weak overall market).

- *Divergence patterns.* Divergence patterns are my favorite technique because they have made me the most money over the years. Divergences (when one market or indicator goes in one direction and another market or indicator goes the opposite direction) between the Dow, S&P, Nasdaq 100, and Russell 2000 indexes tell me where money is flowing and which sector I should be trading.

market selection

Before looking at specific trade examples, let's first discuss a couple of the nuts-and-bolts issues: what to trade and how to time entries and exits.

There are several vehicles you can use to trade these patterns—individual stocks; index tracking stocks like the SPDRs, DIAs, or QQQs; stock index futures; stock index options; or mutual funds. In the following trading examples, it really does not matter which trading weapon would have been used: They all can be effective in exploiting the types of price action I have described.

Regardless of your preferred trading vehicle, the challenge remains the same—understanding price behavior and being in sync with the momentum of the market. In the end, what you trade boils down to your individual risk tolerances and preferences. In the past I have traded stocks, equity and index options, and stock index futures. But at this point in my trading career, I make most of my money trading mutual funds, partly because of their trend persistency compared with other trading vehicles.

entry, exit, and risk control

I am a close-of-the-day trader, which means my trading decisions are based on the entire day's trading action. I make my trades right before the close of trading.

In the past, I used to trade intraday. However, my trading account is hundreds of thousands of dollars to the better since I've moved beyond intraday trading in favor of close-of-the-day trading. This approach has allowed me to capture much more of the gains from the great bull market of the past decade than darting in and out on a daily basis.

As mentioned earlier, my price patterns are short-term and are intended to exploit immediate further strength (or weakness) over the next few trading days. As a trader, I never cut my profits short or set price objectives. My sell criterion is very simple: If the expected strength fails to materialize the next trading session, I exit my position on the close—no hoping, praying, or wishing.

Once I am in a profitable trade, I will add to that position as the market moves in my favor. This is a scale-up trading strategy I learned from master traders such as Jesse Livermore and Nicholas Darvas.

On initial purchases, I do not risk more than 1 percent to 2 percent of account equity. Then, if the trade moves in my favor, I will add to my position on each 1 percent to 2 percent incremental price advance.

Livermore and Darvas also believed in trailing their stops as prices rose, so once the market retraced a certain percentage from their highs, they were taken out with a profit. I usually get out if the market moves 3 percent to 4 percent off any recent high since I have been in. If these percentages seem to suggest I don't give the market much room for error, it is because I focus on trading mutual funds moving upward in tight, rising channels with few or no reactions along the way. (This part of my strategy is one of the key elements of my success.)

in the trenches

Enough of the explanations. Here are some real-life examples that illustrate how to trade these momentum and divergence patterns.

weekend break

The Dow had been in correction mode from August through mid-October 1999, declining more than 11 percent. This correction reached its nadir with a 266-point (2 percent) decline Friday, October 15. Doom and gloom pervaded the Street after the close that Friday, with forecasts of another sharp decline and a break of the critical 10,000 level on Monday, October 18.

But a funny thing happened when the market reopened that Monday: Instead of suffering follow-through selling, the Dow chopped around most of the day, flipping between positive and negative territory (see Figure 5.1). Then, in the last 90 minutes of trading, the Dow shot up 116 points, closing ahead 96 points for the session.

It was a classic example of the Friday-to-Monday momentum break pattern. Coming after a period of declining prices, October 18 marked a major bottom in the market and launched a rally that resulted in the Nasdaq 100 gaining 57 percent by the end of the year.

Over the years, Friday-to-Monday momentum break patterns have marked several significant lows. Both the Friday-to-Monday momentum break patterns of April 14, 1997, and January 12, 1998, led to 30 percent advances in the major indexes over a period of a few months. Other Friday-to-Monday momentum break patterns have led to smaller, but still significant, price moves.

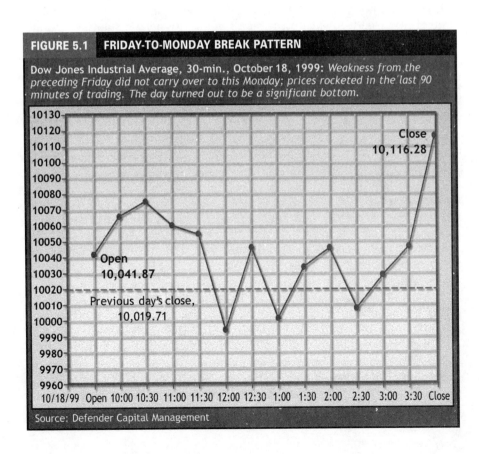

FIGURE 5.1 FRIDAY-TO-MONDAY BREAK PATTERN

Dow Jones Industrial Average, 30-min., October 18, 1999: *Weakness from the preceding Friday did not carry over to this Monday; prices rocketed in the last 90 minutes of trading. The day turned out to be a significant bottom.*

Close
10,116.28

Open
10,041.87

Previous day's close,
10,019.71

10/18/99 Open 10:00 10:30 11:00 11:30 12:00 12:30 1:00 1:30 2:00 2:30 3:00 3:30 Close

Source: Defender Capital Management

As with any of my trading patterns, I trade Friday-to-Monday momentum break patterns instinctively. Trading is not about analyzing or rationalizing, it is about being quick, flexible, and capable of reacting to changes in the market.

On October 18, 1999, however, I was not quick or flexible. I was psychologically unable to make the trade because I got bogged down in bearish analysis. That was my loss: The Dow rallied nearly 300 points the following two trading days. (The lesson: Even experienced traders need to be vigilant about adhering to sound trading practices. You have to be able to execute your game plan to profit from it.) Fortunately, another trading pattern—extreme price momentum—got me in the market on Thursday, October 21.

momentum extreme

On that Thursday, the Nasdaq 100 dropped more than 60 points in the first hour of trading. (This was a reaction to some adverse news that technology giant IBM announced after the previous day's close.) Beginning with the second hour of trading, the Nasdaq 100 gradually traded higher throughout the day (trade not pictured). Then, in the last hour of trading, it surged upward to close 10 points higher on the day. I found this type of extreme daily momentum in the tech-heavy index especially significant because IBM was getting pummeled in trading on the NYSE. As a result of its extreme price momentum off the morning lows and also its divergence with IBM and the Dow (which closed lower by 94 points), I took a position before the close in the INVESCO Technology fund.

As I expected, prices rallied the next day (October 22) and then traded sideways for a few days. But on Wednesday, October 27, this time in the Dow, another momentum pattern triggered—the late-day price surge.

surging market

On this day, the Dow had been trading around the breakeven level for most of that session when it suddenly broke out and staged a 100-point rally in the last hour (see Figure 5.2). This also was a day when the Dow Jones Utilities index was making one of it best advances in several years.

Buoyed by the late-day price surge in the Dow and the out-of-the-ordinary price action in the Utilities, I increased my technology fund position before the close on October 27. The Dow rallied more than 300 points the following two days, with technology leading the way.

While this would have been a completely acceptable two-day trade, I continued (as I do whenever I am in a winning position) to increase my technology mutual fund position as the Nasdaq 100 and other tech-related indexes moved steadily higher over the next two months.

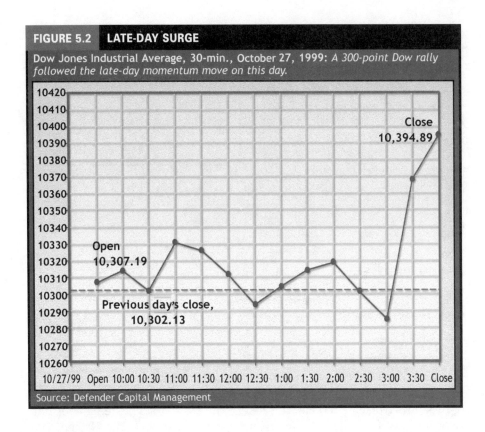

FIGURE 5.2 **LATE-DAY SURGE**

Dow Jones Industrial Average, 30-min., October 27, 1999: *A 300-point Dow rally followed the late-day momentum move on this day.*

Source: Defender Capital Management

mixed signals

My favorite patterns are divergences between the Dow, S&P, Nasdaq 100, and Russell 2000 indexes. By telling you which sectors—large cap, technology, or small cap—are the strongest, divergences provide a good indication of where you should put your money.

Table 5.1 shows the performance of the Dow and the Nasdaq 100 for the seven trading days from October 28 through November 5, 1999. At the time, a one-point move in the Nasdaq 100 equaled a 4.23-point move in the Dow (computed by dividing the Dow by the Nasdaq 100).

It was pretty obvious beginning October 28 where the strength was in the market and, hence, where to be invested—the Nasdaq 100 and technology sector. This divergence between the Nasdaq 100 and the large-cap stocks was particularly notable October 29, when the Nasdaq 100 rose the equivalent of 412 Dow points. It also was glaring November 2 when the Dow closed down for the day in the face of a strong Nasdaq 100.

Many traders began backing away from the Nasdaq 100 around the time shown in Table 5.1 because most traditional technical indicators

TABLE 5.1	DOW AND NASDAQ 100 PERFORMANCE— OCTOBER 28– NOVEMBER 5, 1999	
	Dow	Nasdaq 100
Oct. 28	+227.64	+82.47
Oct. 29	+107.33	+97.51
Nov. 1	(-81.35)	(-21.08)
Nov. 2	(-66.67)	+10.63
Nov. 3	+27.22	+45.73
Nov. 4	+30.58	+30.39
Nov. 5	+64.84	+52.59
Totals	+309.59	+298.24 (1,261.55 Dow pts.)

TABLE 5.2	NEGATIVE DIVERGENCE— APRIL 12–APRIL 14, 1999	
	Dow	Nasdaq 100
April 12	+165.67	(-13.26)
April 13	+55.50	(-44.03)
April 14	+16.65	(-76.22)

were flashing "overbought" signals. However, the extreme divergence between the Nasdaq 100 and the rest of the market suggested something very big was brewing. And far from being overbought, the Nasdaq 100 rocketed ahead another 900-plus points from the close of trading November 5 through the end of December.

The rule regarding diverging markets is to always buy the strong market. If you find yourself in a sector that suddenly begins to diverge negatively from the other indexes, get out as quickly as possible and redeploy your capital in the sector diverging positively.

A classic example of negative divergence occurred in early April 1999. As shown in Table 5.2, there was a vicious rotation out of tech stocks and into large-cap Dow and value stocks beginning April 12. I was in technology during this rotation and exited part of my position on April 12 and the remainder on April 13.

I repositioned myself in the value sector of the market. As it turned out, the Dow and other value stocks continued soaring through the month, while technology went nowhere.

catching the bottom

The V-bottom upside reversal pattern does not occur very often, but when it occurs, get ready for some fireworks. The last notable V-bottom reversal I traded was the major market bottom of October 8, 1998. That day marked the culmination of the summer meltdown, which took most indexes 20 percent or more off their summer highs.

It looked like the market was about to fall deeper into the abyss that day, opening lower and continuing to plummet (see Figure 5.3). By 2 P.M. EST, the Dow was down 274 points, or almost 4 percent. Around that time, I had to leave home to conduct some personal business, never imagining I would soon be moving money into the market. But when I returned home near the end of the trading session, the Dow had made a miraculous turnaround. Right before the close it briefly pushed into positive territory, then drifted back to close marginally lower, down only 9 points.

Even though I was bearish, I had no choice but to trade this pattern. Although I doubted it was a bottom, I thought there would have to be some carryover buying. That is, in fact, how the situation unfolded: The Dow rallied 235 points over the next four trading days. Again, this would

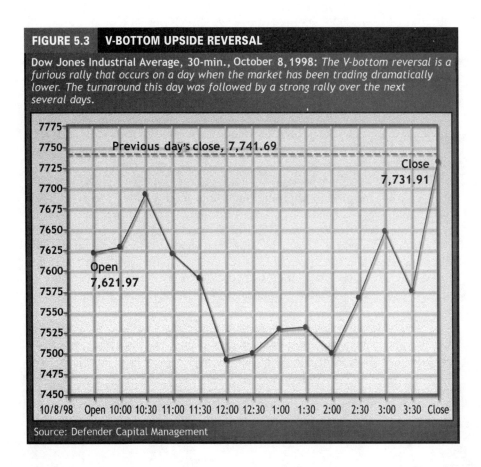

FIGURE 5.3 V-BOTTOM UPSIDE REVERSAL

Dow Jones Industrial Average, 30-min., October 8, 1998: *The V-bottom reversal is a furious rally that occurs on a day when the market has been trading dramatically lower. The turnaround this day was followed by a strong rally over the next several days.*

Source: Defender Capital Management

have been another great short-term trade, but this 235-point rally was luckily only a prelude to the explosion that was about to occur. On Thursday, October 15, shortly before 3 P.M., the Fed unexpectedly lowered the discount rate. After the surprise Fed announcement, the Dow surged a stunning 220 points during the last 60 minutes of trading and closed up 330 points for the day.

This was another example of extreme price momentum—the kind of out-of-the-ordinary price action that invariably leads to much larger gains in the days and, sometimes, weeks ahead. Some traders, intimidated by extreme momentum, retreat to the sidelines awaiting price pullbacks that never occur. As with all my trading patterns, whenever I see an extreme momentum day, I don't think, analyze, or reason—I simply buy. From the close of October 15, the Dow ran up another 900 points through the end of the year.

the short side

I have only one sell-side momentum pattern: the 1-percent-true-selling day. True selling for me is when all the indexes—the Dow, S&P, Nasdaq 100, and Russell 2000—concurrently decline 1 percent or more on the same trading day. Although this is my least reliable trading pattern, most likely because of the historical upward bias in stock prices, it nevertheless has given me some excellent sell signals. For example, the summer 1998 top on July 21 came in the form of a 1-percent-true-selling day. Another 1-percent-true-selling day occurred two days later on July 23. Usually, I will sell up to 50 percent of my position on an initial true-selling day, and the remainder of my position on a second true-selling day (or if prices continue trending down). After closing out my remaining positions on July 23, the Dow sank nearly 1,600 points through the end of August.

Incidentally, my 1-percent-true-selling day pattern also got me out of the market in mid-October 1997, when two such days occurred back-to-back on October 16 and 17. That effectively ended the spring and summer rally in technology and small caps, and enabled me to avoid the minicrash of October 27 (as well as the weakness leading up to that debacle). However, because the 1-percent-true-selling day is my least accurate pattern, there have been occasions when I have exited only to reenter a day or two later when one of my other momentum patterns kicked in on the upside.

The patterns we have analyzed share several common traits: They are simple, based purely on easily observable price action and easy to trade. By focusing on price action and momentum, and avoiding perceptual filters like charts and indicators that can adversely influence trade decisions, I have been able to develop short-term strategies that identify highly profitable trade opportunities in the stock market.

"Keep it simple" may be a shopworn trading concept, but it has been a philosophy I have actively, and profitably, practiced for years.

psychology in action:
inside the mind of a trader

Gary Smith

Trading success rarely comes easily or quickly. For most traders, there is a considerable learning curve, one involved primarily with understanding the true nature of trading psychology rather than finding the perfect entry strategy.

The groundwork for my trading methodology was laid when I read Nicholas Darvas's book, *How I Made Two Million Dollars in the Stock Market* in the early 1960s. But it took me nearly 20 years from my first trade in 1966 to figure out the trading game and enjoy success on a consistent level.

My slow progress wasn't because I had misinterpreted Darvas's ideas. Rather, it was the result of my inability to master the psychological aspects of trading. My particular trading nemesis was always trying to get rich overnight. It was only after correcting that problem that I was able to begin fulfilling my dream of successfully trading for a living.

I think trading is 90 percent psychological, 10 percent "something else." Most traders spend all their time and energy struggling with that 10 percent, forever searching for the perfect trading tool, system, or method. But instead of obsessing about charts, oscillators, waves, cycles, moving averages, and the like, traders should worry more about trading psychology. In fact, the real reason so few succeed in trading is because the traits required for success are almost exclusively psychological.

Most people don't have a good idea of what trading psychology is really all about. Most of you have probably heard psychology is the most important facet of the trading game. After all, books, seminars, and magazine articles have proliferated on the subject. If you are like me, though, you find much of the conventional wisdom on the psychological aspects of trading to be boring, academic, and, in some cases, flat-out wrong. This shouldn't be surprising, since most of the self-proclaimed experts on trading psychology don't even trade. They all spout similar psychobabble about the importance of being confident and optimistic, how you should not be in trading for the money, how it's all right to lose, and how you must keep your emotions in check.

That's fine, but I want to approach the psychology of trading from a different perspective. By examining my real-time trading in 2000 from May through August, I'll take you into the mind of someone who trades for a living and explain how I deal with the psychological battles of trading. More importantly, you'll get a glimpse into my psychological profile and at what makes me tick as a trader. It's what makes us tick that ultimately determines our success or failure.

By approaching psychology from this vantage point, you'll gain greater insight into the practical challenges of trading, and maybe even discover you aren't psychologically suited for the trading game.

taking a hit: dealing with adversity

I selected May as my starting point because that was, by far, my worst trading month ever. In fact, I probably lost more money in May than in all my other losing months over the past 15 years combined. I gave back almost 45 percent of my year-to-date profits during that month and suffered my worst-ever drawdown. It was a time of true adversity in my trading career.

Entering May, I had been doing well for the year. I had survived— even made money—in March and April during the wreck in the technology sector. That was because I was quick to react to the divergences in the market in mid-March, when technology shares declined and the Dow and other value sectors rose.

May, however, was a struggle from day one, and taking a semivacation during the second week of the month—my first vacation in more than six years—didn't help matters. I was still able to trade during that time, but not with my usual concentration. Part of my trading success is because I make trading the be-all and end-all of my life—a sacrifice most traders aren't willing to make. I am totally focused on trading 24 hours a day. I'm always going over possible market scenarios in my mind and how I might react to them, constantly plotting my response to potential market-moving events. Even when I get up in the middle of the night, my mind is always on the market and what I will do the next trading day if this or that occurs.

You may be thinking I need to get a life. But I have a life, and one of its passions is trading. Most of the conventional wisdom on trading psychology says you need to take breaks and vacations to recharge your batteries. Not this trader—and from what I have seen, not many other successful traders, either. I'm reminded of super trader Bill Lipschutz in the book, *The Mind of a Trader* by Alpesh Patel. In the book, Lipschutz says, "The very best traders don't take a lot of time off." He also says you must be focused on the markets you are involved in day in and day out, week in and week out. Taking time off and vacations simply are not part of my equation for trading success.

Another key point: While I may have a passion for the game, I trade purely for the money, something many academics on trading psychology say is a big no-no. I trade for the money because of the freedom and independence it brings, and because I'm not into the real world of schedules, deadlines, and bosses. I trade for the money because I'm obsessed with a secure retirement and being able someday to indulge my other passions in life.

red-letter day

But let's get back to the May slump. As I returned from my minivacation, I found myself modestly in the red on Monday, May 22, the beginning of the third trading week of the month. That day I saw an opportunity to pull myself into the black. The Nasdaq 100 traced out one of my favorite price patterns—the V-bottom upside reversal (see Figure 5.4). From an intraday low of –231 points, the Nasdaq 100 staged a furious rally and closed up 4 points on the session. Over the years, V-bottom upside reversals—especially coming after several days of falling prices—have been among my most profitable patterns. For example, the October 1998 low was marked by such a pattern where the Dow turned a 274-point decline at 2 P.M. into a 9-point loss by the close.

But I made a fatal psychological mistake in playing the V-bottom reversal on May 22: I put on a trade nearly three times greater than my average initial position. In other words, I was so confident of the trade, I plunged in recklessly with little regard for the risk caused by the size of my initial commitment. The next day, instead of getting the usual follow-through that occurs after V-bottom reversals, the market tanked, with

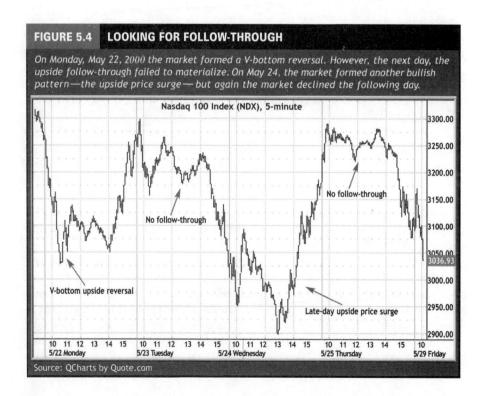

FIGURE 5.4   LOOKING FOR FOLLOW-THROUGH

On Monday, May 22, 2000 the market formed a V-bottom reversal. However, the next day, the upside follow-through failed to materialize. On May 24, the market formed another bullish pattern—the upside price surge—but again the market declined the following day.

Nasdaq 100 Index (NDX), 5-minute

Source: QCharts by Quote.com

the Nasdaq 100 closing down 240 points. I was psychologically devastated by this loss and, as is the case when the markets don't move as I anticipate, I exited my position on the close. One of the few tenets of conventional trading advice that I do adhere to is cutting losses as quickly as possible. If there was any trait that kept me in the trading game while I was learning the ropes in my early years, it was my obsession with always cutting my losses.

And while we're talking about traits necessary for successful trading, let's discuss confidence. After all, it was my confidence that contributed to my large loss May 23. As a rule, I am one of the least confident traders you will ever meet. I believe just about every trade I put on is destined to be an instant loser. Surprised? You might be, considering conventional wisdom holds that it is essential to trade with confidence. Yet over my trading career, it has always been my most confident trades that have cost me the most money. On the other hand, the trades I have had the least confidence in have been my most profitable.

I'm not alone in believing trading with confidence and optimism is a prescription for failure. Trader Larry Williams, in his book *Long-Term Secrets to Short-Term Trading,* had this to say about his belief system: "I believe the current trade I am in will be a loser . . . a big loser at that."

Want more proof? Trading author Max Gunther found that one of the five characteristics common to lucky and successful people was the pessimism paradox: They "nurtured a basic core of pessimism so dense and tough and prickly that it startles you when you first come upon it." As Gunther relates, the successful and lucky of this world not only expect things to go wrong, they expect them to go wrong in the worst possible way. As a successful and lucky trader, I can certainly concur. I just wish I hadn't let my guard down and loaded up on more shares than usual May 22.

On May 24, the day after my huge trading loss, another one of my favorite price action patterns appeared—the late-day upside price surge (see Figure 5.2). All the major indexes surged in the last hours of trading and closed strongly higher for the day. Once again, I plowed into the market in anticipation of follow-through strength the next day. But just as on May 23, May 25 brought no follow-through and the indexes posted precipitous declines. And once again, I immediately closed out my position with another excruciating loss.

I doubt (although I better not get too optimistic here) my trading account will ever again sustain the damage it incurred the week of May 22. Losing months have been rare for me over the years, but May was a doozy and I was completely demoralized. I thought my trading career was doomed and I would never make another dollar. While I don't get emotional over my winning trades, I become an emotional wreck over my losing trades. However, things got worse—much worse—the next week.

bottoming out

On May 30, the day after the Memorial Day holiday, the markets exploded to the upside (see Figure 5.5). The Nasdaq 100 had its greatest one-day percentage gain ever. This type of extreme momentum—especially coming after a period of declining prices—has added considerably to my bottom line over the years.

As with any of my price action patterns, I have been conditioned not to think, analyze, or rationalize—just to react. I've always thought much of my success was because of my quickness and flexibility in entering a trade. But because I was so crushed psychologically from the pounding of my past two failed trades, I was unable to pull the trigger and enter at the close on May 30. Big, big mistake! Although May 31 was quiet, June 1 and 2 saw more explosive upside moves. In fact, on June 2, the up-down volume ratio for the Nasdaq Composite was its second highest since 1978.

Taking on risk—something I was unable to do when I failed to make the trade on May 30—is one of the most important traits of winning traders. Our risk tolerances and attitudes toward risk are ingrained in us from childhood. Some traders, no matter how hard they try, struggle with putting on trades or freeze once in a trade. It's just not in their nature to assume monetary risk. On the other end of the risk spectrum are

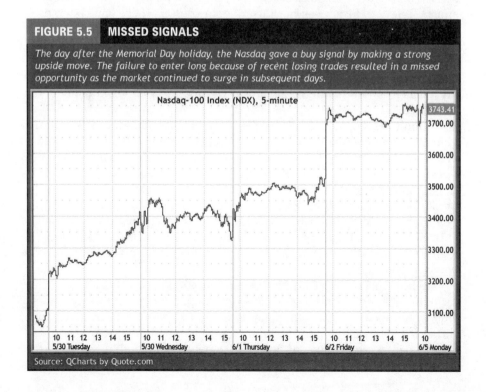

FIGURE 5.5 **MISSED SIGNALS**

The day after the Memorial Day holiday, the Nasdaq gave a buy signal by making a strong upside move. The failure to enter long because of recent losing trades resulted in a missed opportunity as the market continued to surge in subsequent days.

Nasdaq-100 Index (NDX), 5-minute

3743.41

Source: QCharts by Quote.com

the gunslingers and gamblers, those who have no respect whatsoever for risk. They have no trouble putting on trades, but eventually crash and burn because of their go-for-broke mentality. Make no mistake, the delicate balancing of risk and reward is crucial to trading success.

remember the losers

Over the June 3 weekend, I tried to regroup from my worst two weeks ever as a trader. If you believe what the experts tell you, you should put aside your losing trades and missed opportunities and move on. They say it's never productive to fixate on your past losing trades or the trade that could have been.

That's more psychobabble, as far as I'm concerned. My losing trades and missed opportunities eat away at me for days, weeks, months, and even longer. I can't think of a better way to become successful than embracing your trading failures so you will never repeat them again. I can still remember, as if it were yesterday, my worst trades from the early 1970s and 1980s. They still eat away at me. But you know what? The psychological mistakes I made in those trades will never occur again because I will never forget them.

Another reason losing trades eat away at me is my competitive spirit—a spirit nurtured in my early years participating in a variety of sports. I hate to lose, even in Ping-Pong. In trading, there have been days where I have made $10,000 or more. But giving back just a few hundred dollars of those profits the next trading day is gut-wrenching, and damaging to my psyche. Profits never excite or faze me. But any loss, regardless of how small, bothers me because, among other things, I define myself as a trader, much the same way as an artist defines himself by his paintings.

Don't let anyone kid you about trading for a living. It's not the glamorous, easy-money profession often presented by those who pander promises of instant wealth. Traders must endure an enormous amount of physical and mental punishment as they constantly battle the emotional challenges of the trading arena. Robert Rotella said it best in his book *The Elements of Successful Trading:* "Trading is not an occupation, but a love/hate relationship in which the trader constantly struggles with not just making and losing money, but his own gain and loss of identity." You will never make it in this game if you don't know or like yourself very much.

While I may never trade with confidence, and losing trades haunt me for a lifetime, I do persevere—I never give up. There aren't many traders who would have had the emotional stamina to spend 18 years from 1966 through 1984 as a going-nowhere, break-even, part-time trader. And I was able to persevere because of being extremely disciplined, most likely the result of being an avid runner for more than 20 years.

putting the pieces back together

As June began, I thought about how to dig myself out of the worst trading slump of my career. My first course of action was to decide whether I should make any changes in my trading. Should I curtail my trading completely until I regained my composure? Should I cut back my trading size? Or should I keep trading exactly as before?

I decided my best choice was to keep trading as I had, to not skip a beat. After all, it wasn't a changing market that beat me in May—I beat myself. I vowed not to plunge into a trade like the one on May 22 and, most of all, not to get discouraged at failed signals and to keep pulling the trading trigger whenever I saw an opportunity.

My next job was finding a market sector that was suitable for my trading strategy, which is a very basic and simple approach taken from Nicholas Darvas. I buy rising markets or sectors and continually add to my positions as the trend moves in my favor. When the trend reverses, I run like a thief. I knew as soon as I was introduced to this strategy that it was right for me.

Most traders don't have this type of psychological insight to immediately recognize what will work best for them. Instead, they spend a lifetime in the trading game searching for some elusive, magical trading method, losing tens of thousands of dollars or more in the process.

One sector I had traded in and out of without much success earlier in the year had been the realty sector. I liked this sector because of its persistency in trend; once it begins to move, it usually does so in a gradual, yet sustained manner. This is the kind of price movement most adaptable to my trading style. Another thing I liked about the realty sector was its lack of volatility compared with my usual trading sector, technology. This would allow me to be more aggressive in building positions in realty if it trended in my favor.

The tone of the overall market, including realty, had improved since the extreme momentum day of May 30. I therefore made a purchase in the INVESCO Realty Fund on June 6. I purchased more every trading day from June 7 through June 13 as the fund steadily, albeit slowly, trended higher. I was thus well positioned by June 14, when the fund had a 2-percent up day—a big move for the realty sector. I bought even more on June 14, as my experience has been that a big one-day move in realty is followed by even more immediate strength. As shown in Figure 5.6, the INVESCO Realty Fund climbed higher until the end of the month.

The window dressing in the stock market that often occurs on the last trading day of each quarter hit the realty sector hard. However, I wasn't hurt, as I had taken a secondary position the day before in the INVESCO Small Company Growth Fund. (Those who have read my book, *How I Trade for a Living*, know that my favorite one-day trade is to be long small-cap growth the last trading day of each quarter.)

Realty came back from its end-of-the-quarter setback on the first trading day of July and continued its climb throughout the month. My discipline is such that I never set profit objectives, instead believing wealth accumulation is a result of maximizing my winning trades. By the end of July, I had made back all my loss from May, and more. I was feeling better, especially since July had been such a downer for the S&P and Nasdaq 100 indexes. However, I still was not satisfied. Satisfaction in trading leads to complacency and a lessening of the intensity that is needed to stay in peak trading form.

On August 3, we experienced another V-bottom upside reversal as the Nasdaq 100 turned a 150-point intraday loss into a 133-point closing gain—a swing of more than 280 points. Although the V-bottom is one of my favorite patterns, it nonetheless was the pattern that led to my May demise. However, I didn't blink or worry about what had happened in May. My problem then wasn't so much the failing pattern, but the aggressiveness with which I traded it.

Therefore, on August 3, I moved prudently into INVESCO's Technology Fund. This time the V-bottom pattern didn't fail, and technology soared throughout the month (see Figure 5.7). I wasn't so lucky in my

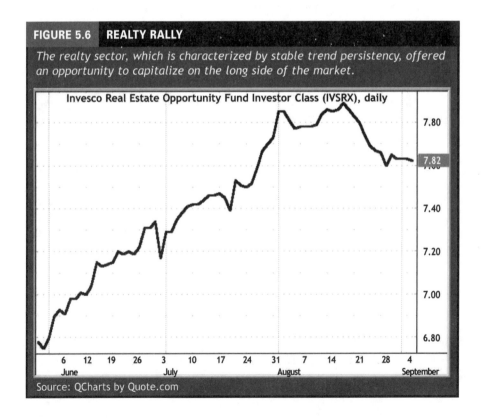

FIGURE 5.6   REALTY RALLY

The realty sector, which is characterized by stable trend persistency, offered an opportunity to capitalize on the long side of the market.

Invesco Real Estate Opportunity Fund Investor Class (IVSRX), daily

Source: QCharts by Quote.com

| FIGURE 5.7 | TECH TRUSTS |

When realty began to falter in August, the technology sector was there to pick up the slack and add to the long-side profits.

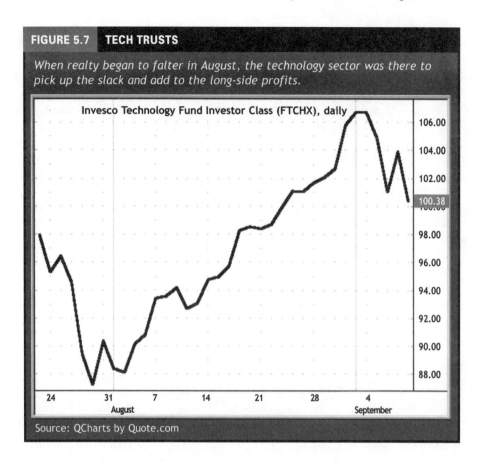

Source: QCharts by Quote.com

realty fund, though, as it hit a brick wall. But as realty began its gradual decline, I continually rolled over my positions there into technology, as that sector continued rising. As August came to a close, the pain of my May losses had finally faded and my June through August profits had exceeded those losses by more than 250 percent. I did nothing differently in that period to overcome my previous trading losses. I simply stuck to my basic trading strategy and kept my psychological miscues to a minimum.

Trading is a very personal and individual process, and we all have different psychological profiles. However, the truly successful traders I've encountered and read about seem to share some commonality in how they approach their profession. Basically, what separates true professionals from part-time hobbyists isn't talent, skill, or intellect, but intensity and obsessiveness. The passion, commitment, perseverance, competitiveness, discipline, fierce independence, and other traits I've discussed burn so much more intensely and obsessively in winners than in losers.

What you don't often read in the trading articles, books, and seminars is that while many may be called to the trading game, few actually possess the psychological traits required to succeed. As Rotella wrote in *The Elements of Successful Trading,* "[T]he reality is that you may never be able to possess these traits, because they cannot simply be learned or developed. . . These traits, or a lack of them, are the product of a variety of factors such as the interaction of our environment, genetics, and biology."

Rotella went on to say how some of these traits are part of our emotional state and have developed from infancy, and possibly earlier in our genetic imprint.

When I say few are able to succeed in the trading game, it's because I deal in reality. It bothers me to see some gurus charge thousands of dollars purporting to train "anyone" to become a successful trader. Not just anyone can become a successful trader, no more than just anyone can make it as a brain surgeon, physicist, or auto mechanic.

But I also believe we should all chase our dreams. Had I not chased my trading dream, I would most likely be toiling away at some dead-end menial job and living from paycheck to paycheck. If trading for a living is your dream, then by all means, go for it. But be prepared and be realistic.

playing the break(out)

Mark Seleznov

A hitter in baseball can fail 70 percent of the time but still make it to the all-star game if he gets enough doubles, triples, and home runs with the other 30 percent of his at-bats. It's the same with trading. In fact, the average successful floor trader is correct only around 30 percent of the time. He stays in business by practicing the old cliché of "cutting losses short and letting profits run." And he does that by developing a sound, systematic trading plan.

Whether they are pattern- or indicator-based, most successful traders use a systematic plan to select their trades. Even floor traders, who basically trade tick by tick, follow a systematic approach.

Short-term and day traders who make hundreds of trades a month have no room for faulty judgment or excessive risk-taking. A trading plan helps guard against these problems by taking the emotion out of trading.

A successful trading plan does not have to be right all the time, or even most of the time, to be profitable. It is the slugging percentage that counts. If your loss when "striking out" is small, but your hits are big, you can be an overall winner.

Think of it this way: Suppose you had a method that triggered 30 trades a day with 50 percent winners and 50 percent losers, but the average win was $600 and the average loss was $300. You would be pretty happy, right? Nevertheless, many inexperienced traders are uncomfortable with being wrong a large percentage of the time.

There is no holy grail in trading. The typical trader usually gravitates toward strategies with very high winning percentages, but often falls prey to black box systems that are limited to one stock or commodity. Many other methods show results for limited time spans, such as periods of great price increases or bull markets. Good trading strategies keep losses small, let profits expand and work over long periods of time in different market conditions.

Before detailing a specific systematic intraday trading approach, let's take a look at some of the common elements of all well-planned trading strategies.

systematic trading plan

A complete systematic trading plan needs seven components: time frame, studies, a setup, trigger, stop, exit, and filters.

All trading plans must start with the *time frame,* which establishes a time span (2-minute, 10-minute, daily, etc.) for the price bar used to determine the patterns and indicators in the approach.

If you are going to buy the highest high of the most recent 20 bars, you must decide whether you are going to look at a 5-minute, 15-minute, daily, or even a weekly bar. You cannot determine appropriate stop levels until you have determined your time frame.

A strategy for which the initial stop-loss is placed below the lowest low of the past three bars would have much more risk on a daily chart than on a 5-minute chart because of the larger range of the daily bars. You must choose a time frame that allows you to place trades that fit your risk tolerance level.

Studies include any calculations or indicators needed to analyze market action, such as moving averages, moving average convergence-divergence (MACD), the commodity channel index (CCI), relative strength index, stochastics, and so on. Studies also include chart analysis tools like trend lines or horizontal support and resistance lines for certain times of the day.

The *setup* is a clearly defined condition (or conditions) that makes it possible to take a trade. If you are using a pattern-based approach, the setup defines the characteristics of the pattern that must be in place before you can take the trade. If you use an indicator like a moving average, an example of a setup might be that price is above or below the moving average (or above or below it by a certain amount).

The *trigger* is the actual entry into the trade. After the setup conditions are met, this trigger signals a buy or sell. There should be no second thoughts about entry. For example, after the setup we just described lays the groundwork for the trade, an entry might be signaled when price exceeds the highest high of the last three bars.

Stops are used to exit a trade that is not performing as expected and can be based on one or multiple conditions. For example, a trader might opt to exit with a $500 loss if the trade has not become profitable after a specific amount of time.

The *exit* is used to liquidate a profitable trade after a certain amount of time has passed. Too many traders exit trades early precisely because they do not have a plan for when and how to get out of positions. Letting winning trades run as much as possible is critical to successful trading.

Filters are additional conditions applied to a trading strategy. A filter can be something as simple as exiting long trades only when the overall market is up. (However, in this case, you would need to decide whether "market" refers to the Dow Jones, Nasdaq, or S&P 500.) Filters can turn a method with average returns into one with above-average results.

market psychology

Any systematic trading approach also should have a "psychological" basis; that is, something that tries to exploit the crowd behavior of the market.

Repetitive crowd behavior is what makes trading work, and recurring price or indicator patterns are visual representations of crowd psychology in action (this will become clearer when we describe our intraday breakout strategy). An effective trading plan allows you to remove emotion from trading and take advantage of such patterns.

One of the primary reasons to use a plan is that it allows you to review trades and evaluate performance. Keep in mind, though, that a trading plan will not do any good unless you follow it. If you entered a trade that did not fit your setup criteria, you did not follow your plan. If you closed out a trade without the stock meeting your exit strategy, you did not follow your plan. Such detours from your game plan may seem like minor lapses at the time, but they can seriously affect your performance.

A trading plan gives you a road map to navigate the markets; if you throw the map out the window, you should not be surprised when you find yourself in the middle of nowhere with an empty gas tank.

intraday breakout system

Now we will take a look at a specific system that incorporates the ideas we have discussed. This system (for Nasdaq stocks only) is the Seleznov Breakout Method No. 8 (SBM8).

This pattern is based on very simple market psychology: When a stock gaps above the previous day's high on the open, new buyers are entering the market, pushing the stock higher. In such situations, there is often some fundamental reason for the higher price: an earnings announcement, a merger, and so on.

When market orders have built up overnight, the market-making firms and specialists gap the stock higher so they can turn around and sell it short, capitalizing on the overzealous buyers piling into the stock. (Remember, in most instances, a market maker or specialist is taking the other side of your trade.) The market maker hopes the stock's rise will bring in other sellers, pushing the stock back down and allowing him to buy back his short position at a profit.

However, sometimes the market makers misjudge the true strength of a price move. If the stock starts to move up again (after the thrust of the initial gap open move), not only will the new buyers be pushing the stock higher, but the market makers and traders who faded the gap opening will need to cover their short positions.

The SBM8 trades in the direction of this trend, as buyers push the stock higher. Here are its components:

Time frame	10-minute bars, normal trading hours.
Studies	None.
Setup	1. The stock opens higher than the previous day's close.
	2. The stock makes at least three consecutive, completed bars (i.e., not partial bars) with equal or lower highs than the previous bars.
Trigger	Buy ⅛ above the high of the previous bar.
Stop	⅛ below the low of the previous bar.
Exit	⅛ below low of two bars ago.
Filters	Only take trades with a maximum risk of one point and do not make trades after 3 P.M. EST.

Let's go over each of these components in detail to make sure they're absolutely clear:

- *Time frame.* A bar starts at 9:30 A.M. EST and runs to 9:40 A.M. to complete. Then the next bar begins.
- *Studies.* Because this is a pattern-based method, there are no studies.
- *Setup.* First, the stock must have opened at least ⅛ higher than the previous day's close. Second, it must make at least three complete down bars, or it can be in a congestion pattern. (The main

part of the setup is that each of the three previous bars must have equal or lower highs than the preceding bars.) What is happening here is that the stock is pausing or pulling back after the initial opening burst.

- *Trigger.* Entry can occur only after a stock has completed at least three 10-minute bars with equal or lower highs (entry must occur on the fourth bar). The filter conditions also must be met (see "Filter," following). What is happening here is the stock is turning back to the upside after its pause or pullback.
- *Stop.* Because most trades will not work out, stops are necessary to keep losses small. If the stock drops ⅛ below the low of the bar previous to the entry bar, exit the trade at the market.
- *Exit.* If the trade works out, stay in it until the price drops ⅛ below the low of the last two bars. Otherwise, all trades are exited "market on close"—no overnight positions.
- *Filter.* To limit risk to a point, the length of the bar prior to entry must have a range of ¾ point or less, because the stop is placed ⅛ below the low of the previous bar.

This is a solid trading plan with good risk-reward characteristics. The filter rule keeps you from trading the pattern in high-priced, riskier stocks. Fortunately, many stocks priced less than $100 provide intraday trade opportunities with manageable risk.

Here are examples of the SBM8 system at work.

Figure 5.8 shows MCI Worldcom (WCOM), which closed at 41⅝ on Friday, January 28, 2000, and opened up the next trading day (Monday, January 31), at 42 (A). The setup began with the 10:10 A.M. bar, which hit a high of 42⅞, and continued over the next four bars, each of which made consecutively lower or equal highs (B). The 11 A.M. bar exceeded the prior bar by ⅛. The 10:50 bar has a range of less than ¾ giving the trade a maximum risk of one point.

The trade is entered at 42½ (C). From this entry at 11 A.M. through the entire day, the stock never traded ⅛ below the low of the last two bars. Exit occurs at the end of the day "market on close" (MOC) at 45¾ (D) for a 3¼-point profit per share.

Figure 5.9 on page 120 shows Sun Microsystems (SUNW), which closed on January 31, 2000, at 78⅝ and opened on February 1 at 78⅞ (A). The stock then moved lower, creating a setup with the three 10-minute bars from 10 A.M. through 10:20 A.M., each of which had a lower or equal high than the previous bar.

The trigger occurred at the 10:30 A.M. bar, ⅛ above the high of the 10:20 A.M. bar at 77⁹⁄₁₆ (B). SUNW rallied with each bar, never falling ⅛ below the low of the previous two bars until the 1:30 P.M. bar, when it fell to 80¼, ⅛ below both the 1:10 P.M. and 1:20 P.M. bars. This exit resulted in 21¹⁄₁₆-point profit on the trade.

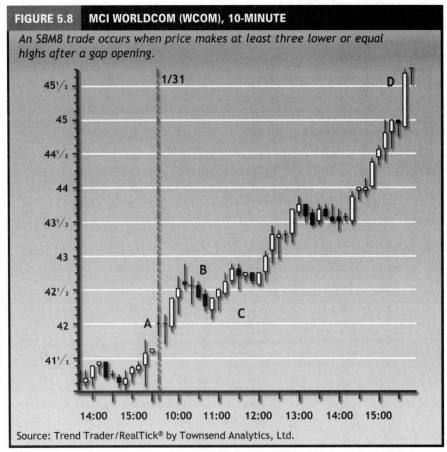

FIGURE 5.8 | MCI WORLDCOM (WCOM), 10-MINUTE

An SBM8 trade occurs when price makes at least three lower or equal highs after a gap opening.

Source: Trend Trader/RealTick® by Townsend Analytics, Ltd.

Figure 5.10 shows a stock with several entries during the day.

Biogen (BGEN) closed at 86¼ on January 31. It opened the next day at 88¹⁵⁄₁₆ (A) and immediately completed four bars with equal or lower highs. At 10:20 A.M. (B), BGEN exceeded the previous bar (which had a range of less than ¾) by ⅛, triggering the trade at 87¹¹⁄₁₆. At 11:10 A.M., the stock slipped ⅛ below the low of the previous two bars, and an exit at 87⅞ closed the trade with a gain of only ³⁄₁₆ (C).

But immediately after this exit, BGEN made four consecutive bars with lower or equal highs. At noon (D), the stock exceeded the previous bar (a bar with a very tight range, less than ¾) by ⅛, at 87⅞, triggering another trade. BGEN rallied immediately, moving higher until 1:50 P.M., when the stock traded ⅛ below the low of the last two bars, signaling an exit at 91¹⁄₁₆ (E), for a nice 3³⁄₁₆ gain on a risk of ½ point.

Finally, late in the day BGEN went into another setup pattern at 3 P.M. (F to G). However, the filter rule to not trade after 3 P.M. keeps us

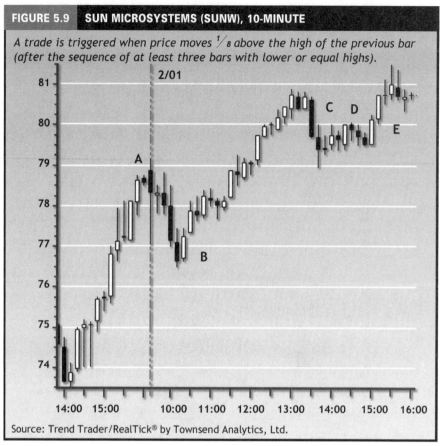

FIGURE 5.9   SUN MICROSYSTEMS (SUNW), 10-MINUTE

A trade is triggered when price moves ⅛ above the high of the previous bar (after the sequence of at least three bars with lower or equal highs).

Source: Trend Trader/RealTick® by Townsend Analytics, Ltd.

out of the market. Still, not a bad trading day, with two winners producing a 3⅜-point profit.

In Figure 5.11 on page 122, USA Networks (USAI) gapped up from its February 2, 2000, close of 49¹⁵⁄₁₆ to open at 51⁹⁄₁₆ (A) and then sold off. After three bars of lower or equal highs, the stock broke above the previous bar by ⅛ at 10:20 A.M., triggering entry at 50⅞. The previous bar had a ¼-point range, giving the trade a ½-point risk (B).

USAI ran for the next 90 minutes before an exit signaled (at 11:50 A.M.) at 51⅝, for a gain of ¹¹⁄₁₆. (Although this was a *wiggle stop,* one that just touches the exit point, you have to get out—rules are rules.)

From 12:20 P.M. through 12:50 P.M., the stock made three lower or equal highs, a congestion pattern that qualifies under all of our rules (C). A trade is triggered at 52³⁄₁₆, and with the previous bar having a range of only ⅛, the risk on this trade is only ⅜.

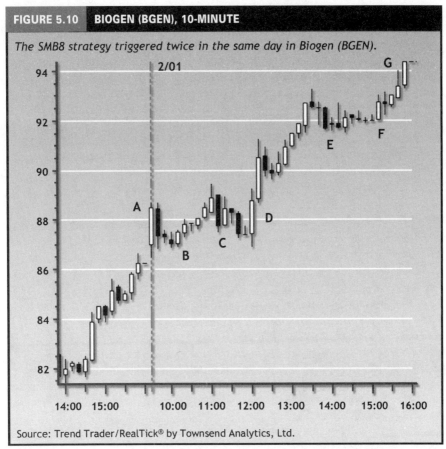

FIGURE 5.10 BIOGEN (BGEN), 10-MINUTE

The SMB8 strategy triggered twice in the same day in Biogen (BGEN).

Source: Trend Trader/RealTick® by Townsend Analytics, Ltd.

USAI rallied strongly until the exit rule closed the position at 53¾ at 2:10 P.M. with a 1⁹⁄₁₆-point gain (D).

The bottom line in trading is to design a plan and stick to it. This gives you the best chance of racking up enough doubles, triples, and home runs to more than offset your strikeouts.

clear-cut chart pattern trading

Mark Etzkorn

One of the criticisms of chart analysis is that patterns are in the eye of the beholder: A dozen traders could look at the same chart and give a

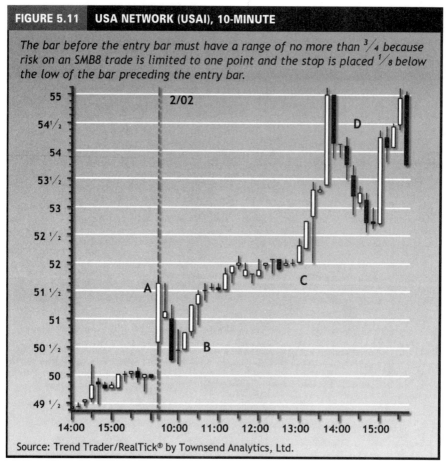

FIGURE 5.11   USA NETWORK (USAI), 10-MINUTE

The bar before the entry bar must have a range of no more than $^3/_4$ because risk on an SMB8 trade is limited to one point and the stop is placed $^1/_8$ below the low of the bar preceding the entry bar.

Source: Trend Trader/RealTick® by Townsend Analytics, Ltd.

dozen distinct interpretations of the different price formations and their implications for the future of a stock:

- "It's a head-and-shoulders."
- "No, it's a modified triple top."
- "No, it's a slightly bumpy rounded-top."
- "That trendline isn't valid!"

And so on.

In that sense, spike days and reversal days have a distinct advantage over other chart-pattern signals because they can be quantified quite easily. While different traders may come up with their own mathematical definitions, it is at least possible for anyone to construct a formula he or she can consistently apply over time to identify these patterns of momentum extremes and sentiment swings useful in short-term trading.

spikes and reversal days: momentum extremes

A spike is a bar with a high significantly higher (or a low significantly lower) than the surrounding highs (or lows). A reversal day occurs when price makes a new high (in an up move) and closes below the previous day's close, or when price makes a new low (in a down move) and closes above the previous day's close. Figure 5.12 illustrates the two patterns.

Spike days and reversal days reflect price climaxes and intraday sentiment shifts, respectively, and imply price corrections or consolidations. A spike is a price extreme—the kind of dramatic move often followed by a reaction or full-fledged reversal. (The astute chartist will note that a spike can only be identified in retrospect; a spike followed by a continuation instead of a reversal is another kind of one-bar pattern, the "wide-range day.")

Reversal days are similar: Price (for a reversal high day) establishes a new high—typically a sign of strength—only to reverse intraday and close below the open, a sign of weakness.

The definitions of these patterns are still a little vague. How much higher or lower than the preceding bars must a bar be to qualify as a spike? And, while the basic reversal day definition is clearer, it certainly could be argued that a reversal high day that closes strongly below the previous day's close—or alternately, below the previous day's low—

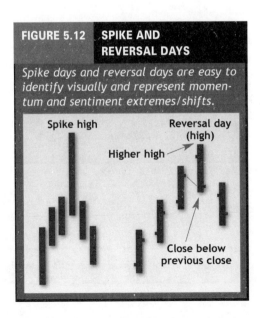

FIGURE 5.12 SPIKE AND REVERSAL DAYS

Spike days and reversal days are easy to identify visually and represent momentum and sentiment extremes/shifts.

Spike high

Reversal day (high)

Higher high

Close below previous close

indicates an even greater momentum and sentiment shift and, thus, a greater likelihood of immediate follow-through.

Not surprisingly, one of the drawbacks of these two patterns as they are typically defined and interpreted is their tendency to produce a multitude of false signals. Reversal days especially are common to the point of being meaningless.

In Figure 5.13, every bar that qualifies as a standard reversal high or reversal low day is marked with a dot above or below it, respectively. These are not high-quality trade signals, in terms of the price action that follows them. Yes, there are good opportunities here and there, but for the most part, these are outnumbered by useless signals.

defining the patterns

This is where things get good, though, for two reasons. First, part of the problem can be solved by coming up with specific formulas to objectively define both spike and reversal bars.

Spikes are a straightforward proposition: How much should a high or low exceed the preceding highs or lows to qualify as a spike (disregarding, for the time being, what happens after the spike bar)? A simple

FIGURE 5.13   FALSE SIGNALS: REVERSAL DAYS

The standard reversal day definition identifies some acceptable trade signals but far more false signals.

Source: TradeStation by Omega Research

approach is to use a percentage of the previous high price. For example, you could define a spike high as one 10 percent higher than the previous high. For a stock that has just made a high of 50, the next bar would have to hit 55 to qualify as a spike (that's a big spike, by the way).

There is room for individual interpretation and discretion. While you want to exclude as many meaningless signals as possible, you can't make the requirements too stringent (e.g., 25 percent) or you won't get any signals at all. You can establish a representative level simply by analyzing past spikes.

Reversal days allow for a little more experimentation. The goal here is to emphasize the momentum of the intraday reversal. A couple of ways to quantify this might be to require that the close occur at the absolute low of the day (or in the lowest *n* percent of the bar), or that the bar close below the low of the previous day.

The second, and even better, reason is the spike and reversal day concepts complement each other very well. When they occur at the same time, in the same bar, the likelihood of a reversal increases. A spike-reversal high bar would be a bar that is *n* percent higher than the preceding bar that closes below the previous day's close, in essence, a reversal bar that is significantly higher than the preceding bars (see Figure 5.14).

What's happening when such a bar appears? In terms of a spike-reversal high day, price is making an extreme up-thrust and reversing the same day, suggesting a potential buying climax, exhaustion, and the potential for a move in the opposite direction. Using the definitions outlined

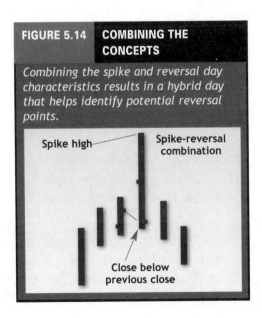

FIGURE 5.14 | COMBINING THE CONCEPTS

Combining the spike and reversal day characteristics results in a hybrid day that helps identify potential reversal points.

Spike high

Spike-reversal combination

Close below previous close

earlier, it's easy to categorize and identify these days. Here's a simple example:

- Spike-reversal high = Today's high must be *n* percent higher than yesterday's high and today's close must be below yesterday's close.

- Spike-reversal low = Today's low must be *n* percent lower than yesterday's low and today's close must be above yesterday's close.

These are fairly loose rules. You could decrease the number of signals by requiring a close above or below the previous day's high or low, or by using a similar filter. (Additionally, you could require the subsequent bar's high or low to be a particular amount below or above the spike bar to confirm the pattern.)

Figure 5.15 shows such points for the same price data as in Figure 5.13 using a 3 percent increase or decrease (from the previous high or low) to determine the high or low of the spike-reversal bar, and an accompanying close above or below the close of the previous bar.

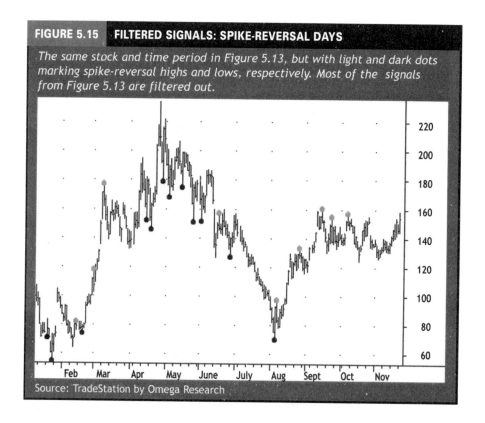

FIGURE 5.15   FILTERED SIGNALS: SPIKE-REVERSAL DAYS

The same stock and time period in Figure 5.13, but with light and dark dots marking spike-reversal highs and lows, respectively. Most of the signals from Figure 5.13 are filtered out.

Source: TradeStation by Omega Research

The most obvious difference is there are far fewer signals in Figure 5.15 than in Figure 5.13 (a good thing, considering the latter's overabundance of bad signals). Some good signals are lost, but far more false signals are eliminated in the process.

Notice also that most of these points are, in fact, spikes (of one magnitude or another) and not wide-range days, which means the intraday reversal element of the pattern is usually followed by a move in the same direction. Overall, combining the spike and reversal day concepts appears to have the benefit of filtering out many of the lower-probability trade signals.

developing a strategy

But is this superficially better looking mousetrap any good at catching mice? The only way to find out is to see if it's possible to develop a viable trading strategy based on the new hybrid spike-reversal day bar.

One of the interesting characteristics of many of the spike-reversal days in Figure 5.15 is that they precede short-term retracements, or pullbacks, in the prevailing trend—indicating (not surprisingly) that thrusts in the direction of the trend are more forceful than reactions against them.

A simple strategy to capitalize on the inherent characteristics of the spike-reversal day would be to enter short on the close of spike-reversal high days and enter long on the close of spike-reversal low days in anticipation of quick follow-through in the direction of the close. (This technique would require real-time monitoring of market conditions to know whether the current close satisfies the trade entry criteria. An entry on the next day's open could also be used.)

Table 5.3 shows the average results of a test of the spike-reversal day pattern on the 30 Dow Jones Industrial Average (DJIA) stocks from

TABLE 5.3	SPIKE-REVERSAL DAY STRATEGY, DJIA STOCKS		
January 1990 to February 2000			
	Profit factor	Average trade (%)	Percent profitable
Average, all stocks	1.03	0.041	51.19
Maximum	2.08	1.2	60.94
Minimum	0.52	-1.06	39.66

January 1990 to February 2000. The following spike and reversal combinations were tested:

- Spike moves ranging from 0.1 percent to 0.4 percent higher or lower than the preceding high or low.
- Close-to-close reversals from 0.1 percent to 0.4 percent higher or lower than the previous close.

These levels, while quite low (especially in terms of defining spikes), were used to generate as many signals as possible to get an idea of the average performance of this technique over time. Also, the test was conducted on the "mature" stocks of the DJIA, which are less volatile than many stocks (the majority of Internet stocks, for example). A test conducted on the latter stocks would benefit from larger percentages (perhaps in the 1 percent to 4 percent range to define spikes) to reflect their higher volatility.

The results: The percentage of winners is slightly more than 50 percent and the profit factor (total profit/total loss) is above 1. Using more stringent definitions for reversal and spike days than those used in the test, especially, would likely generate fewer, but better-performing, signals. But considering no stops were used and the exit was arbitrary (all trades were exited after eight days), the results suggest the basic spike-reversal day, while hardly perfect, helps find potential short-term swing points.

Such points are only the beginning of the journey, not the destination. Exit and risk-control rules are necessary to transform a trading idea into a trading plan. Any short-term strategy that operates independently of (or in opposition to) the prevailing trend must have a method to control losses and take profits, or both, to be profitable.

Techniques to improve performance include always trading in the direction of the underlying trend, combining the spike-reversal entry with a trailing stop technique, and trading only those signals that are preceded by a large, fast price move (which would again increase the likelihood of catching a short-term exhaustion point).

A quick visual inspection of Figure 5.15 suggests a quicker exit might be a step in the right direction. Price often follows through immediately (in the first one to three bars), but then reverses. A trailing stop would prevent giving back these quick profits and increase the strategy's winning percentage (but would also frequently take you out of potentially big trades early). Also, requiring a more significant spike would isolate better trade opportunities.

Chart patterns can be difficult to trade on a mechanical basis, but spike-reversal days present an opportunity to clearly identify short-term swing points based on common-sense price dynamics and market action.

chapter 6

market tendencies and short-term techniques

playing the seasonals

Steve Moore, Jerry Toepke, and Nick Colley

October has a well-deserved reputation for spectacular stock-market declines, the crashes of 1929 and 1987 being obvious examples. Less well
known—but far more consistent—has been the month's historical tendency to launch a market upswing.

The Chicago Mercantile Exchange (CME) has been trading S&P 500
futures since 1982. Although the market has been in bull mode since
then, certain annual, cyclic, or seasonal tendencies have recurred with
enough regularity to warrant their own nicknames. How often, for example, have you heard analysts discuss the "summer rally," or the so-called
"January effect"?

Such phenomena not only can be observed, but can also be quantified. In sifting through fourth-quarter price data for the S&P futures over
the past 18 years, certain seasonal tendencies became apparent that also
were evident in the S&P cash index for the past 50 years. Perhaps the
most intriguing discovery is a tendency for October to be the starting
month of a year-end rally—a phenomenon that has been consistent for
at least the past five decades.

Rather than simply accept the results of the study, however, let us
briefly examine the principles on which it is based. Experienced traders
know that markets move most dramatically when anticipating fundamental change and adjust equally as dramatically when the change actually occurs.

seasonal principles

Seasonal analysis originates from the premise that each market has its own unique fundamental forces that act on it every year. These conditions are not limited to the weather (in the case of commodity markets) but also include fiscal calendars, commercial buying/selling schedules, tax liability, quarterly Treasury refundings, and consumer preferences. If empirical evidence shows a pattern of market reaction to such forces, and it does, then one can more broadly define seasonality as a tendency to repeat similar price movement. As such, it becomes a valid analytical tool for any market.

A seasonal pattern for any market evolves from consistent price responses to annually recurring conditions. Thus, each market tends to create a seasonal pattern unique to itself, making it possible to construct a pattern for any futures contract, cash index, or individual equity using daily price activity over a designated number of years.

In our study of the S&P futures data, each day of every year is assigned a percentage value based on its position from the low to the high of the 12-month price range. The formula is:

$$\text{Daily Relational Value (DRV)} = \frac{DP - LPP}{HPP - LPP}$$

where   DP = Daily price
        LPP = Low price of period
        HPP = High price of period

Those values (rather than raw prices) for a particular day are then added together and divided by the number of occurrences (in this case 18, one for each year in the study period) to arrive at the Average Daily Relational Value (ADRV). The ADRV is a better reflection of historical behavior.

The results of the study show distinct times when the market tends to peak, bottom, and trend during the year, and as such can suggest the normal timing and direction of future price movement.

Figure 6.1 shows what this looks like for the S&P 500 index, when examined over the past 50 and 18 years. As you can see, the similarities between the two data sets are striking. The numerical scale to the right of the chart indicates the historical tendency of the market to make its seasonal high or seasonal low. A reading near 100 occurs when prices have most consistently been high during the year, and a reading of 0 occurs when they have been most consistently low. For example, a reading of 20 indicates that during that particular time, prices have tended to be in the lower 20 percent of each year's price range.

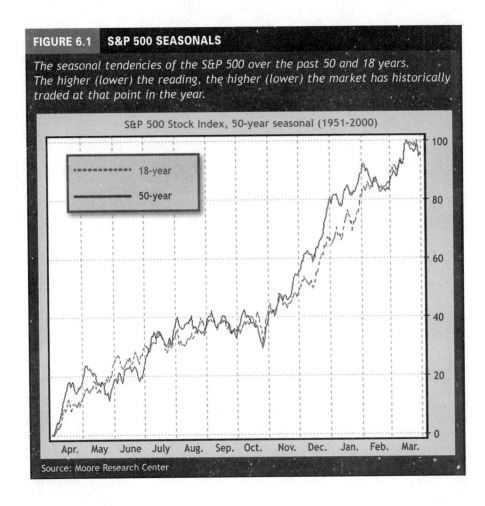

FIGURE 6.1   **S&P 500 SEASONALS**

The seasonal tendencies of the S&P 500 over the past 50 and 18 years.
The higher (lower) the reading, the higher (lower) the market has historically
traded at that point in the year.

S&P 500 Stock Index, 50-year seasonal (1951-2000)

Source: Moore Research Center

Figure 6.2 shows the same phenomenon for the March S&P 500 futures contract. The price chart of the March S&P futures, at the bottom, shows that seasonal tendencies cannot be discovered on a price chart.

seasonal strategies

Although the previous study allows us to see the most productive months, we need to dig deeper to find the most historically reliable and productive trading periods. Using daily settlement prices, computers can simulate every possible combination to select historically optimum entry/exit dates. Table 6.1 shows the results from such a simulation run for the past 18 years of trading in the March S&P 500 futures contract, and the past 50 years of the S&P 500 cash index.

FIGURE 6.2   A FUTURES MARKET COMPARISON

A standard price chart (bottom) does not reveal seasonal price patterns. The seasonal chart (top) highlights when the market is likely to peak, bottom and trend. For example, notice the tendency of the market to rally after bottoming in October.

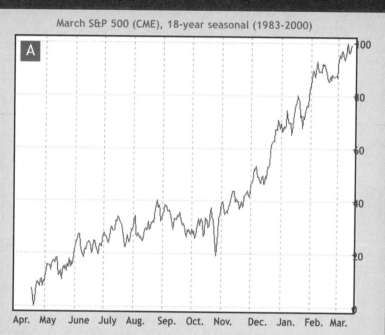

March S&P 500 (CME), 18-year seasonal (1983-2000)

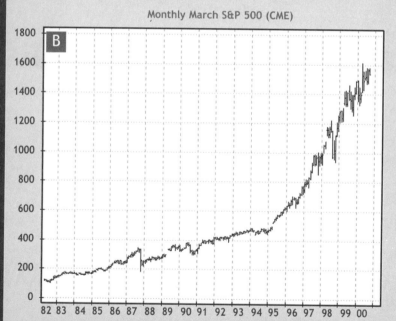

Monthly March S&P 500 (CME)

Source: Moore Research Center Inc.

TABLE 6.1	TRADING OPPORTUNITIES

The performance of entry and exit dates for the S&P 500 and DJIA based on the tendencies revealed in the seasonal analysis.

Market/position	Entry date	Exit date	Win pct	Win years	Loss years	Total years	Average profit
S&P 500 INDEX AND DJIA STRATEGIES							
Strategy 1 - Buy on approximately 10/17							
Long March S&P 500(CME)	10/17	12/29	83	15	3	18	$8,138(5.32%)
Long S&P 500 Stock Index	10/17	12/29	82	41	9	50	3.64%
Long DJIA Index	10/17	12/29	80	40	10	50	3.31%
Strategy 2 - Buy on approximately 10/26							
Long March S&P 500(CME)	10/26	1/19	94	17	1	18	$9,685(6.63%)
Long S&P 500 Stock Index	10/26	1/19	88	44	6	50	5.23%
Long DJIA Index	10/26	1/19	88	44	6	50	5.04%
Strategy 3 - Buy on approximately 12/14							
Long March S&P 500(CME)	12/14	2/08	89	16	2	18	$5,912(4.71%)
Long S&P 500 Stock Index	12/14	2/08	70	35	15	50	3.39%
Long DJIA Index	12/14	2/08	68	34	16	50	3.20%
50-year 90% Strategy for S&P 500 Cash Index							
Long S&P 500 Stock Index	10/27	1/5	90	45	5	50	4.80%
Long DJIA Index	10/27	1/5	84	42	8	50	4.73%

Source: Moore Research Center Inc.

The table simply lists statistics. For example, the second line states that the S&P 500 stock index has closed higher on or about December 29 than on or about October 17 in 41 of the past 50 years—a win-loss percentage of 82 percent that generated an average return of 3.64 percent.

Some veteran traders may associate strength into January with the bull market that began in the early 1980s. However, this research illustrates the existence of this powerful year-end phenomenon back to at least 1950, a tendency also suggested by statistics for the Dow Jones Industrials Average (DJIA) cash index.

These tendencies also are confirmed in Table 6.2 by the Nasdaq 100 index, Russell 2000 index, and Value Line index. However, in these instances we have to be a bit more careful with the interpretations as the entire shorter sample is from a bull market only.

To make sure each strategy isn't solely dependent on the results of a few very good years, but is the work of a truly recurrent event, it also is important to look at the individual yearly statistics. Table 6.3 shows the results of a strategy consisting of being long the March S&P 500 futures between October 26 and January 19. As you can see, there was only one losing trade (1990) since 1982.

Interestingly enough, however, the loss in 1990 was not confirmed by the S&P 500 index or the DJIA. In fact, the DJIA has managed to produce a profitable trade between these dates for the past 22 years, while the S&P 500 index isn't far behind with 18 profitable trades in a row.

Table 6.4 shows a set of similar statistics for trades on the Nasdaq 100 between December 14 and February 8. In this case, there again was

TABLE 6.2 — MORE TRADING OPPORTUNITIES

The performance of various strategies in the Nasdaq 100, Russell 2000 and Value Line indices support the tendencies exhibited by the S&P 500 and DJIA

	Market/position	Entry date	Exit date	Win pct	Win years	Loss years	Total years	Average profit
Trade 1	Long NASDAQ 100 Index	10/17	12/29	73	11	4	15	9.52
Trade 2	Long NASDAQ 100 Index	10/26	01/19	87	13	2	15	15.49
Trade 3	Long NASDAQ 100 Index	12/14	02/08	93	14	1	15	12.58
Trade 4	Long NASDAQ 100 Index	10/27	01/05	87	13	2	15	11.83
Trade 1	Long Russell 2000 Index	10/17	12/29	52	11	10	21	3.43
Trade 2	Long Russell 2000 Index	10/26	01/19	90	19	2	21	8.69
Trade 3	Long Russell 2000 Index	12/14	02/08	86	18	3	21	7.63
Trade 4	Long Russell 2000 Index	10/27	01/05	90	19	2	21	6.69
Trade 1	Long Value Line Index	10/17	12/29	65	11	6	17	3.30
Trade 2	Long Value Line Index	10/26	01/19	94	16	1	17	7.66
Trade 3	Long Value Line Index	12/14	02/08	88	15	2	17	7.08
Trade 4	Long Value Line Index	10/27	01/05	88	15	2	17	6.50

Source: Moore Research Center Inc.

TABLE 6.3 — S&P SEASONAL TRADING STRATEGY

The year-by-year results of the seasonal strategy as traded on the March S&P futures contract.

SEASONAL STRATEGY FOR MARCH S&P 500 (CME)
Enter on approximately 10/26 - Exit on approximately 1/19   Contract size: 250 x index

Cont year	Entry date	Entry price level	Exit date	Exit price level	Profit	Profit amount (%)	Best equity date	Best equity amount (%)	Worst equity date	Worst equity amount (%)
2000	10/26/99	1301.70	1/19/00	1472.50	170.80	13.12	12/31/99	14.02		
1999	10/26/98	1090.20	1/19/99	1257.00	166.80	15.30	1/8/99	18.05	10/28/98	-0.89
1998	10/27/97	884.40	1/16/98	968.40	84.00	9.50	12/5/97	12.81		
1997	10/28/96	706.75	1/17/97	780.75	74.00	10.47	1/17/97	10.47		
1996	10/26/95	583.35	1/19/96	614.15	30.80	5.28	12/13/95	7.58		
1995	10/26/94	466.50	1/19/95	468.60	2.10	.45	10/28/94	2.77	12/8/94	-3.78
1994	10/26/93	465.50	1/19/94	474.15	8.65	1.86	1/10/94	2.26	11/4/93	-1.31
1993	10/26/92	418.30	1/19/93	435.55	17.25	4.12	12/22/92	5.65	11/4/92	-0.39
1992	10/28/91	392.90	1/17/92	419.30	26.40	6.72	1/14/92	7.32	11/22/91	-3.95
1991	10/26/90	308.85	1/18/91	333.90	25.05	8.11	12/21/90	8.39	10/29/90	-0.76
1990	10/26/89	343.65	1/19/90	342.20	-1.45	-0.42	1/2/90	5.49	11/6/89	-1.75
1989	10/26/88	285.35	1/19/89	289.25	3.90	1.37	1/19/89	1.37	11/17/88	-6.31
1988	10/26/87	222.00	1/19/88	249.25	27.25	12.27	1/7/88	18.40		
1987	10/27/86	240.05	1/19/87	271.40	31.35	13.06	1/19/87	13.06	11/18/86	-1.02
1986	10/28/85	189.75	1/17/86	208.10	18.35	9.67	1/7/86	13.86		
1985	10/26/84	171.10	1/18/85	173.40	2.30	1.34	11/6/84	2.72	12/13/84	-3.71
1984	10/26/83	168.80	1/19/84	169.15	0.35	0.21	11/29/83	1.33	12/15/83	-2.52
1983	10/26/82	136.80	1/19/83	146.25	9.45	6.91	1/10/83	8.70	11/23/82	-2.56
Percentage Correct						94%				
Average Profit on Winning Trades						7.04%	Winners		17	
Average Loss on Trades						-0.42%	Losers		1	
Average Net Profit Per Trade						6.63%	Total trades		18	

Source: Moore Research Center Inc.

TABLE 6.4	NASDAQ 100 SEASONAL TRADING STRATEGY

Annual performance figures for the Nasdaq 100 seasonal strategy. Like the S&P strategy, there was only one losing trade.

				SEASONAL STRATEGY FOR NASDAQ 100 INDEX Enter on approximately 12/14 - Exit on approximately 2/8					
Entry Date	Entry Price level	Exit Date	Exit Price level	Profit	Profit Amount (%)	Best Equity Date	Best Equity Amount (%)	Worst Equity Date	Worst Equity Amount (%)
12/14/99	3167.29	2/8/00	4062.77	895.48	28.27	2/8/00	28.27		
12/14/98	1614.09	2/8/99	2034.21	420.12	26.03	2/1/99	32.02		
12/15/97	984.38	2/6/98	1134.32	149.94	15.23	2/6/98	15.23	12/24/97	-4.61
12/16/96	804.62	2/7/97	899.84	95.22	11.83	1/22/97	15.03		
12/14/95	566.29	2/8/96	623.79	57.50	10.15	2/8/96	10.15	1/9/96	-5.63
12/14/94	391.65	2/8/95	425.66	34.01	8.68	2/8/95	8.68	12/19/94	-0.31
12/14/93	382.83	2/8/94	401.46	18.63	4.87	1/31/94	8.14		
12/14/92	349.40	2/8/93	365.72	16.32	4.67	1/14/93	9.14	12/15/92	-0.70
12/16/91	303.02	2/7/92	346.80	43.78	14.45	1/15/92	17.35	12/19/92	-2.81
12/14/90	196.13	2/8/91	244.47	48.34	24.65	2/6/91	25.96	1/9/91	-2.27
12/14/89	216.40	2/8/90	207.20	-9.20	-4.25	1/2/90	5.22	1/30/90	-8.64
12/14/88	170.90	2/8/89	190.10	19.20	11.23	2/7/89	12.40		
12/14/87	146.10	2/8/88	157.90	11.80	8.08	1/7/88	15.47		
12/15/86	144.10	2/6/87	174.60	30.50	21.17	2/5/87	21.17	12/31/86	-1.87
12/16/85	132.60	2/7/86	137.40	4.80	3.62	2/7/86	3.62	1/9/86	-2.87
Percentage Correct					93%				
Average Profit on Winning Trades					13.78%		Winners		14
Average Loss on Trades					-4.25%		Losers		1
Average Net Profit Per Trade					12.58%		Total trades		15

Source: Moore Research Center Inc.

only one losing trade (in 1989). In recent years, not only was this trade profitable, but in many cases it also managed to get closed out without giving back any of its open profits (e.g., 1997 and 1999) or move into negative territory at all (e.g., 1998 and 1999).

possible explanations

Certainly, a number of fundamental conditions and events coincide with the October rally. For example, the U.S. fiscal year begins October 1. Does this cause a flow of federal funds into the economy? Do caps on annual Social Security payments make more private funds available for investment late in the year? Is the market anticipating a flood of year-end bonuses?

Technical analysts, however, should leave such fundamental speculation to others. Nonetheless, although statistics are limited to more recent years, a further seasonal coincidence is that a 23-year pattern for

December T-Bond futures depicts a distinct bottom in late October that launches a rally into late November, early December. The initial thrust upward especially stands out.

In fact, it can be shown that December T-Bonds have closed higher on or about October 31 than on or about October 23 for the past 15 years. Further study shows that futures trading has regularly favored the long end of the yield curve from October into November and December, which is a dynamic normally indicative of easing interest rates.

Studies of cash stock indexes do not translate directly into futures trading and vice versa. Nonetheless, strategies may be devised for both futures instruments and index tracking stocks that seek to take advantage of historical tendencies in the stock market. When stock indexes have observed those same tendencies for 50 years, through good times and bad, bull and bear markets, they reinforce the credibility of seasonal patterns observed in more recent years.

more bang for your buck: patterns within patterns

Mark Etzkorn

What makes a good trade? Well, in retrospect, most traders would say a nice profit makes a good trade. But when you're putting a position on, the outcome is unpredictable. We'd all like to know a trade will be good in advance, but alas, the markets are not so accommodating.

What you look for when you're getting in a trade is an entry point where the odds of a move in your favor are better than average. Then, by having a plan that determines when and where you'll exit with either a loss or a profit, you try to structure a trade where the potential reward is greater than the known risk.

The advantage of trading breakouts of congestion patterns such as trading ranges, triangles, flags, and pennants is that these formations allow you to logically define the risk on your trades. For example, if a stock moves into a trading range after a rally, you may look to buy an upside breakout of the range in anticipation of a continuation of the uptrend. The logical place to put an initial protective stop is below the low of the trading range, because a downside reversal through the support of the range would be a bearish development.

Figure 6.3 provides an example. In late June 2000, Microsoft (MSFT) established a relatively narrow trading range after approximately a 16-point rally. The stock broke out of the upside of the range (around 80⅛) on July 6. The initial protective stop would have been placed just below the support level of the trading range, around 76½. A

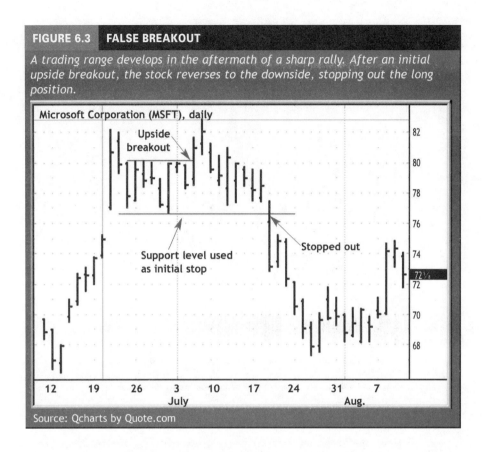

FIGURE 6.3   FALSE BREAKOUT

A trading range develops in the aftermath of a sharp rally. After an initial upside breakout, the stock reverses to the downside, stopping out the long position.

Microsoft Corporation (MSFT), daily

Source: Qcharts by Quote.com

move back below this level would suggest the upside thrust was actually a false breakout and that the trade should be exited.

That's exactly what happened. Two days after entry, the stock had pulled back into the trading range. It moved sideways to lower over the next several days before, on July 19, penetrating the downside of the range and stopping out the long trade.

The risk on this trade was a moderate 3⅝ points. But what do you do when a trading range is much wider and a stop based on either the support or resistance level represents too large a risk? Figure 6.4 shows a much more volatile trading range than that in Figure 6.3. Using the same approach as in the previous example—buying on an upside break-out of the trading range and placing an initial protective stop below the low of the range—would represent considerable risk.

As a result, some traders place the initial stop in the middle of the trading range. This more conservative method is based on the idea that a strong breakout move should follow through immediately and not re-verse back into the trading range. Another way to reduce risk on breakout

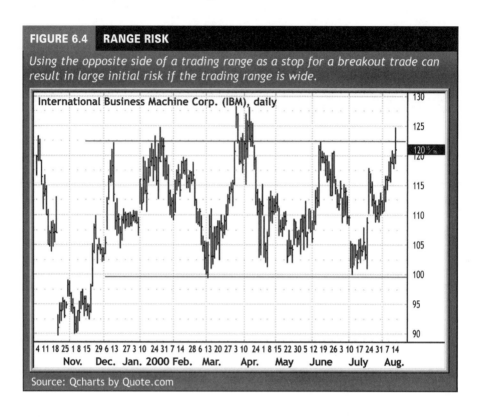

FIGURE 6.4   RANGE RISK

Using the opposite side of a trading range as a stop for a breakout trade can result in large initial risk if the trading range is wide.

Source: Qcharts by Quote.com

trades is to look for shorter term patterns within larger patterns that allow you to place your initial stop-loss closer to your entry point.

patterns within patterns

When the risk implied by a particular trading range is exceptionally large, you can look for smaller congestion patterns near the support or resistance levels of the range. Basing entry and stop points on the levels defined by the smaller pattern can reduce the risk on the trade as well as provide the opportunity for early entry into the position.

Figure 6.5 shows the formation of a wide trading range in Oracle (ORCL) at the beginning of 2000. A trader looking to enter long on an upside breakout of this range would have to accept a risk of more than 16 points, assuming the bottom of the range was used for the initial stop-loss.

However, a much narrower trading range developed in February. Using this range as the basis of an upside breakout trade would have offered the same entry point but a much closer stop. In this case, placing a stop one tick below the low of the narrower trading range would have

FIGURE 6.5   CONGESTION WITHIN CONGESTION

A shorter, narrower trading range forms just at the resistance level of a larger range. Using the support level of the smaller range as a protective level for an upside breakout substantially reduces the trade's initial risk.

Oracle Corporation (ORCL), daily

Wider trading range

Narrow range

Source: Qcharts by Quote.com

reduced the risk to 6¾ points. For a short-term trader, this represents a large stop, but it's still a dramatic improvement and the profit potential for the move out of the larger trading range is still intact. (Later, we'll look at the practical risk-reward impact this can have on a trade.)

Figure 6.6 provides another example. In this case, EMC Corporation (EMC) repeatedly pulled back from resistance around 72½. Because a well-defined horizontal trading range did not develop (the stock swung back and forth in an increasingly wider range), the most recent swing low around 51 would be the reference point for the initial stop-loss—a risk of more than 20 points.

However, as the stock bounced off that low and made another run at the resistance level, it formed a flag consolidation from June 7 to June 12 with a high around 69⅞ (the highs of the bars in the flags were within ¹/₁₆ of each other) and a low around 66¹³/₁₆. The upside breakout of this flag provided an early entry to the subsequent surge that pushed the stock past the 72½ resistance level to new highs.

FIGURE 6.6   FLAG NEAR RESISTANCE

A small flag forms just below a well-defined resistance level, offering early entry into the upside thrust move.

Source: Qcharts by Quote.com

Figure 6.7 shows a 15-minute chart of the Nasdaq 100 tracking stock (QQQ). The stock formed a large bottoming pattern (a head-and-shoulders bottom pattern; the preceding sell-off is not shown) with resistance around $82\frac{5}{8}$. As the stock approached the resistance level for the second time, on May 30, 2000, it consolidated in a narrow flag pattern with resistance around $82\frac{7}{32}$ and support around $81\frac{5}{8}$. Playing an upside breakout of this pattern and using its support level for the initial stop (rather than the most recent swing low around 76) reduced the risk on a long trade to less than a point.

A final example is shown in Figure 6.8. Here, in the middle of a larger trading range with resistance around $32\frac{3}{8}$, Motorola (MOT) formed a flag consolidation in late-October 1999 that offered the opportunity to trade an upside move with lower risk. The stock gapped out of the flag (a bullish sign) above $31\frac{1}{2}$ and continued to run past the resistance of the larger trading range. Placing a stop just below the flag support at $29\frac{15}{16}$ would

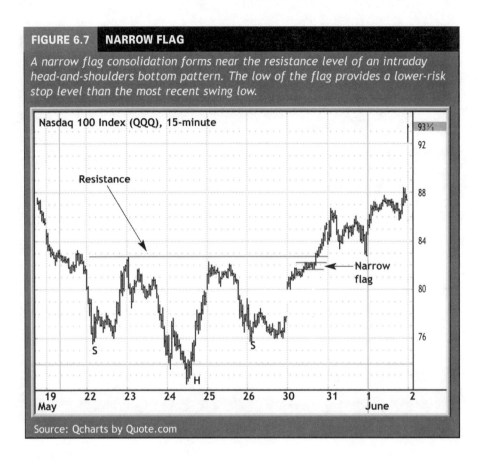

FIGURE 6.7   NARROW FLAG

A narrow flag consolidation forms near the resistance level of an intraday head-and-shoulders bottom pattern. The low of the flag provides a lower-risk stop level than the most recent swing low.

Source: Qcharts by Quote.com

have reduced the initial risk on the trade to less than two points. As was the case with Figure 6.6, the smaller pattern allowed you to both use a tighter stop and get in earlier on an upside breakout.

structuring a trade

Figure 6.5 provides a good example of how this approach can work in the context of a complete trade plan. The rally from the late-October 1999 low to the early-January 2000 high was $41\frac{7}{32}$. The stock then moved sideways, forming the larger trading range. A trader looking to buy on an upside breakout of the range could use the *measured move* approach, whereby the size of the previous price move is added to the current price, to project a price target. Adding the size of the price move preceding the trading range to the low of the larger trading range (around $46\frac{5}{8}$) results in an upside target of $87\frac{27}{32}$.

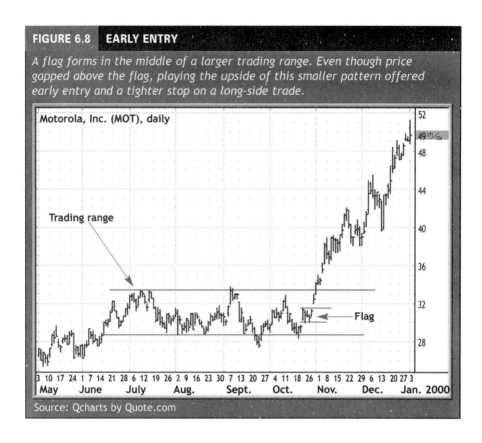

FIGURE 6.8   EARLY ENTRY

A flag forms in the middle of a larger trading range. Even though price gapped above the flag, playing the upside of this smaller pattern offered early entry and a tighter stop on a long-side trade.

Source: Qcharts by Quote.com

Using the measured move approach on the smaller price swing from the January 28 low of 46⅝ to the February 14 high of 64¾ (18⅛ points) sets up a shorter term price target of 77⁷⁄₁₆. This level would mark a good spot to take at least partial profits on the position and raise the stop on the balance of the position. The stock actually formed another flag after hitting a high of 76½ on February 28. This consolidation marked an opportunity to exit part of the position with a profit; the stop on the remainder of the position could then be moved up to the breakeven point, locking in a profit on the trade. The bottom line: The development of the smaller trading range allowed the establishment of a trade with a price target based on the larger, longer term price pattern with a risk based on the smaller, shorter term price pattern.

Another general advantage of this approach is that it increases your flexibility. Even if you are stopped out on a move through the support of the smaller congestion pattern, you can still reenter a long position if the market reverses again and breaks out above resistance a second time. For example, a trader who went long on the intraday upside thrust above resistance (say, at 62⅝) on February 14 and used the low of the smaller trading range (around 58⅝) as the stop level, would have been stopped out on the intraday downside thrust on February 22. However, as mentioned earlier, this loss is much smaller than the one that would have occurred had the stop been placed below the low of the larger trading range, which was nearly 12 points lower.

These patterns may develop relatively infrequently, but they fulfill the primary goals of smart trading: They allow you to establish trades with shorter term risk and longer term profit potential.

a matter of timing

Robert Krausz

Trading is not necessarily easy, but it is a much simpler process than most people imagine. The problem, ironically, is that gaining this understanding often requires a long, complicated journey—kind of like walking out your front door and traveling a few thousand miles to get to your back yard.

New traders especially tend to run into difficulties because they believe that more—indicators, charts, statistics, and so on—is better.

The truth is, simple approaches can yield good results if your analysis is based on a solid frame of reference. Here we will explain a simple, but powerful, concept—multiple time-frame analysis—and show how it will enhance your trading by providing a well-defined framework in which to operate.

trend on different levels

The basis of multiple time-frame analysis is that every time period has its own trend and its own support and resistance levels.

By simple inspection, you can see the trend and support and resistance levels on a 10-minute bar chart are different than levels on a daily bar chart.

However, the trend and support and resistance levels of the 10-minute time frame are still part of the daily trend; the trend of the 10-minute bars obviously shapes the trend of the daily bars. While any time period is a self-contained universe, it still functions as part of a larger structure. longer term price action provides a context for shorter term price action—the frame of reference every trader needs to make good decisions.

The context provided by these different time frames determines how, when, and in what direction to trade.

time frame trading structure

The first step in our trading approach is to define three time frames that will provide the trading structure we operate in.

The time frame we will trade is the "own" time frame. The longer time frame is the "next" time frame. Finally, the longest time frame is simply the "high" time frame. For example, the setup for trading 30-minute bars might be:

30-minute bars = *Own* period

Daily bars = *Next* period

Weekly bars = *High* period

For trading daily bars, the definitions might break down as follows:

Daily bars = *Own* period

Weekly bars = *Next* period

Monthly bars = *High* period

For most practical purposes you only need to focus on two time frames, own and next.

The next time frame indicates the direction of the tradable trend and the support and resistance levels for trading. When the next time frame indicates an uptrend, we will trade from the long side; when the next time frame indicates a downtrend, we will trade from the short side.

Let's walk through some examples using America Online (AOL). Figure 6.9 is a daily bar chart of AOL.

The line plotted in a step formation is the weekly *balance step,* a five-week moving average of the weekly closes (Friday-to-Friday only). In essence, we are overlaying a moving average of weekly price action on a daily chart, making it possible to monitor both time frames simultaneously. The daily bars represent the own time frame (the time frame we will trade) while the weekly balance step functions as the next time frame (the time frame that indicates the tradable trend). What does this multiple time frame analysis reveal?

First, in late September 1999, there were two consecutive closes above the weekly balance step (point A). Second, in early October 1999, the weekly balance step turned up (point B) and continued to rise each week until the end of the year when it turned down for the first time (point F). This highlights that the next time frame was in an uptrend throughout this period from points A to F, and the safest trades to make using daily bars (the own time frame) would have been on the long side, that is, in conjunction with the longer term trend.

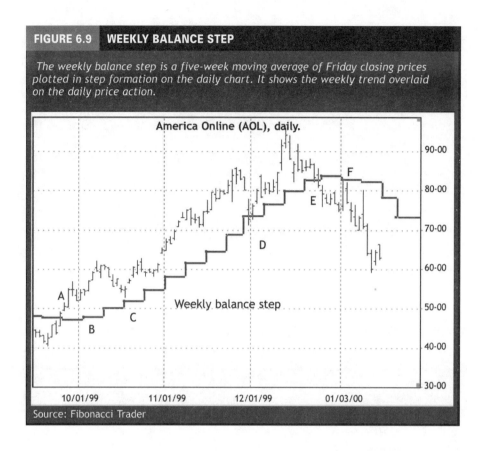

FIGURE 6.9   WEEKLY BALANCE STEP

The weekly balance step is a five-week moving average of Friday closing prices plotted in step formation on the daily chart. It shows the weekly trend overlaid on the daily price action.

America Online (AOL), daily.

Weekly balance step

Source: Fibonacci Trader

This is a straightforward concept. Trading with the trend of the next time frame is like having the wind at your back. Keep in mind that the trend can only change when the direction of the next time frame changes.

Also notice that at points C, D, and E in Figure 6.9 the balance step functions as support and resistance; closing above the balance step is a positive sign. At point C, AOL tests the near-term support defined by the balance step and rallies sharply from this level. Point D marks a similar instance. Point E is a major warning the trend may be changing: The stock breaks support by closing below the balance step for two consecutive bars.

intraday analysis

The same principles outlined in our first example are equally applicable to shorter time frames. Let's drop down in time and take a look at an intraday view of AOL using 78-minute bars (one-fifth of the 390-minute normal trading day) and additional technical indicators to help filter trades.

Figure 6.10 uses the 78-minute bars as the own time period, daily bars as the next time period, and weekly bars as the high time period. Both weekly and daily balance step lines are plotted, and both indicators are calculated over five-bar periods. The daily balance step uses the daily closing prices.

Why did we add the daily balance step? Because we always use the next time frame to determine the tradable trend. Let's look for signs of the market topping using our multiple frame approach on an intraday basis.

Our first warning came when the daily balance step (the next time frame) turned down for the first time (point H). In addition, at point E, the stock closed below the weekly balance step, another negative indication. Adding to the bearishness, the daily balance step crossed below the

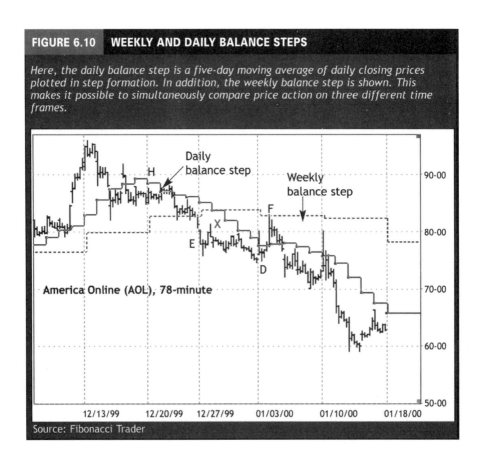

FIGURE 6.10 **WEEKLY AND DAILY BALANCE STEPS**

Here, the daily balance step is a five-day moving average of daily closing prices plotted in step formation. In addition, the weekly balance step is shown. This makes it possible to simultaneously compare price action on three different time frames.

Source: Fibonacci Trader

weekly balance step at point X. Finally, at point F (the same point F from Figure 6.9), the weekly balance step—the high time frame—turned down for the first time, pointing to lower prices as well.

adding a filter

To take things a step further and look for trading opportunities, we will introduce additional technical indicators.

The first is the Ergodic Candlestick Oscillator (ECO), designed by William Blau and detailed in his book *Momentum, Direction, and Divergence.* This momentum indicator is a *double-smoothed* (the application of two moving averages—one very long term and the other shorter term) ratio of the difference between the closing (C) and opening (O) prices of each bar and the difference between the high (H) and low (L) prices for each bar:

$$\text{ECO} = \frac{\text{EMA1}[\text{EMA2}(C - O)]}{\text{EMA1}[\text{EMA2}(H - L)]} \times 100$$

where EMA1 is a longer term exponential moving average (e.g., 26 days), and EMA2 is a shorter term exponential moving average (e.g., 5 days).

Figure 6.11 is the same as Figure 6.10 except that the ECO (calculated on the 78-minute bars, the own time frame) is plotted below the price series as a histogram. The ECO functions as a filter: Readings below zero confirm the trend is down for the own time frame and readings above zero confirm the trend is up.

Look at point G: The ECO actually turned negative prior to the daily balance step turning down. When the daily balance step turned down at point H (same as Figure 6.10), the ECO had been negative for some time and therefore confirmed this change in the trend of the next time period.

When price rallied above the daily balance step at point J, the ECO only rallied above the zero line for one day, or five 78-minute bars, before returning to a negative trend. After point J, the ECO also reconfirmed the downtrend.

putting on trades

Having outlined the concept of using a multiple time frame approach to determine the trend and support and resistance levels, let's see what happens if we take a trade when the trend changes direction, as determined by a change in the next time period (the daily balance step). We'll use the intraday (78-minute bar) time frame.

Now that we are trading, though, we also must give thought to risk control: We will want to have some kind of trailing stop to lock in our

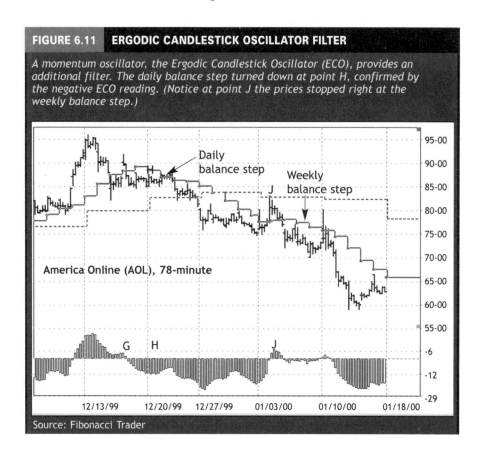

FIGURE 6.11   ERGODIC CANDLESTICK OSCILLATOR FILTER

A momentum oscillator, the Ergodic Candlestick Oscillator (ECO), provides an additional filter. The daily balance step turned down at point H, confirmed by the negative ECO reading. (Notice at point J the prices stopped right at the weekly balance step.)

Source: Fibonacci Trader

profits. For that purpose, we will introduce another indicator, the HiLo Activator, based on the own time period.

The HiLo Activator is a 21-period moving average of the lows or highs. If price closes above the HiLo Activator, the indicator is a moving average of the lows; when the market closes below the HiLo Activator, the indicator flips to being a moving average of the highs. The HiLo Activator is above prices in a downtrending market and below prices in an uptrending market, providing a trailing stop point as the position progresses.

Figure 6.12 shows that a short sell signal in AOL occurred on the close of December 17, 1999, at a price of 85 when the daily balance step clearly turned down. The HiLo Activator is trailing above the prices and the ECO also has confirmed the downtrend by dropping below zero.

Prices continued to fall until January 3, 2000, when the market rallied above the HiLo Activator and penetrated the daily balance step. (You can take profits when price penetrates the balance step and the

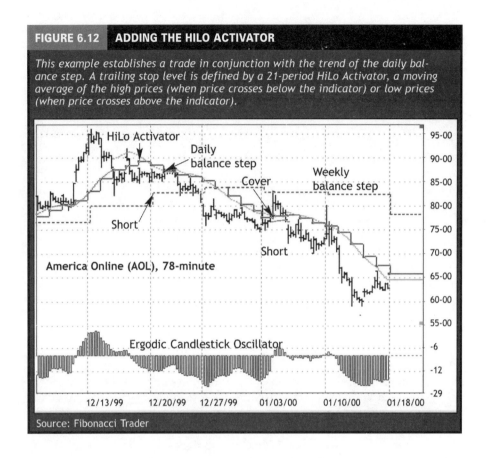

| FIGURE 6.12 | ADDING THE HILO ACTIVATOR |

This example establishes a trade in conjunction with the trend of the daily balance step. A trailing stop level is defined by a 21-period HiLo Activator, a moving average of the high prices (when price crosses below the indicator) or low prices (when price crosses above the indicator).

Source: Fibonacci Trader

HiLo Activator by more than a point.) However, notice that the stock stopped right at the resistance level of the weekly balance step. The daily balance step went into a flat period.

The next day, the downtrend resumed with the daily balance step turning down. Had you gone flat, you could have gone short again because the HiLo Activator flipped again on the close of the first 78-minute bar. Prices were below the daily balance step, which turned down at the close, triggering a short trade at 73½.

A multiple time frame approach is a way of filtering price information through different windows of time. By using weekly bar-based indicators for trading daily bars, you avoid the noise of the daily bars.

Likewise, if you are trading intraday bars, you should filter your trades with daily bar-based indicators, trading when indicators on both time frames are in concert. This is a simple, yet powerful frame of reference for enhancing your trading opportunities.

trading the Wyckoff way: buying springs and selling upthrusts

Henry O. (Hank) Pruden

Before the rudiments of technical analysis were spreading like wildfire via the Internet, bookstores, and television, the general public or the crowd would join a trend only after it had been well underway.

Nowadays, however, the crowd often rushes into a stock, a sector, or a market at the first clue of a price breakout from a congestion zone. But as Joseph Granville, a famous technical analyst and trader, once said, "[In the markets], whatever is obvious is obviously wrong."

So, if the crowd is rushing in at breakout time, who is left to take the other side of the trade? The answer is the better-informed professionals, who have conditioned themselves to act in accordance with another old saying, "One should fear to tread where fools rush in." Hence, if you want to trade like the professionals, and not count yourself among the fools, you may want to sell a breakout rather than buy it—especially when the popular stocks of the day are under consideration.

To avoid being caught with the crowd, you should contemplate buying springs and selling upthrusts—two insightful, but often overlooked, principles of Richard D. Wyckoff, an early advocate of technical analysis who codified the best practices of the famous traders of the early 1900s. His principles and procedures, which came to be known as "the Wyckoff method," are based on reading chart patterns.

Don't expect to discover a set of precise mechanical rules with the Wyckoff method; instead, you'll discover insights, general principles, and guidelines that will help you interpret market behavior.

the patterns

A *spring* is a price move below the support level of a trading range that quickly reverses and moves back into the range. A spring is an example of a *bear trap* because the drop below support appears to signal resumption of the downtrend. In reality, though, the drop marks the end of the downtrend, thus trapping the late sellers, or bears. The extent of supply, or the strength of the sellers, can be judged by the depth of the price move to new lows and the relative level of volume on that penetration.

An *upthrust* is the opposite of a spring. It's a price move above the resistance level of a trading range that quickly reverses itself and moves back into the trading range. An upthrust is a *bull trap:* It appears to signal a start of an uptrend but in reality marks the end of the up move. The magnitude of the upthrust can be determined by the extent of the price move to new highs and the relative level of volume on that movement.

Springs and upthrusts are divided into three types—No. 3, No. 2, and No. 1.

the rules

A No. 3 spring occurs when a modest penetration of support is accompanied by volume that is relatively light compared with the volume of prior down moves. The shallow price penetration and low volume indicate sellers are exhausted. No. 3 springs should be bought immediately.

No. 2 springs penetrate more deeply below support with greater comparative volume than No. 3 springs. This indicates sellers are still abundant during the break. Therefore, a second test of support is necessary before a buy can be signaled. After the initial break below support, price should move back about one-third into the trading range. Ideally, the volume for this up move should be higher than during the immediately preceding downswing, and also greater than volume of previous rallies within the trading range. The secondary test consists of a down move that, on comparatively light volume, usually retraces less than half the rally off the low established on the first downside penetration.

No. 1 springs are wholesale breakdowns below support on volume that is much larger than that of prior downswings within the trading range. Do not buy No. 1 springs; rather, look to sell short if the subsequent rally stops at or below the prior support (now resistance) level, especially if the move back to this level occurs on approximately half the volume of the initial breakdown.

Upthrusts are essentially mirror images of springs. A No. 3 upthrust is completed when, after penetrating resistance on large relative volume, price returns immediately to the average level of closing prices within the preceding range. The No. 3 upthrust is referred to as an "upthrust after distribution." Sell No. 3 upthrusts immediately.

The No. 2 upthrust usually consists of a larger rally past resistance on greater comparative volume than No. 3 upthrusts. Like its No. 2 spring counterpart, however, a secondary test must be conducted before a sell signal is activated. After resistance is crossed initially, price should move back about one-third into the trading range. Volume for this move ideally should be greater than during the preceding upswing and higher than volume during the previous down moves. The secondary test consists of a rally that, on comparatively light volume, often retraces less than half the reaction from the immediately preceding high.

No. 1 upthrusts are legitimate upside breakouts that denote the start or resumption of an uptrend, and are usually accompanied by high volume. Rather than attempting to sell short, look to buy on a pullback that halts at or above prior resistance (now support), especially if the coinciding volume is no more than half the volume of the initial breakout.

in practice

Let's see how these patterns develop in real market situations. The first case involves Broadvision Inc. (BVSN), which formed a No. 2 spring in late January 2000 (see Figure 6.13).

Price fell below support to 37⅜ on high volume on January 31 before springing back to the middle of the trading range at 51¾ on February 3. A buy order was signaled when the stock fell back below 50 on light volume the next two trading days (the secondary test required of the No. 2 spring), with a stop-loss at the most recent low of 37⅜. After breaking back above 50 on February 8, Broadvision subsequently skyrocketed to 90 by early March.

The next two examples are in Lucent Technologies (LU). Figure 6.14 shows that Lucent, in late May 1999, fell below previously defined support near 56 on very light volume, immediately signaling a good buying

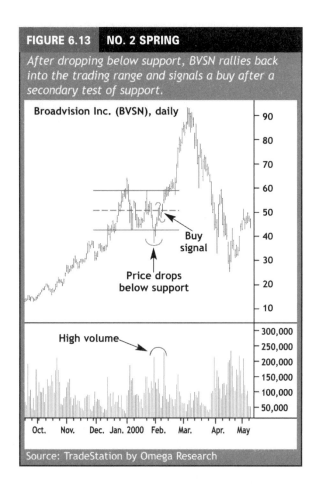

FIGURE 6.13   NO. 2 SPRING

After dropping below support, BVSN rallies back into the trading range and signals a buy after a secondary test of support.

Broadvision Inc. (BVSN), daily

Buy signal

Price drops below support

High volume

Source: TradeStation by Omega Research

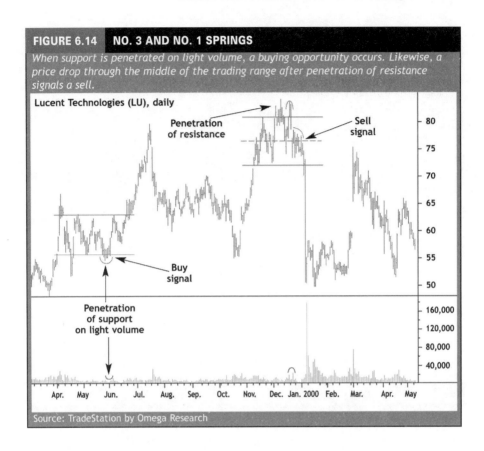

FIGURE 6.14   NO. 3 AND NO. 1 SPRINGS

When support is penetrated on light volume, a buying opportunity occurs. Likewise, a price drop through the middle of the trading range after penetration of resistance signals a sell.

Lucent Technologies (LU), daily

Source: TradeStation by Omega Research

opportunity in accordance with the rules for a No. 3 spring. The stock rallied strongly into July. Although Lucent slumped after the big increase, the stop-loss was never hit.

A new trading range developed in early November, with the stock trading between 72 and 82. When the resistance level was penetrated in mid-December, a short sale could have been executed around 78, the point where the rally began to falter on relatively decreased volume. But a few days later, when the market fell through the approximate halfway point of the trading range, the sell signal was confirmed, with an accompanying stop-loss around the preceding high of 84³⁄₁₆.

Two more examples involve Computer Network Tech. Corporation (CMNT). These setups are practically identical, although they occurred at different times. Figure 6.15 shows CMNT formed a trading range in the 20 to 25 region during November and December 1999.

The stock penetrated resistance toward the end of the year on increased volume, but soon fell back down below 22. The stock again

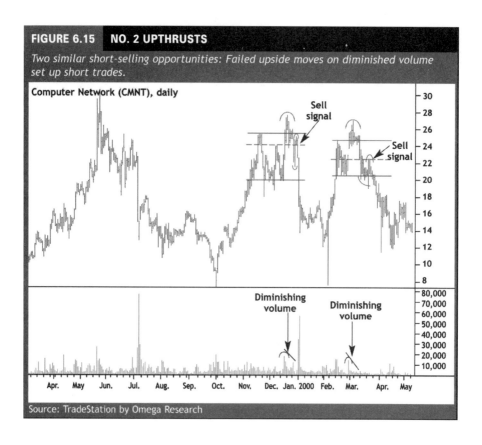

FIGURE 6.15   NO. 2 UPTHRUSTS

Two similar short-selling opportunities: Failed upside moves on diminished volume set up short trades.

Source: TradeStation by Omega Research

attempted to rally, with price reaching 25⅛ on December 30, but it did so on diminishing volume. This failed rally completed the setup sequence for a No. 2 upthrust.

Another similar setup developed in February and March 2000. A selling opportunity arose when price began to decrease past the halfway point of the trading range in mid-March on decreasing volume. In both CMNT examples, stop-loss orders are placed at or just above the preceding highs.

Figure 6.16 shows the final examples, which involve Amazon.com (AMZN) and are a case of several intertwining situations. First, the stock formed a massive trading range between 62 and 110 from late September 1999 to mid-April 2000. When the stock rose above 110 with a burst of volume in early December, only to turn back down again, it could have constituted a No. 3 upthrust and a sell short order could have been placed around 101 (where resistance for a much smaller trading range

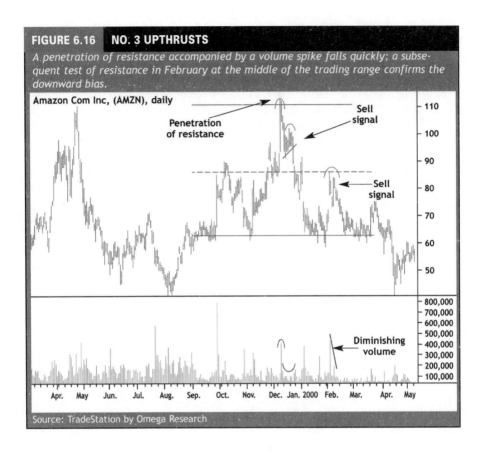

FIGURE 6.16   NO. 3 UPTHRUSTS

A penetration of resistance accompanied by a volume spike falls quickly; a subsequent test of resistance in February at the middle of the trading range confirms the downward bias.

Source: TradeStation by Omega Research

had formed). In early February, another short-selling opportunity presented itself when the market once again failed to rally past the halfway point of the range on diminishing volume.

conclusion

By dividing upthrusts and springs into three separate categories, traders who study the Wyckoff method will be better able to evaluate market behavior around bear and bull traps.

The important thing to remember is that bottom fishing or top picking should not always be avoided or considered dangerous. Recognizing and understanding springs and upthrusts can help you locate reasonably high-reward, low-risk opportunities near the bottoms and tops of trading ranges.

anticipating breakouts and beating slippage

Steve Wendlandt

One of the most important aspects of short-term stock trading is something you almost never hear about: slippage.

Slippage is the difference between where you expect, or want, to be filled on a trade and where your order is actually executed. If you don't understand this concept, try to enter a market order with a browser-based online broker the first day of a hot IPO and see what happens. That's slippage! Slippage can be caused by several factors: Poor execution by a broker, communication failure or other technical problems, or fast market conditions.

While we all try to keep our costs down to the bare minimum without sacrificing service or technology, slippage is probably the most overlooked and significant cost in trading. But through a little-known tendency, you can make slippage work for you instead of bleeding you dry. In fact, if most of your trading techniques are breakout related, you can use this trick on almost every trade you enter. But first, let's look at why it works.

one tick at a time

Tom DeMark, a highly regarded trading system developer who has worked with such top traders as George Soros, Paul Tudor Jones, and Steve Cohen, wrote a book (his second) called *New Market Timing Techniques: Innovative Studies in Market Rhythm and Price Exhaustion.* In it, he explained what probably is one of the most significant discoveries in the markets: the TD One-Tick, One-Time Rule.

This rule states if a market makes a new high or low just once (a single print) and backs off from that point, that new high or low should hold for a significant period of time. In fact, most significant highs and lows only print one time at the extreme price.

It makes sense that the opposite also is true: If a price prints more than once at a certain high or low, then that high or low will be broken in short order almost every time. From that, it follows the more a particular level is tested, the weaker it becomes.

In a layperson's terms, if a stock continually prints or finds support or resistance at a certain price, the odds are extremely good that price level will be broken shortly. That is invaluable information for any trader who uses breakouts as part of his or her strategy.

Figure 6.17 is a five-minute chart of CMGI. The stock bounced off support at 50 six times (and who knows how many prints actually occurred at that level). Every time a stock tests a support or resistance

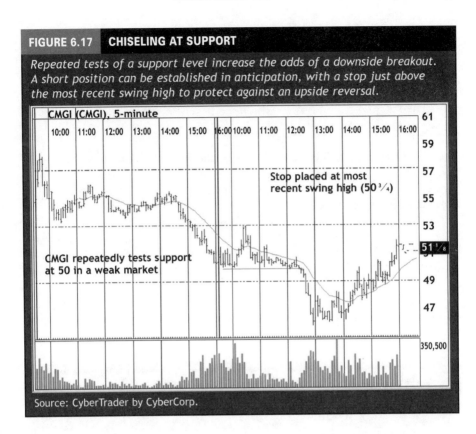

FIGURE 6.17   CHISELING AT SUPPORT

Repeated tests of a support level increase the odds of a downside breakout. A short position can be established in anticipation, with a stop just above the most recent swing high to protect against an upside reversal.

CMGI (CMGI), 5-minute

Stop placed at most recent swing high (50 ³/₄)

CMGI repeatedly tests support at 50 in a weak market

Source: CyberTrader by CyberCorp.

level, that level gets weaker and weaker, as if a hammer and chisel were chipping away at it.

Most people view support levels as opportunities to go long, while breakout traders view tests of support as fuel to propel an eventual breakout. In this example, not only are traders establishing new long positions with their stops just below the support level at 50, many traders also are waiting to short the stock once it does break down. Don't forget that all the people who bought the stock around $50 will either be stopped out or will wait for an opportunity to break even on their trades. The bottom line is that when support at 50 is penetrated it quickly turns into significant resistance.

Here's the question: If, because of repeated tests of the support level, the odds are very good the 50 level will be broken (and the broader market indexes support this view), why wait for the breakout? Doing so increases the odds of having to chase the market or missing the trade. In this case, if you wait for the stock to trade at $49^{15}/_{16}$ and then try to establish a short position, you'll probably end up missing the trade waiting for an uptick.

Let's look at a second example. In Figure 6.18, Netro Corporation (NTRO) was bouncing off the 82½ level for about two weeks. The day it finally broke that support level (March 30, 2000) was a very weak day in the broader market indexes, which helped the stock to finally break down. A good opportunity to short NTRO came at the prior day's close when NTRO closed right at the support level for the second day in a row. The next morning NTRO gapped lower and continued to drop dramatically. It would have been difficult to get short after the market opened for trading on the day of the breakdown (although, there were some upticks in the premarket).

All breakout traders know it's very difficult to get short once a stock breaks through support, if the trade is any good. You must either wait for an uptick (which may not happen) or offer it short ¹⁄₁₆ higher than the inside bid (for Nasdaq stocks). But if the stock is dropping like a rock, who is going to hit your offer?

The bottom line is that if you want to trade a stock when the overall market is trending in the direction of your potential trade, and the stock

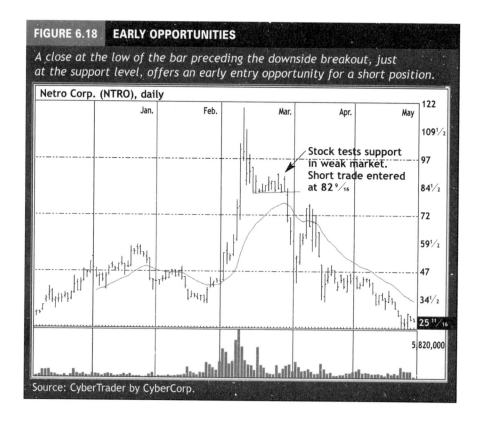

FIGURE 6.18   EARLY OPPORTUNITIES

A close at the low of the bar preceding the downside breakout, just at the support level, offers an early entry opportunity for a short position.

Netro Corp. (NTRO), daily

Stock tests support in weak market. Short trade entered at 82 ⁹⁄₁₆

Source: CyberTrader by CyberCorp.

repeatedly tests a support or resistance level, you should enter *before* the breakout. Most times, you even can avoid paying the spread because the stock will be whipsawing back and forth between the bid and offer. If you wait until the stock breaks out, you are almost always forced to pay the spread—if you can get it at all.

But, you may ask, what if the stock never breaks out? Should you hold the position until it does, or should you exit the position on the close? One approach to reduce risk is to use the last swing low or high as your initial stop-loss point. In the CMGI example, you could have placed an initial stop loss at 50¾ which was the last swing high on the five-minute chart. With a stop in place, you can simply wait for the breakout to materialize. The only reason not to hold the position is if the overall market begins to move counter to the trade (i.e., you're long, waiting for the breakout, and the market begins to drop precipitously).

But you must use caution when entering breakout trades early; you never want to enter a trade that is counter to the overall market momentum. For example, before entering the CMGI trade on the short side, you

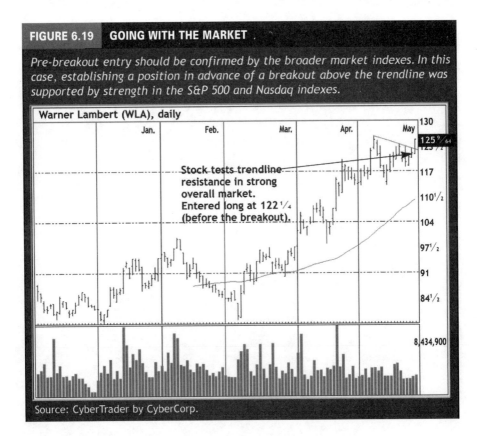

FIGURE 6.19   GOING WITH THE MARKET

Pre-breakout entry should be confirmed by the broader market indexes. In this case, establishing a position in advance of a breakout above the trendline was supported by strength in the S&P 500 and Nasdaq indexes.

Warner Lambert (WLA), daily

Stock tests trendline resistance in strong overall market. Entered long at 122¼ (before the breakout).

Source: CyberTrader by CyberCorp.

should have checked to make sure the Nasdaq and S&P 500 were both
weak on the day and trending lower. The weakness of these indexes
would help pull the stock below the support level.

Figure 6.19 shows one last example. On May 25, 2000, Warner
Lambert (WLA) opened for trading at 121½, just under the down trendline of a nice triangle pattern. The preopening call was for the Nasdaq
and S&P 500 to go higher that morning, and they both began to rally from
the open.

This created a setup to go long before the actual breakout above
the trendline. As soon as WLA began to move toward the trendline, a buy
order was entered at 122¼, well before the 123¹⁄₁₆ breakout point. Not

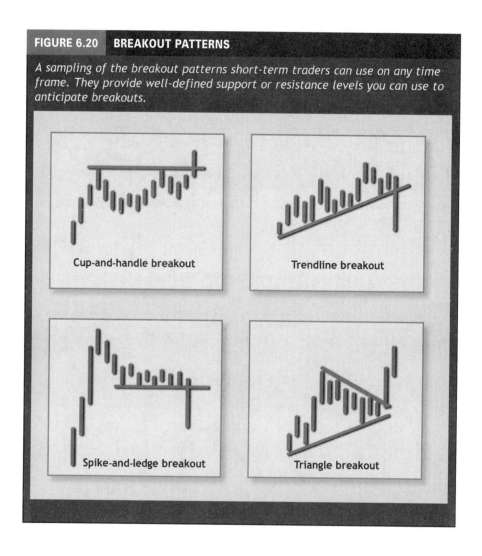

FIGURE 6.20   BREAKOUT PATTERNS

*A sampling of the breakout patterns short-term traders can use on any time
frame. They provide well-defined support or resistance levels you can use to
anticipate breakouts.*

Cup-and-handle breakout

Trendline breakout

Spike-and-ledge breakout

Triangle breakout

long after, the overall market strength helped pull WLA through the trendline; it continued to rally for the rest of the day.

Had you waited for WLA to print at 123⅛₆, you would have been filled at a minimum of ¹³⁄₁₆ worse than the early entry price. Those extra fractions add up quickly. You can usually gain an extra ⅛ (sometimes as much as a point) simply by realizing that support and resistance almost always get broken. Try the following experiment: Multiply 50 percent of all the shares you have traded over a given time period by ⅛ and see what you come up with. That's being conservative.

You can use this entry technique on any breakout-related trade in any time frame, including breakouts from daily and intraday cup-and-handle patterns, triangles, trendline breakouts, and spike-and-ledge patterns (see Figure 6.20). Very rarely should you wait for the actual breakouts to materialize on any of these patterns. Remember, slippage affects you even when you make a profit on the trade. Most traders don't think about the effect of slippage on their winning trades; they only think about the losers. And don't forget about the trades you missed completely because the stock just ripped through the support or resistance level and you couldn't even get a partial fill.

We tend to forget about those missed opportunities completely, but those are usually the most potentially profitable trades because the stock is moving so forcefully. This approach will also help you on the breakout trades that don't materialize because you'll have a better entry price and may even be able to still garner a small profit or, at worst, scratch a trade from these false breakouts.

No approach is without risk, but in certain situations entering early can yield excellent trading results.

chapter 7

more swing trading, day trading, and options strategies

trading the bow tie pattern

Dave Landry

Because markets are prone to long-term continuation moves and false reversals, trying to pick tops and bottoms can be a costly trading approach. On the other hand, blindly jumping on an established trend also has its drawbacks, because every trend has its occasional corrections.

It is useful to have a way to detect when a new trend may be developing and a plan for timing entry based on a price thrust in the direction of the trend. The "bow tie" pattern is a swing trade setup designed to do this by using multiple moving averages and a countertrend correction.

moving average background

The bow tie strategy uses three moving averages: A 10-period simple moving average (SMA), which is simply the sum of the preceding 10 closing prices divided by 10, and 20- and 30-period exponential moving averages (EMAs). An EMA weights the current prices more than prior prices. The theory is that the most recent price action is more relevant than the more distant price action.

An SMA is the sum of the prices over a given period divided by the number of days (or minutes, or weeks, etc.) in the period. Weighted and exponential averages, on the other hand, use calculations that emphasize more recent prices.

Table 7.1 shows how a basic five-day weighted moving average would be calculated. The most recent day is given a weight of 5, the next most recent day a weight of 4, and so on. The closing prices on these days are multiplied by the weighting factors. These results are then added together and divided by the sum of the weighting factors, in this case 15. The result is a weighted average value of 14.42, compared to a simple average value of 13.

The exponential moving average (EMA) weights prices using the following formula:

$$EMA = SC \times Price + (1 - SC) \times EMA(yesterday)$$

where SC is a smoothing constant between 0 and 1.

You can approximate a particular moving average length for an exponential moving average using a smoothing constant according to the following formula:

$$SC = \frac{2}{n+1}$$

where n = The number of days in a simple moving average of approximately equivalent length.

TABLE 7.1	SIMPLE VERSUS WEIGHTED MOVING AVERAGES		
Day	Closing price	Weighting factor	Weighted closing price
Day 1	10	1	10
Day 2	10.5	2	21
Day 3	11.25	3	33.75
Day 4	14.75	4	59
Day 5 (most recent day)	18.5	5	92.5
Simple 5-day average (average of closing prices):	13		
Sum of weighting factors:		15	
Sum of weighted closes			216.25
Weighted 5-day average (sum of weighted closing prices divided by sum of weighting factors):			14.42

For example, a 20-day exponential moving average would use a smoothing constant of .095. The larger n is, the smaller the constant, and the smaller the constant, the less impact the most recent price action will have on the EMA.

In practice, virtually all software programs allow you to simply choose how many days you want in your moving average and select simple, weighted, or exponential calculations.

As a result of their *front-weighting,* EMAs tend to *catch up* to prices faster, reacting more quickly to price swings than simple moving averages. One type of average is not necessarily better than the other. Both have their purposes, which is why both are used in this approach.

A 10-period SMA is used because it gives a true representation of the average price over the past two weeks (10 trading days). The 20- and 30-period EMAs give a rough representation of performance over the past month and six weeks, respectively. (But these are personal preferences: there's no harm in modifying them to suit your ideas.)

the order of the averages

Moving averages follow price moves relative to the number of days in the average. Faster (shorter term) moving averages tend to track price more closely while slower (longer term) moving averages tend to lag price action. During consolidations, prices tend to fluctuate (whipsaw) above and below the moving averages. Faster moving averages tend to remain above slower moving averages during uptrends, and below slower moving averages during downtrends.

Figure 7.1 is a daily chart of Emulex (EMLX) with a 10-day SMA, and 20- and 30-day EMAs. During the consolidation, price bounces around the moving averages and the averages are in no particular order. But once price begins to trend, the 10-day SMA climbs (and stays) above the 20-day EMA and the 20-day EMA climbs (and stays) above the 30-day EMA. This condition of 10-day SMA > 20-day EMA > 30-day EMA is the proper order for uptrends. Conversely, 10-day SMA < 20-day EMA < 30-day EMA is the proper order for downtrends.

the bow tie pattern

When a market makes the transition from an uptrend to a downtrend (or vice versa), the moving averages converge and then spread out again, giving the appearance of a bow tie (note the period in late March and early April in Figure 7.1). For the ideal bow tie setup, the convergence (the middle of the bow tie) should be very tight (the moving averages all should be close in value) and the averages should spread out quickly. In a perfect setup, the transition from proper downtrend order to proper

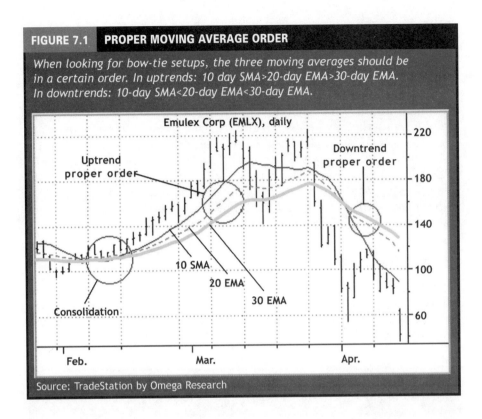

FIGURE 7.1 **PROPER MOVING AVERAGE ORDER**

When looking for bow-tie setups, the three moving averages should be in a certain order. In uptrends: 10 day SMA>20-day EMA>30-day EMA. In downtrends: 10-day SMA<20-day EMA<30-day EMA.

Source: TradeStation by Omega Research

uptrend order (or the opposite for short sales) should occur over a maximum of three to four days.

the setup

Using a 10-period SMA, 20-period EMA, and 30-period EMA, there are six rules for a buy setup (short sales are reversed):

1. The moving averages should converge and spread out again, giving the appearance of a bow tie. At this point the moving averages should be in proper uptrend order: 10-day SMA > 20-day EMA > 30-day EMA.
2. Today's low must be lower than yesterday's low.
3. Go long on a move ⅛ above today's high.
4. If not filled, continue to work a buy order ⅛ above the prior day's high until either filled or the low trades below the 20-day EMA.

5. Once filled, place an initial protective stop ⅛ below low of the bar in step 2.

6. Trail a stop until stopped out (and/or exit in two to six days).

Figure 7.2 shows an example in Concord Communications (CCRD). On June 8 and 9, 2000, the moving averages converge and spread out again, forming the bow tie as the stock makes the transition from downtrend to uptrend (point 1). The moving averages are in the proper order: 10-day SMA > 20-day EMA > 30-day EMA. Next, the stock makes a lower low on June 12 (point 2). Two days later, on June 14, a buy is triggered when the stock trades ⅛ above the June 12 high of 32 (point 3). An initial stop is placed ⅛ below the June 12 low of 30⁹⁄₁₆. The stock traded up more than seven points to 39¹⁵⁄₁₆ over the next four days.

strategy logic

The basis for this approach is straightforward. When moving averages of different lengths converge, as they do at the middle of the bow tie formation, it suggests the longer- and shorter term cycles are coming together. When they spread out again, it suggests a new trend is developing.

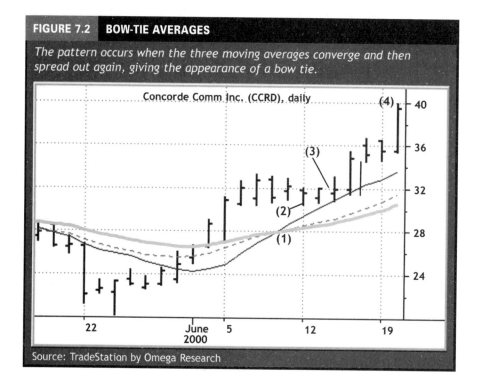

FIGURE 7.2   BOW-TIE AVERAGES

The pattern occurs when the three moving averages converge and then spread out again, giving the appearance of a bow tie.

Concorde Comm Inc. (CCRD), daily

Source: TradeStation by Omega Research

However, simply trading moving average crossovers is risky. Despite what many books on technical analysis will tell you, moving average crossovers do not work. During nontrending periods, crossovers will produce many false signals as the market chops up and down. (In their defense, many of these books were written before nearly everyone had a computer. Before computers, crossover signals worked much better.)

By waiting for a countertrend move (Rule 2, a lower low for buys or a higher high for short sales) and only entering if the trend reasserts itself (Rule 3) you can often avoid false moves. Conceptually, this is no different than waiting for a pullback. Essentially, you are looking for thrust or trend, a correction, and then resumption of trend.

If a market comes all the way back to its 20-day EMA, it's possible that what appeared to be a new trend is really a false move. This doesn't mean that the market isn't tradable; in trading there are no exacts. However, when using any pattern, you should have a rule for when you should step back and reevaluate your analysis. That's the function of Rule 4. On the other hand, it's normal, and likely healthy, for a market to pull back to its 10-day SMA.

The pattern also works on markets coming out of consolidations or bases where the moving averages will form a "half bow tie." These seem to work, but the "rollover" pattern (when the market makes the transition from uptrend to downtrend or vice versa) presents a better opportunity because players may still be trapped on the wrong side of the market. This will add fuel to the move.

market examples

Let's look at a couple more examples. Figure 7.3 shows a long trade in Lynx Technologies (LYNX):

1. The three moving averages converge and begin to spread out on June 12.
2. The stock makes a lower low on June 15.
3. A long trade is triggered at 32¼, ⅛ above the high of (2). The initial stop is placed at 29⅜, ⅛ below the low of (2).
4. The stock rallies nearly 14 points over the next three days.

Figure 7.4 provides an example on the short side of the market in Nanogen (NGEN):

1. The three moving averages converge and begin to spread out on March 22 and March 23.
2. The stock makes a higher high on March 23.

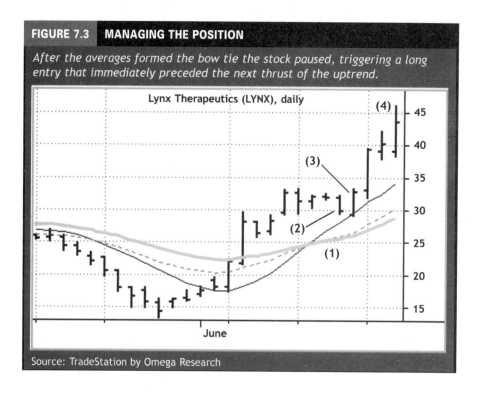

FIGURE 7.3   MANAGING THE POSITION

After the averages formed the bow tie the stock paused, triggering a long entry that immediately preceded the next thrust of the uptrend.

Lynx Therapeutics (LYNX), daily

June

Source: TradeStation by Omega Research

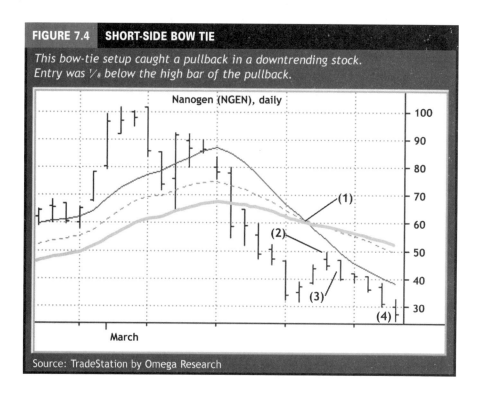

FIGURE 7.4   SHORT-SIDE BOW TIE

This bow-tie setup caught a pullback in a downtrending stock. Entry was 1/8 below the high bar of the pullback.

Nanogen (NGEN), daily

March

Source: TradeStation by Omega Research

3. A short trade is triggered at 43¼, ⅛ below the high of (2). The initial stop is placed at 49½, ⅛ above the high of (2).

4. The stock trades as low as 24¹⁵⁄₁₆ over the next four days.

Bow ties allow you to catch high-probability, shorter term moves when markets are potentially embarking on new trends. By waiting for a countertrend move and then a thrust back in the direction of the trend, you can avoid many false moves and limit the risk on your trades.

what you see is (not) what you get

Dewey Burchett

Over the past few years, thousands of potential traders have set up shop at day-trading firms, only to have their capital wiped out in a matter of weeks or months.

It would almost seem that you could simply study what these traders did and do the reverse. Think of it this way: How many times have you said, "If I had just done the opposite of what I actually did, I would have made money"?

If you are an avid Nasdaq Level II screen user, this may be a valid question. Trading is difficult no matter how you look at it, but if you are learning to do the wrong things, it can make it next to impossible to make money.

What you will soon discover is that some of the "basics" currently being taught about Level II are wrong. We'll take a look at some of the realities of using Level II quotes and outline a few trading strategies that are rarely discussed in any books or trading classes. In fact, just one of the ideas to be revealed will increase the odds of a winning trade dramatically. But let's start out reviewing some of the basics.

Level II basics

The basic premise of Level II is very simple. Figure 7.5 shows an example of a Level II screen. The left side of the screen contains information about who is attempting to buy stock. The right side of the screen shows who is attempting to sell. On both sides of the screen, you can see at which price each participant is buying or selling, and what size (how many shares).

In addition to market makers such as Merrill Lynch (MLCO), First Boston (FBCO), and Goldman Sachs (GSCO), Electronic Communications Networks (ECNs) such as Island (ISLAND/ISLD) and Archipelago (ARCA/ARCHIP) are represented on the Level II screen. These ECNs are primarily

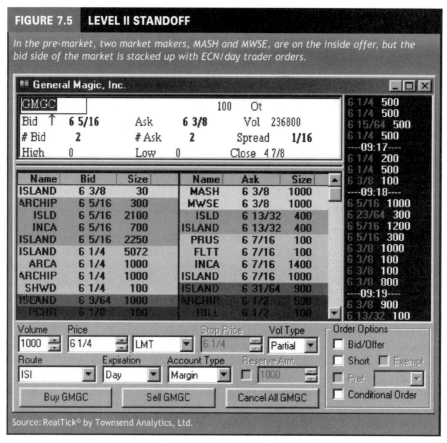

FIGURE 7.5   LEVEL II STANDOFF

In the pre-market, two market makers, MASH and MWSE, are on the inside offer, but the bid side of the market is stacked up with ECN/day trader orders.

Source: RealTick® by Townsend Analytics, Ltd.

RealTick® graphics used with permission of Townsend Analytics, Ltd. © 1986–2001. All rights reserved.

used by day traders and active traders. Keep in mind that a market maker is always on both sides of the market, although obviously at different price levels.

With the basic premise of Level II in mind, it would be easy to jump to the conclusion that if you knew what the order flow was going to be over the next few minutes based on what was on the screen, making money would be like shooting fish in a barrel. For example, you might assume that if seven market makers were stacked up at high bid, say 50, with only one market maker on the offer at 50¹⁄₁₆, the stock is going up because of the order flow. Conversely, if you saw market makers stacking up on the offer or sell side, it would only make sense to position yourself for a short, or sell a stock that you were long.

For the new trainees at the local day trading firm, this makes total sense, and they can hardly wait to get their accounts up and running. If the Level II screen could really be taken at face value, then theoretically it would take a great deal of effort *not* to make money given the available information.

But, things are not always as they seem.

it's the market makers' turf

Traders need to understand one concept when using Level II: Market makers let you see what they want you to see. In addition, everyone sees the same thing that you are seeing.

Market makers have two main objectives: Execute order flow at the best price for their big clients, and make money scalping the stock for the firm. You may have heard that the "smart money" bets in the last few minutes before a horse race. If someone knows his horse is going to win, he is not going to bet big early and tip off all the other handicappers. If he did, other players would bet the same horse, which would lower the odds and the payoff.

Just as the astute handicapper does not show his hand, neither does the market maker. In fact, it is in the best interest of the market maker to make a strong stock look weak on Level II, and vice versa.

What often ends up happening is that a stock with buying interest looks weak, and a stock with selling interest looks strong. On Level II, you will see market makers stacked up together at the top of the offer, with very few bids—right before the stock makes the next move to the upside. Again, it appears this way because the market makers want to make the market look weak when they have stock to buy so they can get a good price. They would prefer to make the stock seem weak so traders will either sell to them on the bid or lower the current offering price, in which case they will buy it from the new seller. Often they will pull an offer when some of the stock is taken out at that price level.

As soon as you understand that the true intentions of the market makers usually are not reflected on Level II, you can use this information, in conjunction with other trading strategies, to determine the proper entry and exit points for the stocks you are trading. For example, assume you want to go long a particular stock during the day. You decide that you would like to buy on the next pullback based on a technical indicator you are using. If you had listened to much of the popular advice regarding Level II, the last thing you would do is buy a stock when market makers were stacked up on the best offering price. Under such circumstances, you would probably think there is too much selling pressure. But this is the incorrect approach. Instead, you should adhere to your trading signal and make the trade. A good way to play the long side, keeping in mind the tendency of market makers to not reveal their true agenda, is to try to take advantage of this market maker "bluff" by putting in a bid (instead of just lifting the offer). Many times, inexperienced traders will hit your bid when they see the market makers stack up on the offer (this works best using an ECN like Island). This will give you a better entry price, as you are using the market makers' trading tactics to your own advantage.

Keep in mind, however, there are certainly times, such as during heavy trending, when a preponderance of market makers on either side of the market reflects true buying or selling interest. Learning how to read market maker action is something you acquire over time. The message here is that you can't always take what you are seeing on the Level II screen at face value. The more liquid a stock, the more likely you will see a better indication of the true buying or selling interest.

The opposite approach would be used for trading on the short side, although entry is more difficult because of the uptick rule. Viewing Level II from a more realistic standpoint—realizing that what is on your screen is exactly what market makers "want" you to see—will help you minimize losses and enable you to not get thrown off when using other trading strategies. Keep in mind, however, that you should not rely on this information exclusively; you should use it in conjunction with other effective strategies. Also, illiquid stocks are less reliable as there are fewer market participants, and one "big gun" can ultimately control the stock.

be the smart money

One particular strategy tends to yield high-probability trade setups, although these opportunities can be difficult to find at times. The approach is based on the premise that not only do the bigger market makers ultimately control which direction a stock will go, but that day traders, when they act collectively, get on the wrong side of the market at the same time. In this context, day traders represent the "dumb money," to use trading terminology. There is an easy explanation for this phenomenon, as the following example will illustrate.

Dumb money usually comes together around news events such as new product developments, strategic alliances with other companies, and the general fancy press releases that don't really tell you much. In the excitement surrounding the news, and compelled by the greed of making a quick buck, traders will chase the latest hot stock of the day using the ECNs. When this happens, most of the market makers will raise their offers and make the traders pay up for the stock.

Once the chase is on, and day traders begin to outbid each other, the stock may move up swiftly, although it generally will do so on light volume. What ends up appearing on the Level II screen is mostly ECNs on the bid side, accompanied by very few market makers as buyers. Most of the time you will see some trades go through on the offer as well, but few of any significant size, and the down move that follows can be even more violent than the preceding rise as day traders bail out on the stock.

finding the opportunities

To find these potential trades, keep track of stocks with news prior to the market open. These stocks often will trade up significantly in the pre-opening market, and have short-lived runs in the first five minutes of trading as market makers sell the stock to an investing public that only buys when the market opens. Other times, these stocks will fall immediately when the market opens.

The best way to determine how to play these situations is to watch the volume. If the volume continues to be heavy all the way to the opening bell, the stock will likely continue to push slightly higher within the first 5 to 10 minutes of trading. If the volume is relatively light, the stock will most likely immediately get hit with profit-taking. Fortunately, you do not have to wait for an uptick in the premarket to sell the stock short; waiting until after the open of trading will require you to sell on an uptick. Although other news-related events occur throughout the day, most significant news is released before the open, so you have to do your homework early in the day.

Figure 7.5 shows a Level II screen of General Magic, Inc. (GMGC). On this particular day, GMGC signed an agreement with IBM. And as usual, day traders were hard at work bidding the stock up in the premarket, as evidenced by the large number of ECN (ISLD and ARCA/ARCHIP) bids on the left-hand side. Also notice that there is only one market maker (SHWD) on the bid side, two levels down, which means they are not aggressively buying the stock. In addition, most market makers are on the offer side of the market (right-hand side of the screen).

Now, who will ultimately win this standoff? This example shows the time of 9:19—11 minutes prior to the market open. The first question when spotting a situation like this is, where are the resistance levels? Figure 7.6 shows that General Magic has resistance (prior support) in the 6 to 6½ area . It would be logical to expect the stock to meet resistance in this area once it opened; this is where you would look to sell the stock short, given that relatively heavy volume continued to the opening bell.

In this case, volume continued to come in, and within 30 seconds the stock gapped open to the upside and made the high of the day at 6⁷⁄₁₆. Although above-average volume continued in the first 15 minutes, the intraday chart in Figure 7.7 shows the stock quickly pulled back from the high. From then on, it traded as low as 5¾, but managed to close at 5⅞ on the day. For traders looking to scalp a quarter point or more, or 4 to 6 percent, this was a quick, low-risk play.

FIGURE 7.6   RESISTANCE DEFINED

Previous trading defined resistance in GMGC, and a likely place to look for a short trade opportunity.

General Magic (GMGC), daily

Source: Qcharts by Quote.com

One other misconception traders have is that when they see a big buy or sell order, say 10,000-plus shares, they automatically assume it dictates buying or selling pressure. An example would be that you see a buyer (generally a market maker or Instinet) come in with an order of 10,000 shares on the bid side. Traders too often assume this means the stock will immediately rise as the buyer attempts to buy shares. This is generally an incorrect assumption, and it all goes back to the fact market makers are letting you see what they want you to see.

If you wanted to buy 10,000 shares, would you advertise your intentions to the world so they would make you pay up for it? Of course not, and in most situations neither will anyone else. If you really look at such bids and offers, they are generally a couple of levels down from the top of the bid or offer, and usually only appear on the screen for a few seconds. In other words, someone has an agenda, and it's not necessarily one with your best interests in mind. These trading scenarios should be viewed as warning signs. If you understand that things are not as they seem, you can better profit from what really is.

FIGURE 7.7	**GAP OPENING**

The stock quickly established the high of the day (at 6⁷⁄₁₆) and began to decline.

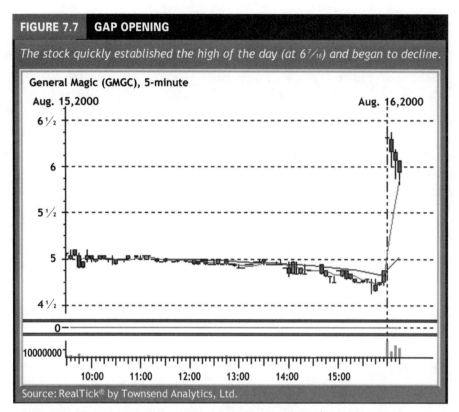

General Magic (GMGC), 5-minute

Aug. 15, 2000   Aug. 16, 2000

Source: RealTick® by Townsend Analytics, Ltd.

taking cover with options

Jerry Wood

There was a time—it seems so long ago—before rocketing initial public offerings and 80 percent Nasdaq returns, when stocks didn't go up every day. It may be hard to believe now, but over the years there have been long stretches when equities have simply refused to double every other month.

The odds are that we will see this kind of environment, which is much more representative of the market's historical norm, once again. When we do, how can an ambitious trader make money under such dire conditions?

One possibility is to dust off a handy option strategy that worked well during the dark days of trading ranges and single-digit annual returns: the covered call.

the stock-option combination

A covered call position is the short sale of one call option for every 100 shares of underlying stock. You can either sell the call and buy the stock at the same time or sell the call on stock you already own. Here's a simple example of a covered call position in America Online (AOL):

Trade date: Jan. 14, 2000

Stock position: Own 100 shares AOL at 63	$6,300
Option position: Sell 1 April 65 AOL call at 8½	($850)
Total cost of trade:	$5,450

As the seller (also referred to as the *option writer*) of the April 65 call, you receive $850 cash from the buyer. In return, you are obligated to sell your 100 shares of AOL to the buyer (at the *strike price,* or the price at which the underlying stock may be purchased or sold by the option holder upon exercise of the option contract, in this case $65 a share), if he chooses to exercise his option. This obligation lasts until the April option expiration date.

advantages

Because the call buyer does not take the full risk of stock ownership (or the interest cost associated with that ownership), he pays a premium—in this case $850—for the right to buy your stock. This premium is the golden goose of covered call selling. It enables you to reap the two main benefits of the position:

1. Increased return on investment. You immediately receive income—$850, in our example. Regardless of the stock's movement over the life span of the option, that money is yours to keep.
2. Greater downside protection for your stock position. The money you get from selling the call effectively lowers the purchase price of the stock. In this case, the total cost of the position is only $5,450. If the stock price drops, you will lose substantially less than if you purchased the 100 shares outright for $6,300 and did not sell the call.

disadvantages

The premium you receive for selling the option does not come without a catch. Your obligation to sell the stock at the strike price has two intertwining disadvantages:

1. Risk of being forced to sell stock. When the stock moves above the strike price, you risk having to sell your stock to the call buyer who exercises his option. There are ways to mitigate this risk, but if you own a stock that you simply cannot bear to sell (possibly because of tax consequences), think long and hard before selling calls against it.

2. Loss of upside profits. If you are forced to sell your stock, you will give up the potential profits of any increase in your stock above the strike price. For example, if AOL was to climb to $90 at April expiration, you would still be obligated to sell your stock to the call buyer at the $65 strike price.

Stocks you are neutral or moderately bullish about are the best candidates for covered calls. While the maximum profit will always occur when the stock price finishes above the strike, selling calls against a stock that you are strongly bullish on is not a good idea, as you will not profit more from a larger price increase. Conversely, stay away from stocks you feel will drop significantly. Although the premium you received for the call will reduce your losses, a loss is still a loss and such stocks are best avoided altogether. The next step is to consider the details that will determine the position's likelihood of success: the strike price and the expiration date of the call option.

choosing the best strike price

The most important decision when putting on a covered call position is whether to sell the in-the-money (ITM), at-the-money (ATM), or out-of-the-money (OTM) calls against your stock.

The following are just a few of the choices you would have faced had you wished to sell calls on January 14 against AOL stock trading at $63 a share:

- *In-the-money call.* Sell April 55; call at 14.
- *At-the-money call.* Sell April 62.5; call at 9¾.
- *Out-of-the-money call.* Sell April 70; call at 6¾.

Which one should you have sold against your stock? That would depend, frankly, on your opinion about the direction of AOL over the course of the next three months. Sell the ITM call if you are slightly bearish, the ATM call if you are neutral, and the OTM call if you are moderately bullish.

In this example, if you think AOL might drop, the best call to sell would be the April 55 option (the ITM strike price). Because the downside break-even point of the covered call position is the stock price minus the call price, the April 55 covered write would result in a break-even price of $49 at April expiration ($63 – $14 = $49). The downside break-even levels for the April 62.5 (ATM) call and the April 70 (OTM) call would be 53¼ and 56¼, respectively.

However, if you like the near-term prospects of the stock, but are not wildly bullish (in which case selling any call would not be prudent), the April 70 would provide the greatest possible profit potential: $70 (strike price) – $63 (stock price) + $6.75 (call price) = $13.75. Selling the ATM 62.5 calls would reflect a neutral stance on the stock. Figure 7.8 better illustrates the risk-reward trade-offs inherent in choosing a particular strike price in a covered call position.

choosing the best expiration date

As an option moves closer to its expiration date, it continues to lose time premium (call price above intrinsic value, which is the amount by which an option is in the money). This is called *time decay,* and it is always working in the call seller's favor. This decay, however, does not occur at a steady, linear pace. It increases as the option gets closer to expiration. For this reason, covered-call positions soon to expire offer

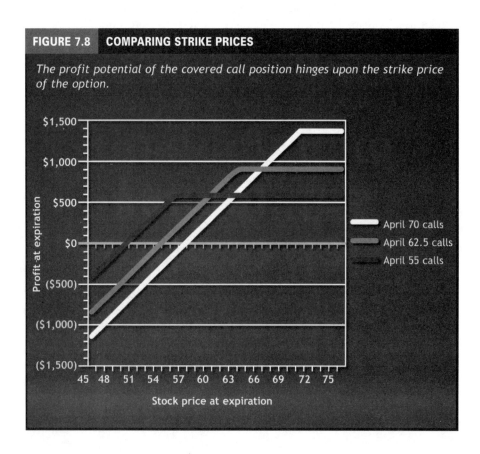

FIGURE 7.8   COMPARING STRIKE PRICES

The profit potential of the covered call position hinges upon the strike price of the option.

April 70 calls
April 62.5 calls
April 55 calls

Profit at expiration

Stock price at expiration

faster profits. The problem is that the smaller call price also offers less downside protection.

These trade-offs must be considered when determining which expiration month to sell. Generally, the most attractive covered call opportunities will exist within two to six months before expiration. This offers a good compromise between risk and reward.

calculating return on the strategy

Perhaps the best way to examine call-writing opportunities is to compute the percentage returns, both simple and annual, that various strategies will yield. Simple returns are fine when evaluating positions with the same expiration date, but return on investment should be annualized when comparing positions expiring on different dates.

The trader should compute two figures for each position. The first is the return if the stock is unchanged at expiration from the original purchase price. The second is the return if the option is exercised (the stock closes above the strike price at expiration). Table 7.2 demonstrates how the *return if unchanged* would be computed for the three possible AOL covered-call candidates.

Because the 55 and the 62.5 calls both finished in the money, or with a strike price below the market price of the underlying stock, the *return if exercised* is the same as the *return if unchanged*. However, the return if exercised for the 70 covered-call position will be different. If the stock closes above the 70 strike at expiration, it will be sold at $70 a share, resulting in $700 more profit than if the stock was unchanged at expiration. This would raise the profit to $1,375 and result in a return on investment of 24.4 percent.

TABLE 7.2	COVERED CALLS: RETURN IF UNCHANGED		
Strike price	55	62.5	70
Expiration value of 100 shares AOL @ $63	$5,500 (exercised)	$6,250 (exercised)	$6,300 (call expires)
Subtract net investment ($6,300 minus proceeds of one AOL call)	- 4,900	-5,325	-5,625
Net profit	$600	$925	$675
Return to expiration (profit/net investment)	12.2 %	17.4%	12.0%

These numbers, for simplicity, ignore commissions and dividends. Yes, some firms still do pay dividends (though AOL does not), and payments received during the duration of the position should be added to the net profit figure. Conversely, commissions should be deducted.

Also, the use of margin to buy stock will increase your returns, but keep in mind that margin is a double-edged sword and will accentuate your negative returns if the stock falls significantly.

evaluating your rate of return

While you always can increase the possible rate of return by selling cheap far OTM calls, this would greatly dilute the two main objectives of the strategy: increased income and greater downside protection. Ultimately, what creates the profit potential in covered-call writing is the amount of *time premium* that exists in the calls you sell. The higher the call's premium, the greater the return.

The variables that influence call premium and, in turn, the rate of return of a covered call are:

- The distance of stock from strike price.
- Time remaining until expiration.
- Dividend payments.
- Prevailing interest rates.
- Volatility of the underlying stock.

The most important of these pricing variables and the key to evaluating covered-call opportunities is volatility. If the market expects large future price swings in a stock, then that volatility assumption (the *implied volatility*) will be reflected in higher call prices—and greater rates of return and downside protection for the covered writer. These payoffs come at a price. A volatile stock is more likely to move out of the profit range of the position and result in a loss for the trader.

For example, a three-month rate of return of more than 17.4 percent on our ATM AOL position is high. This works out to a 68 percent annual return—very rich, even by today's standards. That high return arises because predicting the price of a volatile stock like AOL three months in the future is very difficult indeed.

The trick for the covered call writer is to sell calls on a stock that is likely to experience less actual volatility in the coming months than the implied volatility is forecasting. You can generate superior above-market returns if you do this consistently. Using a stock that has recently made a large move and appears to be settling into a trading range is often the best way to take advantage of this volatility discrepancy.

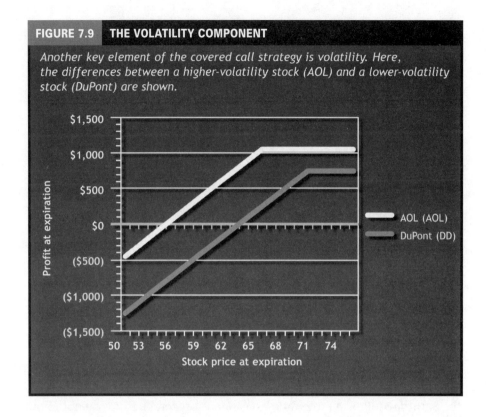

FIGURE 7.9 THE VOLATILITY COMPONENT

Another key element of the covered call strategy is volatility. Here, the differences between a higher-volatility stock (AOL) and a lower-volatility stock (DuPont) are shown.

Figure 7.9 illustrates the disparity of the returns between a high-volatility stock (AOL) and a lower-volatility stock (Du Pont). The differences are obvious. The Du Pont (DD) covered call rate of return is lower and the break-even level is higher, even with the dividend paid by Du Pont factored in. Table 7.3 breaks down the numbers.

TABLE 7.3 AOL VERSUS DUPONT

	Buy 100 AOL @ 63 & Sell 1 April 65 Call @ 8$^1/_2$	Buy 100 DD @ 67$^1/_2$ & Sell 1 April 70 Call @ 4$^1/_2$
Expiration value	$6,500	$7,000
Cost of position	(Stock price − Call price) 5,450	[Stock price − Call − Div. Rec. ($35)] 6,265
Net profit	$1,050	$735
Return	(19.2%)	(11.7%)

exercise risk

One of the big worries of novice option traders is the threat of getting short calls exercised and having to sell stock. This is especially troublesome if you will owe significant taxes on the sale of your stock.

The best way to avoid this is to simply buy the call back when the amount of premium above intrinsic value gets small enough.

For example, consider the AOL April 62.5 covered call position. Imagine the stock rallies to $75 a few days before the expiration date, giving the call an intrinsic value of 12½. The calls are trading at 12⅝, which leaves very little profit potential in the position, so you decide to just buy back the calls to avert the possibility of losing the stock.

Remember, equity calls can be exercised anytime, not just on the expiration date. They usually will not be exercised, however, until very close to expiration when the time premium gets very small. After buying back the calls, you can keep the stock and sell calls with a more distant expiration, if you desire.

Alternately, if it's difficult to buy the calls back at a fair price, you can buy an identical number of underlying shares on the open market by expiration day and use that new stock to deliver against the calls. (Important note: You must tell your broker to deliver the newly purchased shares and not the original stock.)

No matter how far out of the money the call is, unless you buy it back, you must hold on to the stock until the option officially expires on the Saturday following expiration day. Most brokerage firms do not allow you to hold uncovered short calls, and if they do, the margin is very high. (Keep this in mind when entering the trade; you must buy the stock first.)

If you are not already long the underlying stock, the best way to minimize your risk is to enter the covered write as a single order. Tell your broker the total cost you want to pay, which is the price of the stock minus the desired price of the short call.

risk protection

There are protective measures you can take if the stock moves too far from the strike price. If the stock moves down to where there is little downside protection value left in the short call, you can buy back the cheap call and sell a more expensive call with a lower strike. Conversely, if the stock rises to a point where almost all the profit potential has been realized, you can buy back your deep ITM call and sell a higher ATM or OTM call to gain additional income.

which position is best?

Numerous software programs claim to unravel the mystery of options and their complex formulas and cryptic Greek terms. Some of them are good at sorting through the immense stacks of equity and index option data, but keep in mind these numbers and percentages are only tools, not magic bullets. They can be employed to assess and compare risk, but will not tell the whole story.

In general, selling ATM or slightly OTM calls with a two- to six-month time frame is the optimum covered call strategy. But ultimately, trading is more art than science and the trader must sort through a full plate of factors, such as stock price expectation and volatility, when determining whether to enter into a trade.

Stock prices can do five things: They can stay the same, go up a little, go up a lot, go down a little, or go down a lot.

The trader or investor who sells covered calls against his stock will likely do better than his stock-only counterpart under four of these five scenarios. Not bad odds considering equity prices just might not explode to the upside forever.

spreading your charting options

Thomas Stridsman

One basic disadvantage to only trading stocks from the long side, or using futures for selling short, is the limited risk protection and decreased ability to tailor a position to suit your specific needs. One way to customize your positions is to use a set of basic and easy-to-implement option strategies that complement a few equally basic technical analysis chart patterns.

If you believe the market will go up, you could simply buy a call option and limit your risk to the amount paid; or you could buy a put option if you believe the market will go down. But what if you could weigh the possibilities of a certain scenario actually happening—say on a three-grade scale (e.g., unlikely, likely, very likely)—and then tailor an options position to fit the scenario and the potential risk-reward ratio you're willing to take on?

The probabilities of chart-pattern analysis can help you choose an appropriate option strategy for a given trading situation.

vertical jump

Consider a situation in which you think the market may rise, but you still want some protection against a potential drop. Instead of just buying a call option, you could buy one call option and sell one call option with a higher strike price to limit your risk.

This position is called a *vertical debit call spread*. Figure 7.10 shows the profit potential for this position. (*Debit* means it will cost money to

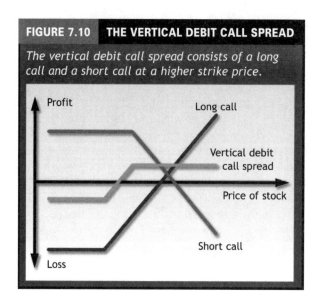

FIGURE 7.10 **THE VERTICAL DEBIT CALL SPREAD**

The vertical debit call spread consists of a long call and a short call at a higher strike price.

put on one of these spreads; you cannot lose more money than the cost of the position.)

Granted, the profit potential will also be limited, but why aim for a higher profit—and thereby also take on more risk—than your market analysis deems reasonable? To establish a similar position in anticipation of falling prices you could put on a *vertical debit put spread,* consisting of one long put option and one short put option with a lower strike.

To implement a vertical debit call spread, you should choose the strike for the short option to be at or slightly above (below for a put spread) the targeted price for the underlying stock. The two options should not be more than two strikes apart because options too far out-of-the-money tend to become very illiquid.

The advantage of a strategy like a vertical debit spread is that you don't have to hold it until expiration. Depending on how the market unfolds, you can get rid of one-half of the position or add even more options to either side of the strategy.

If you place a vertical debit call spread in anticipation of the penetration of a resistance line, you can easily buy back the previously shorted option once the market has moved in your favor, ending up with an outright long call position. Or, if the market goes against you, sell the long option to end up with a short call position that will allow you to take a small profit out of the declining market.

Because it doesn't matter how many total options the spread consists of, as long as it has an equal number on both sides, buying and selling more than one option only adds to the position's flexibility.

Say you bought two call options and sold two call options with a higher strike. Figure 7.10 shows that a vertical debit call spread will become profitable earlier than an outright long option. Once your position has moved into profitable territory, you could then buy back one of the short options to end up with the position shown in Figure 7.11.

This position will not be as profitable as an outright long call position if the market moves very strongly in your favor. Because it becomes profitable sooner, however, it will take a substantial move by the underlying stock before the outright long position will start to outperform this modified vertical debit call spread. Further, if and when this happens, you can always buy back the last remaining short option and end up with two outright longs.

straddling volatility

A vertical debit spread is a useful position when you have a fairly clear opinion about what the market will do next. But what about when you're not so sure—when you think it can take off in either direction?

That's when a long straddle would come in handy. A long straddle consists of one or more long calls and an equal number of long puts with the same strike price. Figure 7.12 shows what this position will look like compared with the performance of an individual long put and long call.

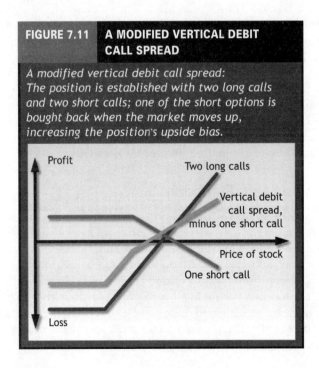

FIGURE 7.11   A MODIFIED VERTICAL DEBIT CALL SPREAD

A modified vertical debit call spread:
The position is established with two long calls and two short calls; one of the short options is bought back when the market moves up, increasing the position's upside bias.

Profit

Two long calls

Vertical debit call spread, minus one short call

Price of stock

One short call

Loss

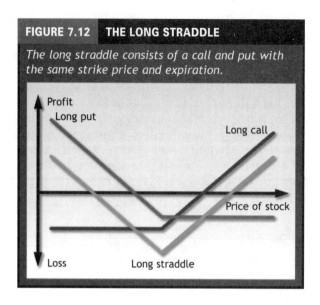

FIGURE 7.12   THE LONG STRADDLE

The long straddle consists of a call and put with the same strike price and expiration.

The straddle will make money if the market makes a substantial move in either direction, but will lose money if volatility decreases and the market drifts in a narrow trading range.

As with the vertical debit spread, the straddle allows you to get rid of the side of the position that loses money once the market takes off; the more options you use for the initial position, the more flexibility you'll have as the price action unfolds. Figure 7.13 shows what a long straddle (initially consisting of two call options and two put options) would look like after selling one of the put options. As you can see, it's now slightly easier to earn a profit on the long side than the short side.

Now let's take a look at the kinds of chart patterns that offer trading opportunities for the option strategies we've discussed.

chart patterns and directional bias

When you get right down to it, there are only four types of chart patterns: those that favor a strong move either up or down; those that favor a more modest move up or down; those that imply a strong move in either direction; and those that don't favor a move in either direction (i.e., price will continue to move sideways).

Most traders are probably better off avoiding the last type. The profit potential is very limited, unless you're a trader who specializes in volatility plays without any regard to the actual price of the underlying market.

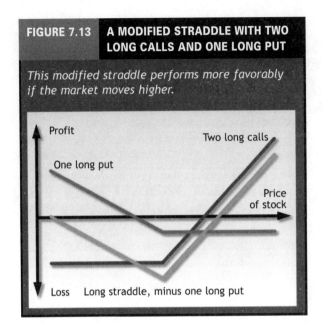

FIGURE 7.13   A MODIFIED STRADDLE WITH TWO LONG CALLS AND ONE LONG PUT

This modified straddle performs more favorably if the market moves higher.

Among the patterns that favor strong moves in a certain direction are top and bottom formations like head-and-shoulders, double tops and bottoms, and wedges. In Figure 7.14, the formation during the fall of 1998 is an example of a double bottom with its most important resistance (often referred to as the *neckline*) at point 1 (the relative high between the two lows of the pattern, which also happens to coincide with the bottom of a consolidation pattern preceding the double bottom).

An upward sloping wedge, which implies a potential top and trend reversal, consists of two upward sloping, converging trendlines. In Figure 7.14, this pattern is forming between trendlines 5 and 8. A downward sloping wedge formed between trendlines 4 and 7.

Other patterns with a strong directional bias are consolidation patterns within trends, such as flags and pennants. Because these occur within the context of an established uptrend, the consolidation patterns at points 2a, 2b, and 2c in Figure 7.14 all favor a break (continuation) to the upside—in the direction of the previous trend. (Such patterns are, in fact, often referred to as *continuation patterns*.)

For these patterns, the magnitude of the subsequent move depends not only on other support and resistance levels present in the market, but also on the move leading into the pattern. To get a rough estimate, look for the move out of the pattern to be similar in size to the move leading into the pattern. That turned out to be fairly accurate for the patterns in Figure 7.14.

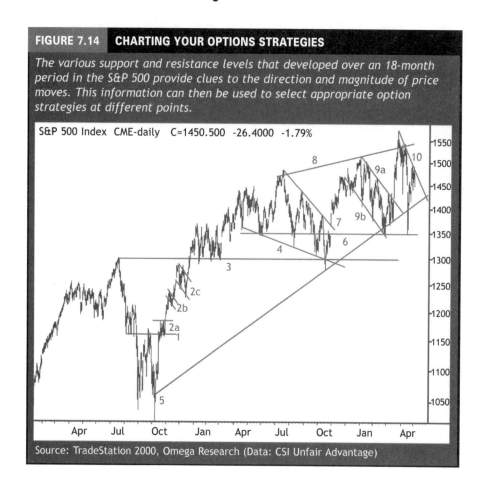

FIGURE 7.14   CHARTING YOUR OPTIONS STRATEGIES

The various support and resistance levels that developed over an 18-month period in the S&P 500 provide clues to the direction and magnitude of price moves. This information can then be used to select appropriate option strategies at different points.

S&P 500 Index CME-daily   C=1450.500 -26.4000 -1.79%

Source: TradeStation 2000, Omega Research (Data: CSI Unfair Advantage)

The patterns on this chart all represent support or resistance of one degree or another. The next step is to consider which option strategies to use to capitalize on the price action they imply.

combining pattern and strategy

The way to trade these patterns is to place a vertical debit spread in anticipation of the move through the support or resistance line in question, then liquidate the losing half of the position after the breakout has occurred.

Ideally, though, you should wait until the market pulls back slightly from the breakout before eliminating the losing half. However, because the market sometimes takes off without looking back, waiting might prevent you from getting out of the unprofitable side. As a result, it's a good idea to consider working with a total of four options. This way, you can get rid of half the losing position as the breakout begins—giving you a position looking like the one in Figure 7.11—and the other half at the pullback, giving you two outright long options.

In the event of a failed breakout, you have two choices: Stay with your recently modified position, or scale it back further so it consists of one long and one short option, which you can sit on in anticipation of a second breakout attempt.

When the market is about to test a major trendline or support or resistance level without any other kind of formation (such as any of the ones mentioned earlier) to indicate possible direction, price is equally likely to take off in either direction, and usually in a rather swift move with large, short-term profit potential for the correctly positioned trader. The magnitude of the move is usually limited to previously defined support or resistance levels and the other extreme of the price channel, such as the ones marked by trendlines 9a and 9b in Figure 7.14.

Another directionally unbiased pattern is the (preferably symmetrical) triangle, which forms with the intersection of two major trendlines, such as trendlines 5 and 10. Directionally neutral patterns like this are opportunities to put on straddles.

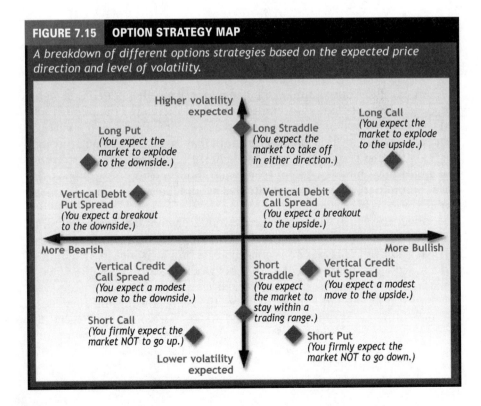

FIGURE 7.15   OPTION STRATEGY MAP

A breakdown of different options strategies based on the expected price direction and level of volatility.

Higher volatility expected

Long Put
(You expect the market to explode to the downside.)

Long Straddle
(You expect the market to take off in either direction.)

Long Call
(You expect the market to explode to the upside.)

Vertical Debit Put Spread
(You expect a breakout to the downside.)

Vertical Debit Call Spread
(You expect a breakout to the upside.)

More Bearish

More Bullish

Vertical Credit Call Spread
(You expect a modest move to the downside.)

Short Straddle
(You expect the market to stay within a trading range.)

Vertical Credit Put Spread
(You expect a modest move to the upside.)

Short Call
(You firmly expect the market NOT to go up.)

Short Put
(You firmly expect the market NOT to go down.)

Lower volatility expected

TABLE 7.4	MATCHING UP: CHART PATTERNS AND OPTION STRATEGIES

Different chart patterns and the option strategies to use to capitalize on them.

Volatility	Strategy	Implementation	Suggested chart patterns
Higher volatility expected	Long call:	Buy one or more calls with the same strike price.	After breaking through a neckline and (preferably) also after a test of support
	Vertical debit call spread:	Buy one or more calls, and sell an equal number of calls with a higher strike price.	In anticipation of breaking through a neckline or consolidation pattern.
	Long straddle:	Buy one or more calls, and an equal number of puts with the same strike price and expiration.	In anticipation of a breakout of a horizontal consolidation area or symmetrical triangle (either direction), or a test of a major trendlines.
	Vertical debit put spread:	Buy one or more puts, and sell an equal number of puts with a lower strike price.	In anticipation of breaking through a neckline or consolidation pattern
	Long put:	Buy one or more puts with the same strike price.	After breaking through a neckline and (preferably) also after test of resistance.
Lower volatility expected	Short put:	Sell one or more puts with the same strike price.	After breaking through a neckline and (preferably) also after test of support.
	Vertical credit put spread:	Sell one or more puts, and sell an equal number of puts with a higher strike price	In anticipation of breaking through a neckline or consolidation pattern.
	Short straddle:	Sell one or more calls, and an equal number of puts with the same strike price and expiration.	When moving into (or when expecting to stay within) a horizontal consolidation area or symmetrical triangle.
	Vertical credit call spread:	Buy one or more calls, and sell an equal number of calls with a lower strike price.	In anticipation of breaking through a neckline or consolidation pattern.
	Short call:	Sell one or more calls with the same strike price.	After breaking through a neckline and (preferably) also after a test of resistance.

An excellent opportunity to place a long straddle occurred in October 1999, when the market attempted to test both support at about 1300, and trendlines 4 and 5. It also would have been possible to add a vertical debit call spread to this position in anticipation of a breakout through the resistance at trendline 6 and the wedge at trendline 7. No matter how you might have handled the outcome and modified the positions as the market unfolded, these two strategies would have positioned you to profit from sizable moves.

Given the apparent longer term wedge developing between trendlines 5 and 8, it could (at the time this was written) be a good place for a vertical debit put spread in anticipation of a breakthrough of trendline 5 and a move back to support at 1350. This would be an acceptable move if the market continued down over the next couple of days.

But if this test failed the first time, the market would be very close to the meeting point of trendlines 5 and 10—a more neutral pattern that would call for a long straddle. Figure 7.15 on page 189 and Table 7.4 give you a quick overview of how and when to place these and a few other basic option strategies.

section three

risk control and money management

The trading and investment industry rankles whenever the word "gambling" is associated with their business. Many brokers and fund managers (understandably) deem the "G word" to be an unwelcome reminder to potential clients of the unavoidable risks of putting money in the market, whether as a long-term investment or as a short-term trade.

But the naked truth is that, in a very important way, all trading and investing is gambling. No one can forecast the future—whether it be the future of the market or the weather—and thus none of us can guarantee profitable returns on our trades and investments. If the future was as neatly predictable as some in the industry would have you believe, we'd have no need for financial markets. Risk simply is unavoidable.

If that's the case, where does it leave the average trader—shaking in his boots on the sidelines? It shouldn't. Risk cannot be avoided, but it can be controlled and managed. Traders who accept risk and take steps to manage it move into the realm of sound *speculation,* which is a very different proposition from gambling. Traders who do not would be better off at the roulette table. In short, trading can be gambling, but it does not *have* to be. Ironically, the only way to prevent your trading from being gambling is to understand and embrace the rules of probability and risk that are common to games of chance as well as the market.

The well-worn platitudes are true: Risk control and money management make or break traders. Take two traders, trading the identical entry and exit rules, with the same amount of capital. After six months, one could be broke (or worse) and the other could be raking in profits. How is this possible? For starters, perhaps the first trader always traded the same number of shares or contracts per trade, regardless of circumstances, and placed stop-loss orders according to what he *felt comfortable* risking—two of the most common practices of unskilled traders (and not a few traders who think of themselves as skilled). The second trader varied his trade size according to his account equity and market volatility (finding the *best* amount to trade at a given time), and based his stops on similar variables. In short, the first trader was really shooting from the hip, and the second trader practiced sound risk control. (And this example only takes into account a couple of the most obvious tools of risk management.)

In this chapter, we'll explain the principles that underlie prudent risk control and effective money management, and then look at various techniques you can use to maximize the potential of your trading strategies—regardless of what they are—and minimize their risk. You'll learn everything from improving your stop-loss placement to understanding the balance of probability and profitability for your trading strategies. These are the concepts every trader must master to have a chance to prosper in the markets.

chapter 8

limiting risk and maximizing profit

reining in risk

Gibbons Burke

Money management is like sex: Everyone does it, one way or another, but not many like to talk about it and some do it better than others. But there's a big difference: Sex sites on the Web proliferate, while sites devoted to the art and science of money management are somewhat difficult to find.

Many financial sites on the Web let you track a portfolio of stocks on a glorified watch list. You enter in your open positions and you get a snapshot, or better yet, a live, real-time update of the status of your stocks based on the site's most recently available prices. Some sites, like Fidelity's, provide tools that tell you how your portfolio is allocated among various asset classes such as stocks, mutual funds, bonds, and cash.

While such sites *get at* the idea of money or portfolio management, the overwhelming majority fail to provide the tools required to answer the central question of money management: "When I make a trade, how *much* do I trade?" (Try to find the topic of money management on the Motley Fool site.)

We'll discuss how to measure and manage trade risk and where to find the tools to help do it in a responsible and profitable manner. The key underlying concept is to limit how much money you are willing to let the market extract from your wallet when you inevitably make losing trades.

When any trader makes a decision to buy or sell (short), he or she must also decide at that time how many shares or contracts to buy or sell; the order form on every brokerage page has a blank spot to specify the size of the order. The essence of risk management is *making a logical decision* about how much to buy or sell when you fill in this blank.

This decision determines the risk of the trade. Accept too much risk and you increase the odds that you will go bust; take too little risk and you will not be rewarded in sufficient quantity to beat the transaction costs and the overhead of your efforts. Good money management practice is about finding the sweet spot between these undesirable extremes.

overtrading and undertrading

Figure 8.1 shows the relationship between the long-term result of a series of trades and the amount of risk taken on a per trade basis.

If you risk too little on each trade, shown by the undertrading zone, the returns will be too low to overcome transaction costs, small losses, and overhead (quote feeds, electricity, rent, subscription to *Active Trader,* etc.) and trading will be a losing proposition.

Risk more and the returns will increase, but the potential drawdown (account losses you will need to endure to get the return—another cost of doing business) always increases as you increase the per trade risk. Returns continue to increase moving into the overtrading zone. Trading at the peak of the potential return curve is difficult

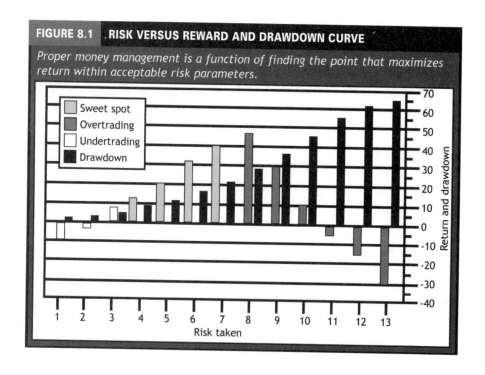

FIGURE 8.1 .RISK VERSUS REWARD AND DRAWDOWN CURVE

Proper money management is a function of finding the point that maximizes return within acceptable risk parameters.

psychologically because the per trade drawdowns can be extremely high, and the margin of safety for dealing with unexpectedly high losing trades is very low. You're getting into territory where one unexpectedly large loser can blow you out.

The best place to live on this curve is the spot where you can deal with the emotional aspect of equity drawdown required to get the maximum return. How much heat can you stand? Money management is a thermostat—a control system for risk that keeps your trading within the comfort zone.

it's more than stops

It's surprising that many active traders and investors have no idea what money management is about. They generally entertain a fuzzy notion that it has to do with setting stops, and that discipline is involved to make sure you execute the stops when they are hit, but their understanding doesn't go much further. Most people seem content to let their brokers track their trades for them, and the tools provided by the brokerage sites are adequate to the task.

But none of the online broker rating services tell you about brokers who provide the tools to help you manage these risks, and none of the traditional online or even most hyperactive day trading brokerage firms seem to cover this important contributor to trading success (or failure).

Why is this? Perhaps it reflects the extended bull run this market has enjoyed since 1982, and the speculative, maniacal extended leg of the bull market fueled by the dot.com land rush since 1997. This type of market—where making money consists of taking a ride on the back of the bull trend and buying the dips—tends to turn the merely bold (and possibly reckless) into market geniuses. The perceived risk in stock market investing has been very low, so the need to manage that risk has not been a pressing concern. Why worry when it will always come back and you can make a killing if you buy more?

More important to success than managing risk has been the ability to charm your broker into getting you into the latest IPO allocation, although interest in this ability has clearly cooled recently.

two types of player

There are really two types of people operating in the financial markets: traders and investors. It is useful to understand the difference between the two—it may explain, in part, why so many people ignore risk management.

Many people who call themselves traders are, in reality, active investors. The typical investor only purchases stocks and buys as many as possible with all the available cash in his or her account. The risk-free position, for the typical investor, is to be fully invested in stocks for the long term, because, as we all know, stocks "always" go up (*sure*). When active investors get more investment cash, they plow it into their mutual funds or buy individual stocks.

The investor's game seems to consist of selective hitchhiking on a freeway that is only going in one direction with the object of getting a ride from the Mercedes driving in the fast lane. They don't know how far the car is going to go and they don't really know when to bail out if the car starts driving in reverse.

These hitchhikers are slow to switch cars when one hits the brakes, runs out of gas, or blows a head gasket. A great amount of hope and faith is involved.

Even active investors don't really pay attention because they operate under the assumption, reinforced by a 20-year-old bull, that the market eventually will go up again and the safe thing to do is hold on or, smarter yet, buy more to lower the cost basis on the position. In this game, it doesn't matter very much whether the car has good brakes or seatbelts—the gas pedal and cruise control are all that matter.

This sort of investing can work in good times, but when the bull turns into a bear, there is going to be a big pileup of fancy cars on the freeway full of drivers who don't know how to deal with the reality of investing risk.

Good *traders* operate differently. If buy-and-hold investing is like hitching a ride on the freeway, short-term, active trading is more like a demolition derby. Traders are not loyal to the stocks they buy and sell. They measure the risk of each trade. They may have profit objectives but more commonly they use strict risk management as brakes and seatbelts to protect them in the melee and allow them to maneuver quickly. Success in this game is often more dependent on the use of brakes than the accelerator pedal.

Bad traders bring the biases and habits of the freeway-hitchhiking investor into the demolition derby of short-term, active trading, which requires completely different skills and a unique way of thinking. These reckless traders go merely beyond simply buying dips and constant-dollar investing with all their cash: They trade on margin, borrowing money from their brokers to buy more dips and invest in more stocks. When they are tapped out on margin, they use credit cards to plow more rental money into stocks with little regard to the risk that goes along with this degree of leverage.

They are entering the demolition derby ring in a *borrowed* V12 Mercedes and, because they are not used to managing risk, they don't understand how to read the speedometer, operate the brakes, or fasten the seatbelts.

money management tasks

You need to perform the following important money management chores to do the job properly:

- Determine how much you are willing to risk on each trade.
- Understand the risk of the trade you are about to take and size the trade appropriately.
- Track the trade going forward.
- Pay attention to your risk points; take small losses before they become big losses.
- Review your performance.

determining per trade risk

The most important decision you need to make is how much you are willing to risk on each trade relative to your entire portfolio. Many of the top traders in Jack Schwager's *Market Wizards* books said they limited this amount to less than 2 percent of their stake.

The reason to keep this number small is to protect yourself from a series of losses that could bring you to the point of ruin. Losing trades are a fact of life when trading—you *will* have them. The key is to limit those losses so that you can endure a string of them and have enough capital to place trades that will be big winners.

understanding trading risk

It's easy to determine how much risk there is in a particular trade. The first step is to decide—before you put the trade on—at what price you will exit the trade if it goes against you. There are two ways to determine this price level.

The first is to use a trading method based on technical analysis that will provide a reversal signal or a stop-loss price for you.

The second is to let money management determine the exit when you don't have a technical or fundamental opinion about where to place the "I was wrong" price point. This is where you draw a line in the sand and tell the market that it cannot take any more money out of your wallet.

No matter what your approach—whether technical, fundamental, astrological, or even a random dartboard pick—you should not trade or invest in anything without knowing, at all times, what your exit price will be. You need to know this price ahead of time so that you don't have to worry about the decision when that price is reached—the action at that point should be automatic. You won't have time to muddle it out when the market is screaming in the opposite direction you thought it would go!

If you are using the first method (where your timing method provides an exit stop automatically), you can use the following formula to determine how many shares of stock to buy or sell:

$$s = \frac{er}{p - x}$$

where s = Size of the trade
e = Portfolio equity (cash and holdings)
r = Maximum risk percentage per trade
p = Entry price on the trade
x = Predetermined stop loss or exit price

For example, Belinda has a trading account with a total value (cash and holdings) of $100,000 and is willing to risk 2 percent of that capital on any one trade. Her trading system gives her a signal to buy DTCM stock trading at $100 per share and the system says that the reversal point on that trade is $95. Plugging this into the formula tells Belinda that she can buy 400 shares of DTCM. The cost of this investment is $40,000, but she is only risking 2 percent of her capital, or $2,000, on the idea.

Belinda then gets a tip from her brother-in-law that KRMA is about to take a nosedive from its lofty perch at $40 because he heard from his barber that earnings of KRMA will be well below expectations. She's willing to go short another $10,000 of her stake on this idea. She studies a KRMA chart and can't see any logical technical points that would be a good place to put in a stop, so she uses the money management method to determine the stop according to this formula:

$$x = \frac{p(i - er)}{i}$$

where x = Predetermined stop loss or exit price
p = Entry price on the trade
i = Investment amount
e = Portfolio equity (cash and holdings)
r = Maximum risk percentage per trade

Since she's shorting KRMA, the value for i, $10,000, should be negative. Plugging these values into the preceding formula would tell Belinda that her stop price on the short sale of KRMA should be 48. If she didn't want to assign a high confidence on this trade, she could reduce the max risk to 1 percent ($r = .01$), which would bring the stop down to 44.

Another worthwhile variation to these methods is to use Ed Seykota's "core equity" for e in the formulas rather than the total value of all holdings in the portfolio. Core equity is what you have left when you subtract the total value at risk in all open positions from the total equity; value at risk in each trade is calculated by multiplying the number of shares in the position by the difference between the current price and the stop price on that trade.

Using the core equity value as the basis for sizing new trades has the desirable effect of automatically reducing the risk exposure on new positions when market volatility in your existing positions increases.

tracking your trades

It is important to watch your positions as they progress and adjust your stop prices as the market moves in your direction.

In the first example, if DTCM moves from $100 to $120 and the stop is left at $95, what started as $2,000 or 2 percent at risk is now $10,000 (9 percent of the total equity) at risk. The mistake most people make is to consider trade winnings on open "house money"; somehow this money is less painful to lose than the money in your back pocket. This is a bad mental habit. If losing 2 percent of equity on a trade would be painful to Belinda when her account was at $100,000, losing 9 percent after the stock has moved to $120 should be several times more so. Moving your stop loss up with the price on a winning trade does several good things: It locks in your profits and if you are using core equity to size new positions, it will allow you to take more risk on new trades.

Never move a stop backward from its initial price—stops should always be moved to reduce, never increase, the amount of risk on a trade.

Past the initial risk you are willing to take, stops should be a one-way valve for the flow of money from the market to your account.

terminating with prejudice

A money management plan will only be useful if you do what it says. As the saying goes, you must plan your trades and trade your plan. If a stop price is hit, you must take that hit. If you find that your system is generating stops that are constantly getting hit, then perhaps you should reexamine the rules of the system; but don't mess with your money! Second-guessing the approach will cause you to take on more risk than you planned, increasing the chances that a bad trading system will ruin you. Once your stop is gone, how will you know when to get out next?

Take your losses when they are small because if you don't they are sure to get large. In this regard, discipline is of the highest importance. It is a cardinal mistake not to take a stop if it is hit. It's even worse if the stock comes back and turns the trade into a winner because now you have been psychologically rewarded for making the mistake.

Get out quickly and reassess the situation. If you think it will come back, put on a new trade with a new stop. Faith, hope, and prayer should be reserved for God—the markets are false and fickle idols.

tools for understanding and practicing good money management

A few Web sites provide software or Web-based tools for understanding money management. Most of the large finance sites do a fair job at letting you track the value of your investments, but none of them are really suited for tracking the performance of a trading program—for that you need a piece of software.

The popular finance software packages, such as Quicken and Microsoft Money, can track the history of your transactions but don't do as good a job at treating these as trades. They're fine for showing you the value of your portfolio and can save you time preparing your tax return, but they are not suited to executing the steps that have been outlined here.

Table 8.1 provides a list of sites and software packages that help with these tasks, some better than others. Money Maximizer, software written by traders for traders, is a good package for managing your trading risk by sizing your trades to the amount of risk you want to take. The interface can be a bit clumsy and the program leaves a few things to be desired, but it's a good overall package; the "Size-It" tool sizes your trades based on risk relative to core equity.

Another software package that showed a great deal of promise—but is no longer produced—is kNOW Software by MoneySoft.com. The Web site provides an excellent online manual and the tutorial is a worthwhile and instructive guide to good money management practices.

The Athena software looks good, too, but has a steep price tag: $12,500. The site is worth a visit: Dr. Van Tharp provides some good information on proper money management.

Excel makes an excellent tool for implementing the previously listed formulas. (It's what I use for my own trading, in combination with Quote.com QCharts live quotes package. The Quote.com QFeed includes an add-in to power Excel spreadsheets with live quotes.

Some of the tools listed are a cross between software and a Web site (Webware). These packages are generally free but are paid for by banner ads displayed in the window of the software. The Medved quote tracker lets you turn off the ads if you register and pay the $60 fee.

Money management is a complex subject that you must master if you want to enjoy a sustained trading career. The books listed under

TABLE 8.1	SOFTWARE SITES SIZING THINGS UP					
Software	Type	Risk Mgmt?	Company	Web Address	Price	Comments
Athena Money Management	Software	Yes	International Institute of Trading Mastery, Inc.	www.iitm.com/software/ii05002.htm	$12,500	Associated with the money management practices of Dr. Van Tharp, an investment psychologist
kNOW Software	Web site	Yes	MoneySoft.com	www.moneys-oftware.com	n/a	Software is no longer available but the site has very good information
Money Maximizer	Software	Yes	Trading Research Design	www.moneymax-imizer.com	free trial; Full $159; Pro $259	Written by a top-rated hedge fund manager
QCharts	Software	Yes	Lycos/Quote.com	www.qcharts.com/	$89/mo.	Quote sheets track stops; calculate trade and portfolio risk updated in real time
Trade Factory.com	Web site	Yes	TradeFactory.com	www.tradefactory.com	$299 + $99/mo.	Based on the famous Turtle Trading methods
Captool	Software	No	Captools Company	http://captools.com	$249 - $3,500	Complete professional tool; includes tax accounting
Fund Manager	Software	No	Beily Software	www.beiley.com/fundman/desc.html	$39; manual $2	Specially suited for tracking mutual fund performance
Money 2000	Software	No	Microsoft	www.microsoft.com	$64.95	
Quicken Deluxe	Software	No	Intuit	www.intuit.com/quicken	$59.95	
Money Deluxe	Web site	No	Microsoft Investor	www.moneycentral.msn.com/investor	$59.30	
Portfolio	Web site	No	Quote.com	www.quote.com	free	Daily portfolio valuations; e-mail alerts
Medved Quote Tracker	Webware	No	2GK Inc.	www.medved.net/QuoteTracker	free; no ads $60	
Stocktick	Webware	No	NAC Consulting	www.nacon-sulting.com	$24.95	
StockVue 2000	Webware	No	NQL Solution	www.stockview2000.com	free; banner advertisements	

"Money Management" in the Appendix of this book provide additional information on this multifaceted topic.

playing it safe

Chuck LeBeau and Terence Tan

Many successful traders often advise less experienced traders to spend more time learning how to exit their trades, rather than obsessing about entry points. After all, your exits determine the success and profitability of your trades. A good exit can salvage a bad entry and a poor exit can easily turn a winning trade into a loss.

There are many types of useful exit techniques, but the simplest and most critical exit is the money-management exit—the classic *stop loss* that protects your trading capital and prevents ruin. If you hope to be successful over the long run, nothing is more important than the preservation of your trading capital.

Stock market investors using a "buy-and-hold" strategy may be able to survive without protective exits (if they pick the right stocks); but short-term traders, especially those who trade futures and other leveraged instruments, who forgo money-management stops are setting themselves up for certain ruin.

Many money managers and traders have lost hundreds of millions of dollars by disregarding prudent money-management techniques. In *The Education of a Speculator,* well-known trader and author Victor Niederhoffer wrote: "I have never used stops, even to bail myself out. Somehow, having a fixed rule to exit provides my adversaries too great an advantage." Soon after, Niederhoffer went on to lose tens of millions of dollars of his clients' money in the 1997 Thai baht crisis.

Although some traders may prefer to avoid fixed stop orders in the markets because of their unusually large positions, many large money managers do keep close track of specific stop points on their positions without actually placing these orders in the markets. When these stop points are reached, all positions are promptly liquidated at the market, just like a regular stop order. This alternative to placing large resting stop orders in the market requires tremendous mental discipline and also very close intraday monitoring of the market.

For the beginner or part-time trader, intraday monitoring may not be feasible, making the placement of resting stop orders in the markets a vital necessity. For the beginning trader, the first priority in trading must always be to preserve trading capital from the risk of catastrophic ruin; everything else is secondary.

The preceding statement says the goal is to *preserve trading capital from the risk of catastrophic ruin,* not to eliminate or reduce the risk of loss. Reasonable losses are an integral part of the trading process and good traders accept losses as a cost of doing business. In fact, it is not uncommon for the best traders to take more losses than bad traders do. The critical issue in this discussion is the size of the losses that are taken. Catastrophic losses must be avoided at all costs. And such losses are easily avoided by always using a simple money-management stop.

Good traders actually need money-management stops more than bad traders do. The truth is that bad traders are going to fail very quickly whether they use money-management stops or not, while good traders will survive and prosper indefinitely. The better you trade, the longer you will trade and the more likely it becomes that you eventually will encounter a potentially catastrophic event. When that event happens, your stops had better be in place.

In addition to the dollars involved, there are also psychological advantages to using stops. A money-management stop establishes a predefined loss point that allows you to exit a losing trade unemotion-ally. Traders who use money-management stops know from the outset they will accept only a limited amount of adverse price action on each trade; after reaching that point, they will cut their losses. Having a well-defined strategy for handling the losing trades eliminates the real-time stress of dealing with losing positions. The trader using money-manage-ment stops will never experience the agony of having to watch a huge loss grow larger day after day.

Disciplined use of money-management stops provides a psycho-logical advantage before putting on a risky trade. Suppose your entry strategy calls for you to take a trade in a highly volatile market. The high volatility presents the opportunity for large profits but also virtu-ally unlimited loss. No knowledgeable trader should be willing to enter such a trade. However, if you have a reasonable money-management stop that defines exactly what your worst loss will be, it is psychologi-cally much easier to confidently enter the trade. You also will be psy-chologically prepared to quickly and decisively accept the loss should it occur, and as a result you will have the confidence to enter high risk-high reward trades.

a better stop approach

The simplest money-management stop is a stop-loss order placed a fixed dollar amount from the entry price. Such "dollar stops" are easy to im-plement, but there are correct and incorrect ways to use a dollar stop in your strategy.

The incorrect way to use dollar stops is to calculate the maximum amount you can "afford" to lose in the trade and set your dollar stop ac-cordingly. There are two problems with this approach: First, the market does not base its adverse price movements on how much money you can afford to lose, and second, there is no point in risking the "maximum" on every trade.

The correct way to set dollar stops is to use market characteristics and your trading experience (or historical testing data) to determine the best stop placement level. For example, dollar stops should not be placed too close to the entry price because random price movement will stop the trade out prematurely (the dreaded *whipsaw* effect). Neither should dollar stops be placed too far away from the market, because that would mean taking a much larger loss than is actually necessary. Fig-ure 8.2 shows a good example of how the latest market bottom can work as a support level suitable for a stop that will help you avoid any cata-strophic events.

Another way to place dollar stops is to use some measure of the current volatility of the market. The goal is to keep your stop outside the

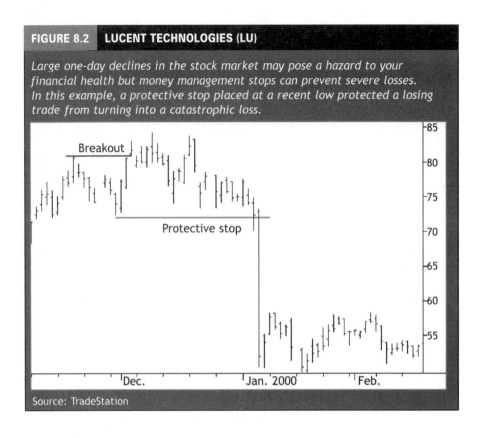

FIGURE 8.2   LUCENT TECHNOLOGIES (LU)

Large one-day declines in the stock market may pose a hazard to your financial health but money management stops can prevent severe losses. In this example, a protective stop placed at a recent low protected a losing trade from turning into a catastrophic loss.

Source: TradeStation

range of the random or natural price movements of the market while still maintaining your goal of capital preservation. For example, if the average daily range of a market is $1,000, the dollar stop on that market should be at least $1,000. It must be emphasized again that adequate system testing and analysis should precede the implementation of any dollar stop to find the appropriate level. Stops should not be picked out of the air.

It's also important to understand the volatility characteristics of each market you trade and not to blindly use the same fixed dollar stop for all markets (or even for the same market, if its volatility characteristics are changing). The challenge is to develop money-management stops that adapt to current market conditions based on some simple measure of market volatility.

One method to adjust the stop to the current market volatility is to look at the average true range (ATR) or the standard deviation of prices over a certain period of time and multiply these measurements by a certain factor to determine how far away the stop should be placed from the entry price. (The ATR is the difference between today's high and low, or the difference between yesterday's close and today's high or low, whichever is the largest.)

When using the ATR method, be careful to place the stop more than one ATR from the entry price to avoid being stopped out by random price movement. The advantage of using a stop determined by ATR is that it is highly adaptive to current market conditions. The distance from your entry point to the stop would increase in periods of high market volatility and decrease in periods of lower volatility. In Figure 8.3, the arrows show where a fixed dollar-based stop would have stopped you out twice in the middle of a nice bull run, while a 1.5 ATR stop would have let you stay in the trade for almost the entire move.

In practice, the downside of using an ATR stop is that the short-term ATR sometimes becomes unusually small and the resulting tight stop gets whipsawed. To avoid this, you can calculate both a short-term ATR (e.g., 3 to 4 days) and a longer term ATR (e.g., 15 to 20 days) and always

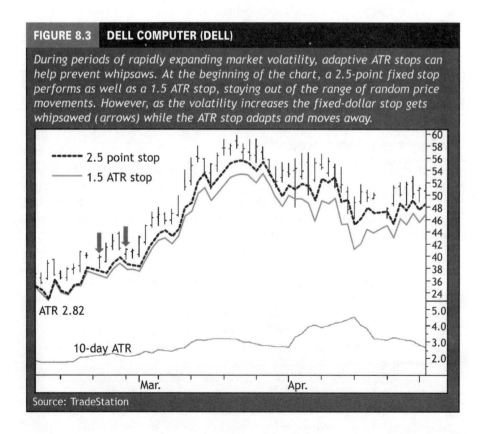

FIGURE 8.3   **DELL COMPUTER (DELL)**

During periods of rapidly expanding market volatility, adaptive ATR stops can help prevent whipsaws. At the beginning of the chart, a 2.5-point fixed stop performs as well as a 1.5 ATR stop, staying out of the range of random price movements. However, as the volatility increases the fixed-dollar stop gets whipsawed (arrows) while the ATR stop adapts and moves away.

----- 2.5 point stop

—— 1.5 ATR stop

ATR 2.82

10-day ATR

Source: TradeStation

set your stops using whichever of the two ATRs is the largest. This procedure allows the stops to move away quickly but prevents them from moving in too close after just a few unusually quiet days.

perfection is not possible

There's no such thing as a perfect stop point, even using an adaptive technique. Most traders who use money-management stops find that the stops are either too close (subject to frequent whipsaws) or too far away (subject to large losses).

Extensive testing has shown that most traders would benefit from using relatively large money-management stops. At first thought, it would appear that using tighter stops (keeping losses small) would lower the expected drawdown. However, this seemingly logical assumption doesn't hold up in testing. In almost all cases, wider stops result in a higher winning percentage and a lower drawdown. Smaller stops are psychologically attractive, but limiting losses too much can actually deteriorate system performance because of frequent whipsaws caused by random and insignificant price movements.

By contrast, wider stops are activated less frequently, and systems with large stops generally tend to demonstrate a higher percentage of winning trades. The downside is that large stops force you to occasionally suffer uncomfortably large losses which, although infrequent, can be psychologically difficult to accept. Is there a compromise solution to this problem? There might just be.

finding the middle ground

An interesting phenomenon connected to using a *good* entry technique is that it is often possible to tighten a money-management stop after giving a trade a certain amount of initial latitude after the entry. The better the entry technique, the larger the money-management stop you can use during the first few bars of a trade. However, after a specific number of bars, the money-management stop can often be reduced to a much smaller amount.

For example, if you use a $5,000 stop when entering a trade in the S&P 500 futures, and this represents an uncomfortably large loss, it may be possible to leave the $5,000 stop in place only for the first few days and then tighten the stop to $2,500 for the remainder of the trade. The chances of being stopped out late in the trade with a $5,000 loss have been eliminated.

The exact stop amounts and the time of implementation would have to be determined by computer research and statistical analysis of your strategy's characteristics. Research has shown that some trend-following strategies can benefit substantially by implementing a larger stop in the beginning of a trade, and then reducing the original stop by as much as 50 percent or more once the trade is underway. Starting off a trade with a large money-management stop allows the trade sufficient opportunity to begin moving in the right direction when there is a high level of confidence in the entry indication. As the trade moves out into the future and the confidence of the entry indication declines, tightening the stop reflects the decreasing confidence in the trade. Figure 8.4 shows such a strategy implemented on a long position in Oracle (ORCL) in early 2000.

There are other possibilities for dealing with the problem of large stops. Break-even stops or profit-protection (trailing) stops that override the money-management stop can easily be implemented in later stages of the trade. Once these stops are activated, the possibility of taking the large original stop loss is substantially reduced or eliminated.

Proper understanding and implementation of the money-management stop is vital to trading survival. A stop effectively limits the maximum loss on a trade, which in turn contributes to the primary goal of

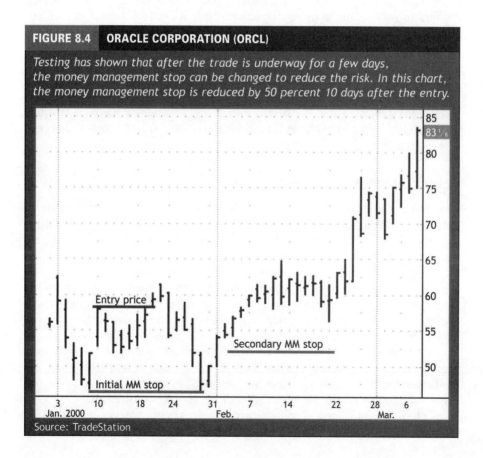

FIGURE 8.4   ORACLE CORPORATION (ORCL)

Testing has shown that after the trade is underway for a few days, the money management stop can be changed to reduce the risk. In this chart, the money management stop is reduced by 50 percent 10 days after the entry.

Source: TradeStation

capital preservation. Trading without a money-management stop exposes you to the risk of catastrophic loss.

The importance of the money-management stop is aptly summed up by Jack Schwager with this statement from his book, *The New Market Wizards:* "If you can't take a small loss, sooner or later you will take the mother of all losses."

exit, trade left

Thomas Stridsman

"If I only had exited that trade on the first signs of trouble, I might have ended up with a small profit instead of this huge loser."

Honestly, how many of us haven't heard that one before? Or worse, how many of us actually have uttered the same phrase ourselves? The truth is, probably the first and most costly lesson we have to learn as traders is no trading strategy is complete if its entry signals aren't accompanied with a.good working exit technique that allows us to hold on to our profits.

A trailing stop—a stop-loss order that follows a trade as the market progresses—is one technique traders use to protect open trade profits and prevent winning trades from turning into losers.

We'll look at a few of the different ways traders approach trailing stops and analyze how these techniques perform when subjected to extensive testing.

defining trends and holding profits

Ever since the earliest days of technical analysis, an uptrend has been defined as a market that continues to move higher without penetrating the low of the most recent retracement, or pullback. For a downtrend, the opposite holds true.

Figure 8.5 shows an extended uptrend: The dashed and solid lines are successive relative highs and relative lows, respectively. In general terms, as long as the market keeps making higher highs and higher lows, the uptrend is still in effect. When this basic rule is violated, the market is either in a consolidation phase or potentially beginning a reversal.

In this example, the relative lows function as support levels and represent a succession of higher stop levels for a long position—a basic trailing stop technique. As the market pushes above another relative high, the most recent relative low becomes the new stop level.

There is, however, a major problem in trying to use this kind of trailing stop strategy: If an uptrend is characterized by continuously

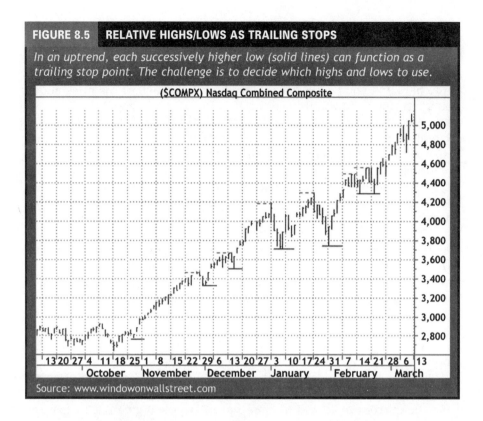

FIGURE 8.5   RELATIVE HIGHS/LOWS AS TRAILING STOPS

In an uptrend, each successively higher low (solid lines) can function as a trailing stop point. The challenge is to decide which highs and lows to use.

Source: www.windowonwallstreet.com

higher highs and higher lows, which highs and lows should we use? Using many of the progressively higher stop levels in Figure 8.5 would result in giving back sizable profits. Also, these levels were chosen visually; others, either of greater or lesser magnitude, could have been selected. Which ones would best limit risk and maximize gain? It may seem obvious in retrospect, but it's impossible to know in real time, as price action is unfolding.

A simple, if not perfect, way to work around this is to use the longest time-frame price bars (15-minute, hourly, daily, weekly, etc.), given your typical trade length. The object is to filter out as much market noise as possible without losing too much of the price information you need to make your trades. For example, if your trades normally last no more than two or three weeks, use only daily bars, comparing the current bar only with the immediately preceding bars as the market evolves. That is, in an uptrend, today's high and low should be higher than yesterday's high and low. If they are not, the market has given you its first warning sign of pending consolidation or trend reversal. In Figure 8.5, notice how (even in this strongly uptrending market) a lower low is more likely to be followed by another lower low than a higher low.

If you're a longer term trader, use only weekly or monthly bars to filter out the noise that comes with the daily price action. In the previous example (with a trade length of a few weeks), you also could have used weekly bars, but then your trades would have lasted for only two or three bars and you would have filtered out too much of the price action you are trying to capitalize on.

The same principle also holds true if you're an intraday trader. For example, if it is possible to achieve essentially the same results (without losing too much detail) using hourly bars as it is 15-minutes bars, use the former.

Using this reasoning, we can construct two trailing-stop strategies. The first strategy simply uses the most recent high or low and will signal an exit for a long position as soon as tomorrow's price moves below today's low (reverse for short positions).

The second strategy is similar to the first, except that it signals an exit on a move below yesterday's close instead of yesterday's high or low. The reason is that the closing price might be more significant than the other price extremes during the day; if the trend is strong enough, it is reasonable to assume that a two-day-old closing price should not be overlapped if the market is going to continue to trend.

A third trailing-stop strategy would be to use a moving average: You would exit your position if price retraced enough to penetrate the moving average. The problem here is because moving averages lag price action, the faster the market moves, the farther away the average will be from the current price and the more profit you will give back when the market turns against you, adding volatility to your account and anxiety to your life. But by using a shorter (faster) average, you will be stopped out too soon or at the least opportune moments. Figure 8.6 shows how a longer term average can expose you to too much risk, while a shorter term average gives you very little breathing room. The problem then becomes one of picking the moving-average length that will allow you to trade as profitably as possible as often as possible.

One way to determine the best moving-average length for a trailing stop is to base it on the size of the market move you're trying to catch and what your most profitable trade length typically is. For most short-term interday trading strategies, the optimum number of bars per trade seems to fall in the 8- to 10-day range. If that holds true for your strategy as well, then chances are this also will be the best look-back period for your moving average and other indicators.

The principle regarding the length of the look-back period can be used to create a fourth trailing-stop strategy. During a nontrending, neutral day, tomorrow's price action is likely to fluctuate about the same amount above and below today's closing price. But if the market is in an uptrend or downtrend, price should fluctuate more than 50 percent of the day's range above or below today's close, respectively.

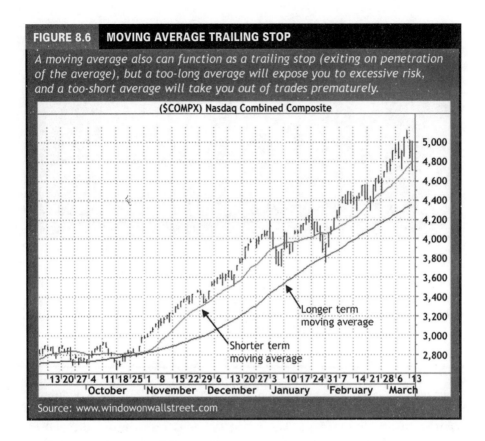

FIGURE 8.6   MOVING AVERAGE TRAILING STOP

A moving average also can function as a trailing stop (exiting on penetration of the average), but a too-long average will expose you to excessive risk, and a too-short average will take you out of trades prematurely.

($COMPX) Nasdaq Combined Composite

Longer term moving average

Shorter term moving average

Source: www.windowonwallstreet.com

These fluctuations can then be compared with the average true range (a volatility calculation; see "True Range" on page 212) for the look-back period in question. If the price fluctuations exceeded what could be expected (based on the average true range) we would have an early warning sign there might be a change of direction on the horizon. In other words, you would exit a long position if the stock moved more than half the average true range below the most recent close (reverse for short positions).

How do these four strategies work in the stock market? Figures 8.7 through 8.10 show the results from testing these four trailing-stop strategies with a *safety factor* (a buffer to the original stop amount) added to each one of them. Each strategy was tested on the 30 Dow Jones Industrial Average stocks from January 1990 to February 2000.

The safety factor was added because many times the market "knows" where the most obvious stop levels are located and takes them out with a swift move before resuming in its original direction. The remedy for this is to take a slightly larger risk by placing the stop a little bit farther away

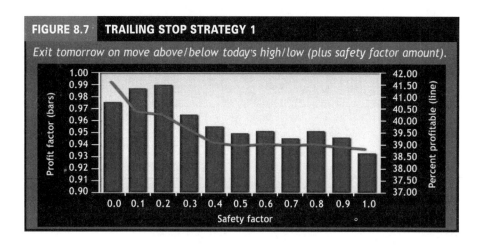

FIGURE 8.7   TRAILING STOP STRATEGY 1

Exit tomorrow on move above/below today's high/low (plus safety factor amount).

from the current price. For example, for a trailing stop that would exit a long trade on a penetration of the lowest low of the last two bars, a safety factor of ¼ could be added, so the stop would become a ¼ point below the lowest low of the last two bars. A safety factor gives each trade a little margin for error and gives you a way of not running with the crowd. For strategies 3 and 4, we used a fixed look-back period of eight days.

To make sure that we really tested the exit techniques and nothing else, we used a random entry technique. No commissions were deducted. To compare and rank our findings, we used the profit factor and the percentage profitable trades. (The profit factor is gross profit divided by gross loss, which means that if it is above 1, we made more money than we lost.)

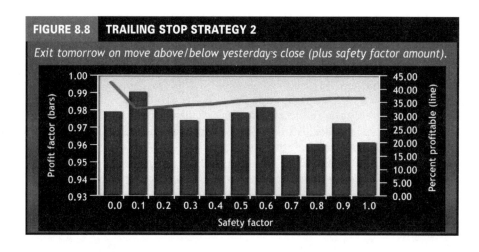

FIGURE 8.8   TRAILING STOP STRATEGY 2

Exit tomorrow on move above/below yesterday's close (plus safety factor amount).

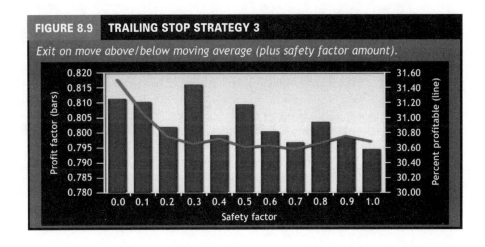

FIGURE 8.9   TRAILING STOP STRATEGY 3

Exit on move above/below moving average (plus safety factor amount).

Exit strategies 1, 2, and 3 didn't work at all—none of the variations we tested had a profit factor of 1 or above, as shown in Figures 8.7 to 8.9. Interestingly, strategies 1 and 3, which are the most basic techniques, used by many traders, did not turn out to be the best strategies in any stock, no matter what safety factor was used. This means that these strategies are very sensitive to the type of entry technique used and should, therefore, only be paired with entries that have a high probability of moving immediately in your direction.

Strategy 3 also suffers from the fact that you need to be on the right side of the moving average when you enter the trade, which makes it very difficult to use in a short-term strategy where it is crucial to pick as

FIGURE 8.10   TRAILING STOP STRATEGY 4

Exit on move more than 50 percent of average true range (plus safety factor amount) above/below the most recent close.

many tops and bottoms as possible. Strategy 4, on the other hand, worked very well, even with a random entry, with a safety factor of 0.5 percent producing the best results.

To see how strategy 4 (with a safety factor of 0.5 percent) might work with a specific entry method, we added it to the entry technique developed in Chapter 5, "clear-cut chart pattern trading." The entry technique uses a combination of spike and reversal days to identify potential swing points. Table 8.2 summarizes the results of testing this combination on the same test data used earlier.

The top half of Table 8.2 shows the combined results for both long and short positions. However, because most people trade primarily on the long side of the market, the bottom half of the table shows the result for long positions only: 46 percent were profitable, for an average profit of $96,614 per year (in today's market value), trading 1,000 stocks per market.

With an initial account balance of $547,876 (calculated as twice the sum of the margin requirements for all the stocks) and taking into account the average time spent in the market (27 percent), this would equal a return of close to 18 percent per year.

Trailing stops represent a trade-off: They can help lock in profits and reduce risk in your trading plan at the expense of overall profitability. The challenge is to find a trailing stop that prevents winning trades from turning into losers but gives winners as much of a chance as possible to reach their maximum profitability.

The tests shown here reveal that some of the more basic techniques used by traders don't leave room for improvement. The trailing-stop technique based on a move that exceeds an amount determined by current volatility (via the true range calculation) showed visible improvement over the other techniques.

true range

True range (TR) is a measure of price movement that takes into account the gaps that occur between price bars. This calculation provides a more accurate reflection of the size of a price move over a given period than

TABLE 8.2	SPIKE-REVERSAL ENTRY WITH TRAILING STOP							
These are the results of a system that enters on a combination spike-reversal day and uses the fourth (volatility-based) trailing stop technique. Results are shown both for all trades and long trades only.								
	Profit factor	Percent winners	Average profit ($)	Trades/ year	Profit/ year ($)			
All trades	0.99	43.70	386	635	11,424			
	Profit factor	Percent winners	Average profit ($)	Trades/ year	Profit/ year ($)	Time in market	Margin ($)	Return on margin (%)
Long trades only	1.17	46.29	6,336	419	96,614	27%	547,876	17.63

the standard range calculation does, which is simply the high of a price bar minus the low of a price bar. The true range calculation was developed by Welles Wilder and discussed in his book *New Concepts in Technical Trading Systems* (Trend Research, 1978).

True range can be calculated on any time frame or price bar—five-minute, hourly, daily, weekly, and so on. The following discussion will use daily price bars for simplicity. True range is the greatest (absolute) distance between the following:

1. Today's high and today's low, when yesterday's close is within today's range.
2. Yesterday's close and today's high, when yesterday's close is below today's low.
3. Yesterday's close and today's low, when yesterday's close is above today's high.

Average true range (ATR) is simply a moving average of the true range over a certain time period. For example, the five-day ATR would be the average of the true range calculations over the past five days.

sizing your trades

Thomas Stridsman

Have you noticed that while many market gurus have no problem letting you know which stocks to buy, they very rarely let you know how many shares you should buy to maximize the risk-reward relationship of your portfolio over the long haul?

This aspect of trading is very important, however, because not only is it possible to trade too conservatively in an effort to minimize risk, it also is fully possible to trade too aggressively in an effort to maximize the reward.

In his book *The Mathematics of Money Management,* Ralph Vince illustrated this with an example of a betting game. There was a 50 percent chance of winning, with the winners being twice as big as the losers. If you win $2 for each win and lose $1 for each loss, the expected outcome (or "mathematical expectation") of each bet in this game would be 50 cents [($2 × 0.5) – ($1 × 0.5)]. With a positive expected outcome for a trading strategy, it is easy to believe that we should invest as much as we can on every trade. Unfortunately, things aren't that simple.

The truth is that, depending on the probabilities of the strategy and the ratio between the dollar values of the winners and the losers (more often referred to as the profit factor), there is an optimal value or fraction (*f*) of your total equity you should risk at each bet. This value can be calculated using a calculation called the Kelly formula:

$$f = \frac{(PF + 1) \times (P - 1)}{PF}$$

where *PF* = Profit factor (gross profit / gross loss)
    P = Probability of winning bet

Plugging in the values from our simple game, we find the most optimal fraction of our total equity to bet is 0.25, [(2 + 1) × 0.5 − 1]/2, or 25 percent. That is, if we bet any less than this, we will not maximize our potential return; but if we bet any more, we will only increase risk without increasing return; and we will actually end up with less money than we would using the optimal trade size.

Twisting the Kelly formula around a little bit can prove this. Instead of solving for the optimal fraction to invest, we can set it to a fixed value, such as 0.5 (or 50 percent) and solve for the profit factor. If the profit factor turns out to be lower than 2, we know we are betting too aggressively, compared with the results we get when betting only 25 percent. If the profit factor also turns out to be lower than 1, we are losing money. Thus, by betting too aggressively, it's possible to take a winning strategy and turn it into a losing one, which happens to be a key reason so many inexperienced traders fail before they even get out of the starting blocks. Conversely, the lower the profit factor, the less you can risk in each trade.

stock market applications

For the stock market, the situation becomes a little more complex because there are now two variables that measure risk. The first measures how much we are prepared to let the price of a stock, future, option, or currency move against us on a percentage basis; the second is how much of our total account equity we're willing to risk as a consequence of the market moving against us. To get a better feel for how this works, consider the following two examples.

In the first, you have an initial equity balance of $200,000 and are considering buying a stock trading at $100. You are willing to let the market move against you 10 percent before you take a loss, which at the current market price would be $10 per share (0.1 × 100). The total amount of capital you're willing to lose on this trade is 0.75 percent of your total equity, which equals $1,500 (0.0075 × 200,000). To limit your loss to $10 per share for a total of $1,500, you will need to buy 150 shares, which means you need to commit a total of $15,000 to the entire position [(1,500/10) × 100]. Dividing the initial account balance with the amount committed to the position tells you that you can have 13 similar trades at the same time (200,000/15,000).

In the second example, you have an initial equity balance of $100,000 and are considering buying a stock trading at $150. Because in this example you have less initial capital, you decide you're now only willing to take a 5 percent move against you at the market for a loss of 0.25 percent of your total capital. This comes out to $7.50 (0.05 × 150) per share traded and $250 (0.0025 × 100,000) for the entire portfolio. To peg your expected worst-case scenario to $7.50 per share for a total of $250, you will need to buy 33 shares, which in turn means you have to commit a total of $5,000 [(250/7.5) × 150]. If you again divide the account balance going into the trade with the amount you need to commit to it, you now find you can have 20 similar positions going at the same time (100,000/5,000).

Now, how can it be that we can have more trades going at the same time even though the stock prices are higher and the initial portfolio balance is lower? Well, the answer can be found in the interplay between the maximum amount that we are willing to risk per stock and the total amount that we're willing to risk for the strategy as a whole. As it turns out, the stock price and the account balance have nothing to do with it. Instead, both mathematical operations can be simplified into the following mathematical expression:

$$\text{Maximum Markets to Trade (MMT)} = \frac{\text{MLS}}{\text{MLP}}$$

where MLS = Maximum loss per stock in percent of initial stock price

MLP = Maximum loss for portfolio in percent of initial account balance

For example, it does not matter if you can stomach market moves against you of 1, 4, or 8 percent if these moves correspond to portfolio risk of 0.25, 1, and 2 percent, respectively, because in all instances the MMT (the number of positions you can trade at the same time) will be 4. If, on the other hand, you have no problem weathering a 10 percent move against you resulting in a 0.25 percent total loss of equity, you can trade 40 positions at the same time. But if you think you can only take a 1 percent move against you for a 1 percent total loss of equity, you can only trade one position at a time.

Figure 8.11 shows the relationship between market moves against you and the amount of equity you are willing to lose. The numbers within the matrix, which show how many positions you can have on at the same time, are simply calculated as MLS divided by MLP, as shown in the previous formula. The more risk you're willing to take per stock traded,

FIGURE 8.11   OPEN POSITIONS

The more you're willing to let the stock move against you, but the less capital you're willing to lose per trade, the more positions you can trade at the same time.

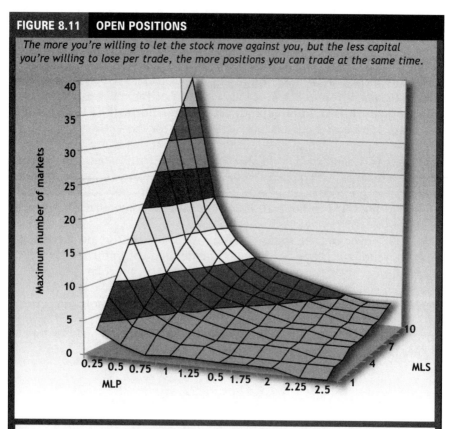

Number of possible open positions at one time

					Maximum loss for portfolio (MLP)					
		0.25	0.5	0.75	1	1.25	1.5	1.75	2	2.25	2.5
	1	4	2	1	1	1	1	1	1	0	0
	2	8	4	3	2	2	1	1	1	1	1
	3	12	6	4	3	2	2	2	2	1	1
	4	16	8	5	4	3	3	2	2	2	2
Maximum loss per stock (MLS)	5	20	10	7	5	4	3	3	3	2	2
	6	24	12	8	6	5	4	3	3	3	2
	7	28	14	9	7	6	5	4	4	3	3
	8	32	16	11	8	6	5	5	4	4	3
	9	36	18	12	9	7	6	5	5	4	4
	10	40	20	13	10	8	7	6	5	4	4

while assuming less risk for your total equity, the more markets you can trade. The highlighted rows and columns give you an idea how much risk you'd have to assume for your entire equity if you follow the guidelines of *Investors Business Daily (IBD)*, which are: (1) don't let a market move against you more than 8 percent; and (2) don't hold open positions in more than six stocks at one time.

According to *IBD,* you should not let the market move against you more than 8 percent (the bolded rows) and not be positioned in more than six stocks at a time (the intersection between the bolded rows and the bolded columns), no matter how much trading or investment capital you might have. To achieve this, you will have to risk between 1.25 percent and 1.5 percent of your total equity per trade.

The amount of total equity you are prepared to risk is not the same as the amount you will have to commit to the trade. To understand how much money you will have tied up in each position, simply reverse the preceding formula:

$$\text{Capital Committed per Trade } \textit{in percent of total equity } (\text{CCT}) = \frac{\text{MLP}}{\text{MLS}}$$

where MLP = Maximum loss for portfolio in percent of initial account balance

MLS = Maximum loss per stock in percent of initial stock price

Figure 8.12 shows what this would look like using the same numbers as in Figure 8.11.

Continuing on the *IBD* example, a 1.25 percent to 1.5 percent risk of total equity per trade means you must have between 16 percent and 21 percent of your total capital committed to each position.

However, while the *IBD* guidelines are good basic rules or starting points, they don't necessarily represent the most optimal solution for your strategy's profit factor and winning percentage. They might be fine for some trading strategies, but totally off the wall for others.

the optimal solution

To determine the proper trade size, you also need to consider your investment or trading style and examine it for criteria such as the estimated average profit per trade, your estimated average and largest losers, and the dispersion of the individual trades (the standard deviation of outcomes—how consistent your trades are).

Further, because you will be buying and selling different stocks trading at completely different levels, it is paramount to use nothing but percentage-based calculations. This should not be a problem if you're a

FIGURE 8.12   **CAPITAL COMMITMENT**

The less you're willing to let the stock move against your position and the more capital you're willing to lose per trade, the larger chunk of your money you will have tied up in each position.

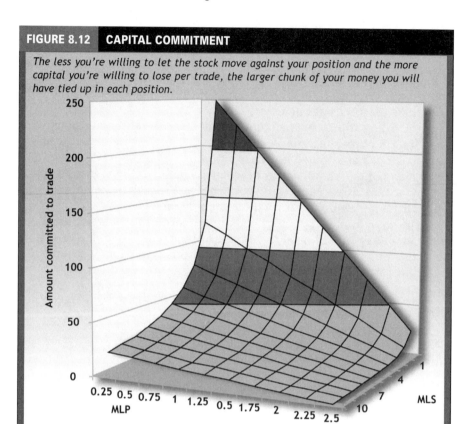

		Percent of total capital committed to one position									
		Maximum loss for portfolio (MLP)									
Maximum loss per stock (MLS)		0.25	0.5	0.75	1	1.25	1.5	1.75	2	2.25	2.5
	1	25	50	75	100	125	150	175	200	225	250
	2	13	25	38	50	63	75	88	100	113	125
	3	8	17	25	33	42	50	58	67	75	83
	4	6	13	19	25	31	38	44	50	56	63
	5	5	10	15	20	25	30	35	40	45	50
	6	4	8	13	17	21	25	29	33	38	42
	7	4	7	11	14	18	21	25	29	32	36
	8	3	6	9	13	16	19	22	25	28	31
	9	3	6	8	11	14	17	19	22	25	28
	10	3	5	8	10	13	15	18	20	23	25

purely systematic or rule-based trader. It is slightly more difficult for discretionary traders, but as long as you have your paperwork in order, you should still be able to calculate these numbers.

From the initial example from *The Mathematics of Money Management,* we concluded that given the same statistical traits of two trading models, a trader who risks more of his trading capital doesn't necessarily make more money in the end. Instead, that trader actually runs a greater risk of going completely broke. The trick then is to find the value that optimizes returns given the more complex environment of trading.

Before we can do that, there are a few other things to understand. The most important is that the day-to-day (or hour-to-hour) activity in the markets is as close to random as something possibly can be. A successful technical trader knows it is not completely random, even if for the longest time the majority of analysts and researchers insisted this was the case. The reason was simply that there were no statistical tests or computers powerful enough around to prove them wrong. Today, even the most bullheaded researchers have had to admit there is something the academics now call "random walk with a drift." Markets do trend, and the trends are persistent.

Nonetheless, there's a major reason to assume randomness when trading with an optimized money management strategy: For a thoroughly researched and correctly designed trading strategy, the outcome of each individual trade should be random, even if the expectancy for the strategy, traded on several different markets over a longer period, happens to be positive. The more certain you can be that each individual trade has a random outcome, provided your strategy has a long-term positive expectation, the more certain you can be you've been able to squeeze out all available information.

By randomness (for a trading strategy), we mean that we have no way of knowing if the outcome of the next trade will be above or below the outcome of our average trade (with the average trade, of course, being positive and large enough to warrant trading in the first place).

Also, even if you know your strategy isn't random, you are better off assuming it is, because assuming a nonrandom model also would assume you should vary your bet size in accordance with the outcome of your preceding (few) trade(s). This might be the best way to go in the short run, but when conditions change you run the risk of betting more on your losing trades and less on your winning trades and, hence, not making as much money and experiencing longer and more severe losses (or "drawdowns") than you should have.

the essential rules of trading

This leaves us with the following essential rule of trading: No matter whether you believe the markets or your strategy to be random, you are better off assuming they are random and, consequently, sticking to risking the exact same percentage of money on each trade. To do that, you can use the following formula to calculate how many shares you can buy at each transaction:

$$\text{Total Amount Committee } in\ dollars\ (\text{TAC}) = \text{NST} \times \text{SP}$$

where NST = Number of stocks to trade = MLP × IAB/MLS × SP
   MLP = Maximum loss for portfolio in percent of initial account
      balance
   IAB = Initial account balance
   MLS = Maximum loss per stock in percent of initial stock price
   SP = Stock price

   In a spreadsheet program (such as Microsoft Excel), the formula will result in something like Table 8.3, where cell D3 holds the formula = C2 × C3, cell D5 holds the formula = C4 × C5, cell D6 holds the formula = D3/D5, and cell D7 holds the formula = D6 × C4.
   Even with this formula, however, we still have to decide what the optimal values are for the MLP and MLS. For the MLS, it's somewhat arbitrary and you could go either with what was the largest historical loss ever experienced by the system, the average historical loss or a theoretical value based on some type of statistical measure such as the standard deviation of historical outcomes. The important thing is that it is a value that makes sense according to the rules of your trading strategy.

TABLE 8.3   STOCK CALCULATOR

To calculate the number of stocks you can trade and how much of your trading capital you will have tied up in a specific position, you will need to decide how much you're willing to risk both as a percentage of the stock price and your initial account balance.

B	C	D
1 Stock calculator		
2 Initial account balance	$100,000.00	
3 Maximum loss (portfolio)	1.50%	$1,500.00
4 Stock price	$100.00	
5 Maximum loss (stock)	8.00%	$8.00
6 Number of shares to trade		188
7 Total amount committed		$18,800.00

Remember though, there is a trade-off here: The smaller the value, the more money you will have tied up in each individual position and the fewer markets you will be able to trade; the fewer markets you can trade, the less diversified you will be and, consequently, the more sensitive your overall trading results will be to the individual markets traded and how you manage to handle them.

the next level

To calculate the optimal risk to assume for the portfolio as a whole, things become a little more complicated. First, you need to assume a specific percentage level of risk—say 1.5 percent per trade. Then you need to calculate what your total, theoretical profit would have been had you been able to take on this risk for all your historical trades. This is done easiest with the help of a spreadsheet program.

First set up a chronological list of all your trades, including the entry price, the stop-loss level, and the outcome of the trade. Tables 8.4A–C show what this can look like in a five-trade example. Table 8.4A shows the total profit after five trades, using a maximum tolerated loss for the portfolio of 1.5 percent, is $895; while with a maximum tolerated loss of 7 percent (Table 8.4B), it's $2,424.

From just viewing these two examples, it seems—because our strategy is a good one—the more we're willing to risk the more we will make in the end. But watch what happens when we increase the maximum tolerated loss to 15 percent (Table 8.4C). Suddenly, we're actually losing money. This is because the combined risk (both from the percentage risked per stock and the percentage of total equity risked) we're taking now is too large to be offset by the percentage gains per stock in each trade, which we obviously cannot change. In fact, in this particular case, the 7 percent of total equity risked turned out to be the most optimal solution with the best risk-reward ratio, given the 8 percent risked per stock. In this case, all other solutions will be suboptimal. (Note: Risking 7 percent of your total equity is a lot and this value is likely to come down with an increasing number of trades.)

Referring to Tables 8.4A–C to calculate the most optimal fraction of your portfolio to risk per trade, you can use the following formulas:

1. In cell E3, type =C3*D3 and then drag it down to fill the entire column.
2. In cell G3, type =Round (D11*D$12/ABS(E3),0)
3. In cell G4, type =Round (I3*D$12/ABS(E4),0) and then drag it down to fill the entire column.
4. In cell H3, type in =G3*F3 and then drag it down to fill the entire column.

TABLES 8.4A–C OPTISIZE IT

Everything else equal, you can optsize the amount of your total equity to risk at each trade in order to maximize your returns. But you have to be careful. If you over optsize it is possible to take a winning strategy and turn it into a losing one.

	B	C	D	E	F	G	H	I
1	Portfolio optimizer A							
2	Date	Entry price	Stop loss	Stop loss	Profit/stock	Stocks traded	Total profit	Account balance
3	01/01/00	$100.00	8.00%	$8.00	($8.00)	188	($1,504.00)	$98,496.00
4	02/02/00	$94.00	8.00%	$7.52	$12.50	196	$2,450.00	$100,946.00
5	03/03/00	$112.00	8.00%	$8.96	$18.00	169	$3,042.00	$103,988.00
6	04/04/00	$140.00	8.00%	$11.20	($11.20)	139	($1,556.00)	$102,431.20
7	05/05/00	$128.00	8.00%	$10.24	($10.24)	150	($1,536.00)	$100,895.20
8	Sum profits:				$1.06		$895.20	
9								
10	Initial (changeable) parameters							
11	Initial account balance: $100,000.00							
12	Maximum loss (portfolio):	1.50%						

Italicized values are calculated **A**

	B	C	D	E	F	G	H	I
1	Portfolio optimizer B							
2	Date	Entry price	Stop loss	Stop loss	Profit/stock	Stocks traded	Total profit	Account balance
3	01/01/00	$100.00	8.00%	$8.00	($8.00)	875	($7,000.00)	$93,000.00
4	02/02/00	$94.00	8.00%	$7.52	$12.50	866	$10,825.00	$103,825.00
5	03/03/00	$112.00	8.00%	$8.96	$18.00	811	$14,598.00	$118,423.00
6	04/04/00	$140.00	8.00%	$11.20	($11.20)	740	($8,288.00)	$110,135.00
7	05/05/00	$128.00	8.00%	$10.24	($10.24)	753	($7,710.72)	$102,424.28
8	Sum profits:				$1.06		$2,424.28	
9								
10	Initial (changeable) parameters							
11	Initial account balance: $100,000.00							
12	Maximum loss (portfolio):	7.00%						

Italicized values are calculated **B**

	B	C	D	E	F	G	H	I
1	Portfolio optimizer C							
2	Date	Entry price	Stop loss	Stop loss	Profit/stock	Stocks traded	Total profit	Account balance
3	01/01/00	$100.00	8.00%	$8.00	($8.00)	1,875	($15,000.00)	$85,000.00
4	02/02/00	$94.00	8.00%	$7.52	$12.50	1,695	$21,187.50	$106,187.50
5	03/03/00	$112.00	8.00%	$8.96	$18.00	1,778	$32,004.00	$138,191.50
6	04/04/00	$140.00	8.00%	$11.20	($11.20)	1,851	($20,731.20)	$117,460.30
7	05/05/00	$128.00	8.00%	$10.24	($10.24)	1,721	($17,623.04)	$99,837.26
8	Sum profits:				$1.06		($162.74)	
9								
10	Initial (changeable) parameters							
11	Initial account balance: $100,000.00							
12	Maximum loss (portfolio):	15.00%						

Italicized values are calculated **C**

5. In cell I3, type in =D11+H3.

6. In cell I4, type in =I3+H4 and then drag it down to fill the entire column.

The procedures outlined here give you a way to determine how many shares to buy to optimize the risk-reward ratio for both an individual strategy and your portfolio as a whole. In this case, however, our portfolio only consists of one stock, which means all trades can be organized in one sequence.

multitrade money management

Thomas Stridsman

In the previous section, we showed that for any trading strategy there is an optimal amount, or fixed fraction, of trading capital that should be risked for each trade. Furthermore, once this amount has been determined, it should not be altered.

To calculate how much capital to risk per trade, you first need to determine how large a point loss you are willing to take on a trade. The larger the point loss, the fewer shares you will be able to buy. Similarly, the smaller the loss you are willing to take, the more shares you will be able to buy.

do the math: dollars versus percentages

For example, assume you have $100,000 available in your trading account and you are risking 2 percent of trading capital ($2,000) per trade. If you're willing to buy a stock at 100 using a stop loss of 90, then you would buy 200 shares [$2,000/(100 – 90)], which would tie up $20,000 of your capital (200 × 100).

The dollar risk is not the same as the dollar amount tied up in the trade. If you're only willing to risk $5 per share (a 95 stop loss), then you would need to buy 400 shares ($2,000/100 – 95), which will tie up $40,000 of your capital.

These two examples used dollar-based calculations to make them more understandable. However, such calculations should be done using percentages rather than dollar amounts. To understand why, let's substitute the $100 stock in the first example, first with a $200 stock and then a $50 stock, but keep the dollar-risk on the trade fixed at $10.

With the $200 stock, you would tie up $40,000 [$2,000/(200 – 190) × 200], but with the $50 stock you only tie up $10,000 [$2,000/(50 – 40) × 50]. The reason is that $10 is a greater percentage of $50 than it is of $200. But the amount of capital tied up in the $100 stock with the 95 stop loss is the same as in the $200 example. This is because the percentage risk in both trades is the same: 5 percent ($5/100 = $10/200 = 0.05). Thus, to ensure all trades influence your bottom line equally—to keep your risk consistent from trade to trade—use percentage-based rather than dollar-based calculations when determining stop-loss levels.

By the same token, it is equally important to increase the dollar amount risked per trade as your trading capital grows. This happens automatically when you risk the same fixed percentage of total account equity per trade. In the preceding examples, we risked $2,000 of a $100,000 account per trade, or 2 percent of total equity. If this actually is the optimal amount to risk (the percentage of equity that maximizes your strategy's profit potential), you should adhere to it. For example, if your account size increases to $200,000, you should risk $4,000 per trade; otherwise you will not optimize the profit potential of your strategy.

how much to risk

Now, when preaching risk control, many analysts and market commentators simply advise you not let a stock's price move against you more than a certain percentage before taking a loss, but that's only one part of the story. The other key element is how much of your total account equity that percentage should correspond to. We'll continue to follow the guidelines of *Investors Business Daily* (*IBD*), which recommend (as mentioned previously) (1) don't let a market move against you more than 8 percent; and (2) don't hold open positions in more than six stocks at one time.

There's a little math involved to calculate how much of your equity 8 percent risk is per stock. As it turns out, it is approximately 1.3 percent.

$$\text{Percentage of portfolio Equity to} \atop \text{Risk per trade (PER)} = \frac{(IAB \times SP \times MLS)}{(IAB \times SP \times NS)} = \frac{MLS}{NS}$$

$$= \frac{0.08}{6} = 0.0133$$

where IAB = Initial account balance
      SP = Stock price
   MLS = Maximum loss for stock in percent
    NS = Number of stocks

That is, provided you're not willing to let any of your positions move against you more than 8 percent (in terms of stock price), and you plan on investing in no more than six stocks at a time, you should not risk more than 1.3 percent of your account equity on any one trade. With these percentages in hand, we now can reconsider the initial examples to calculate how many shares to trade, given a certain stock price and account balance.

The way to calculate it is to divide the dollar amount of the equity you can risk per trade by the point risk of the trade. In this case, if you had a $100,000 account and wanted to buy a stock trading at 100, you would buy 162 shares [($100,000 × 0.013)/($100 × 0.08)], which would tie up $16,200 ($100 × 162) of trading capital. On the other hand, with a $10,000 account and a stock trading at 1¼, you would buy 1,300 shares [($10,000 × 0.013)/($1.25 × 0.08)], tying up $1,625. Both $16,200 and $1,625 represent approximately one-sixth of the available capital in each case, making it possible for you to invest in six stocks, regardless of how much money you have or what the price of the stock is.

avoiding the pitfalls

There are, however, three major drawbacks of doing things this way. First, keeping the MLS at 8 percent is rather rigid, because it doesn't take the current market conditions into account. Nor does it let you place a stop loss at the most logical spot, such as a few ticks under the nearest significant support level within a reasonable distance from the entry price, in the case of a long trade.

The second drawback is this assumes all trades can be placed at the same time, using the same initial amount of account equity for all trades. However, because this would seldom happen (it would only be the case if you always entered and exited all six stocks at the same time), it is necessary to figure out a way to calculate the available capital for each new trade, taking into consideration all open trades at a given time. This is done with the following formula:

Capital to Risk per Stock traded (CRS) = (ACB + MCI + OP) × PER

where ACB = Available cash balance, including closed out profits
  MCI = Money currently invested in other positions
   OP = Open profits
  PER = Percentage of portfolio equity to risk per trade

The third drawback is being limited to trading six stocks only. A better way to trade is to put together a portfolio of stocks (say, up to 30) that you monitor regularly and take trades as soon as they are signaled, buying an appropriate number of shares.

Because there might be days where trades are signaled in more than one stock, it's necessary to divide whatever funds you have between these trades. To do this, the previous formula needs to be modified as follows:

$$CRS = (ACB + MCI + OP) \times PER \times \frac{1}{NES}$$

where NES = Number of stocks with entry signals

Now, based on the maximum loss you're willing to take in regard to the MLS and PER for the previous formulas, you can calculate how many dollars you need to commit to each trade as:

$$TAC_{prel} = \frac{CRS \times SP}{SP \times MLS} = \frac{CRS}{MLS}$$

where TAC = Total amount committed in dollars per trade

But it doesn't stop there. As indicated by the subscript, this TAC value is only preliminary. What if all (or most of) the CRS comes from MCI and OP only (i.e., we're already fully invested, or close to it)? If there isn't any cash, we can't buy the stock. Therefore, the formula needs to be modified to the following:

$$TAC_{final} = \text{Whichever is less of}$$

$$ACB \times \frac{1}{NES}$$

or

$$TAC_{prel}$$

Say you have $50,000 in cash in your account and are willing to risk 5 percent of your equity per trade ($2,500). If you have another $30,000 tied up in one or several positions with an open loss of $8,000, and you get a signal to buy three additional stocks, then your CRS should be no more than $1,200 per trade [($50,000 + $30,000 − $8,000) × 1/3 × 0.05], in which case the TAC$_{prel}$ would be $20,000 for each trade. However, because you have only $50,000 in cash, and $50,000 divided by 3 is less than $20,000, you can only commit approximately $16,650 ($50,000/3).

This means there will be situations where you're not risking the full CRS amount. Specifically, this happens when you either don't have enough cash available in your account, or when you get several signals the same day, in which case the CRS will be divided among all the signals for that day. From this perspective, the PER and CRS values should be looked at more as values to strive for than to follow rigorously.

The important relationships to remember are that the better the system, the higher PER you can use, and the higher the expected profits. But, the higher PER you use, the sooner you will be fully invested and the more trades you might have to skip or take at a less than optimal level, and consequently, the lower the expected profits. The trick then, is to find the best balance.

a practical example

Theoretically, you now can be in as many stocks as you want with this particular strategy and trading account. This is especially helpful if you're a short-term, systematic trader, accustomed to monitoring and trading a rather large portfolio of stocks. The only limitation is that occasionally you will be fully invested, having no additional cash to spare. However, the shorter term you trade, the more likely it is that recently closed out trades will free up trading capital.

Let's take a look at how this can work during a short sequence of trades using the index tracking stocks QQQ, DIA, and SPY as examples. In this case, we're starting out with $100,000, risking 5 percent of equity per trade, and deducting $20 for commissions. The particular trading strategy is irrelevant. We'll use a short series of representative trades that illustrate how the money management principles we've outlined can improve the performance of any strategy.

Table 8.5 shows that on July 14, 1999, there was a signal to enter the DIA at 112.31 (all prices have been converted to decimals and rounded), with the maximum risk set to $1.50 per share. On this day, there were also signals to enter the QQQ and SPY at different levels and risk amounts. The amount risked for this strategy has nothing to do with the level at which the market is trading; instead of sticking to a fixed MLS, we're letting it fluctuate according to the most recent market activity. At the end of that day, the DIA trade showed an open loss of –$0.657. Four days later, the trade was closed out with a loss of –$1.032.

Table 8.6 shows each trade's corresponding dollar value for the total positions after calculating the number of shares we need to buy for each and how much capital we need to tie up. For example, for the

TABLE 8.5 SAMPLE TRADES

On July 14, there were signals to enter three trades in the sample portfolio. For the DIAs, the system calculated the maximum amount to lose per share as $1.5. At the end of that day, DIA was down 0.657 points. At the end of the next day, the trades in the QQQs and SPYs were closed out with profits of $0.625 and $0.781 per share, respectively.

Date	Amounts per share traded (DIA)				Amounts per share traded (QQQ)				Amounts per share traded (SPY)			
	Entry price ($)	CRS risk ($)	Open profit ($)	Closed profit ($)	Entry price ($)	CRS risk ($)	Open profit ($)	Closed profit ($)	Entry price ($)	CRS risk($)	Open profit ($)	Closed profit ($)
7/7/99	0	0	0	0	0	0	0	0	0	0	0	0
7/8/99	0	0	0	0	58.75	0.812	0.5	0	0	0	0	0
7/9/99	0	0	0	0	0	0		0.719	0	0	0	0
7/12/99	0	0	0	0	0	0		0	0	0	0	0
7/13/99	0	0	0	0	0	0	0	0	0	0	0	0
7/14/99	112.313	1.5	-0.657	0	59.844	1.063	0.406	0	140	1.344	0.156	0
7/15/99	112.313	1.5	-0.61	0	0	0	0	0.625	0	0	0	0.781
7/16/99	112.313	1.5	-0.282	0	0	0	0	0	0	0	0	0
7/19/99	112.313	1.5	-0.547	0	0	0	0	0	0	0	0	0
7/20/99	0	0	0	-1.032	0	0	0	0	0	0	0	0

TABLE 8.6   FOR THE TOTAL POSITION

This shows the amount of capital committed for the trades in Table 8.5, as well as the open and closed profits. The total value of the QQQ and SPY trades closed out on July 15 came out to $332 and $168, respectively. The DIA trade, which lasted five days, eventually was closed out with a loss of $330.

Date	Amounts for total position (DIA)			Amounts for total position (QQQ)			Amounts for total position (SPY)		
	Final TAC ($)	Open profit ($)	Closed profit ($)	Final TAC ($)	Open profit ($)	Closed profit ($)	Final TAC ($)	Open profit ($)	Closed profit ($)
7/7/99	0	0	0	0	0	0	0	0	0
7/8/99	0	0	0	100,000	831	0	0	0	0
7/9/99	0	0	0	0	0	1,204	0	0	0
7/12/99	0	0	0	0	0	0	0	0	0
7/13/99	0	0	0	0	0	0	0	0	0
7/14/99	33,735	-217	0	33,735	209	0	33,735	18	0
7/15/99	33,735	-203	0	0	0	332	0	0	168
7/16/99	33,735	-105	0	0	0	0	0	0	0
7/19/99	33,735	-184	0	0	0	0	0	0	0
7/20/99	0	0	-330	0	0	0	0	0	0

DIA trade we had to tie up $33,735 (ACB × (1/NES) = $101,204/3), which means that we had to buy 300 shares ($33,735/112.3). The $101,204 comes from the available capital at the end of July 13 (see Table 8.7). At the end of the first day, the open loss was –$217 (300 × $0.657 + 20), and four days later the trade closed out with a loss of –$330 (300 × 1.032 + 20). The same calculations can be done for the SPY and QQQ trades as well.

Table 8.7 shows what the summary for the portfolio as a whole would look like when it is marked to market at the end of each trading

TABLE 8.7   PORTFOLIO SUMMARY

At the end of July 13, all the portfolio equity is in the form of available cash to use in trading the next day. At the end of July 15, there was a total open loss from all positions of $203 and a total closed-out profit of $501. Of all our total equity, $67,970 was available for trading the next day.

Date	New positions	MCI ($)	Open profit ($)	Closed profits ($)	ACB + MCI + OP ($)	ACB ($)	Equity top ($)	Drawdown (%)	Flat time
7/7/99	1				100,000	100,000			
7/8/99	0	100,000	831		100,831		100,831	0.00	0
7/9/99	0			1,204	101,204	101,204	101,204	0.00	0
7/12/99	0				101,204	101,204	101,204	0.00	0
7/13/99	0				101,204	101,204	101,204	0.00	0
7/14/99	3	101,204	9		101,213		101,213	0.00	0
7/15/99	0	33,735	(203)	501	101,501	67,970	101,501	0.00	0
7/16/99	0	33,735	(105)		101,600	67,970	101,600	0.00	0
7/19/99	0	33,735	(184)		101,520	67,970	101,600	-0.08	1
7/20/99	0			(330)	101,374	101,374	101,600	-0.22	2

day. At the end of July 13, the portfolio had a total value of $101,204, all of which was available for new positions (meaning there were no open positions tying up trading capital).

At the end of July 14, there were three open positions tying up all previously available capital. The combined open profit from these three positions is $9, making the value of the portfolio equal to $101,213, none of which is available for new positions the following day.

At the end of this short trading sequence (July 20, when all the positions had been closed out), the total value of the portfolio is $101,374, all of which is available for trading the next day. Table 8.7 shows that the account currently is in a 0.22 percent drawdown that has lasted for two days. In this case, the return on the account is 1.37 percent after 10 days of trading. This shows how different trades interact within your portfolio and how you can go about determining how much to risk and how much capital to commit to your trades in a dynamic, systematic fashion.

Trading is much more than just identifying the most opportune buying and selling points. Applying a little research before you start trading—and using the right money management techniques—will add considerably to your bottom line.

section four

traders on trading

There is no profession in which mentoring is more important than trading. And there are no better teachers than those with first-hand experience. This chapter features several interviews with traders, analysts, and trading coaches from various corners of the trading world. Some are household names; others are not. They range from Wall Street money managers to individual traders working out of their homes, from stock traders to futures traders, from systematic traders to discretionary ones. They offer excellent insights into how successful market players go about their business each day, regardless of their backgrounds or specific approaches.

chapter 9

views from the front line

interviews by Mark Etzkorn

Dr. Ari Kiev
entering the trading zone

Given his past career as a consultant to Olympic athletes, it's not surprising that psychiatrist and trading coach Dr. Ari Kiev draws frequent parallels between success on the athletic playing field and success in the market.

In discussing whether market success at the "super-trader" level is about innate talent or learned skills, Kiev says, "If you think of it in terms of sports, Michael Jordan probably has some extra God-given talent, which was further developed by coaching and training. Not everybody who makes it to the pros is Michael Jordan, but they still have certain requisite skills."

The New York-based Kiev has helped more than a few of the Jordans of the trading world (mostly top institutional traders and hedge fund managers) develop their "requisite skills." Among his clients is Steve Cohen, head of SAC Capital Management, LLC, and one of the top-performing stock traders on the Street.

For Kiev, 66, who has degrees in medicine and law, his work in the trading field is just the latest chapter in a multifaceted professional life, which includes authoring a dozen books on psychiatry and anthropology (including *A Strategy for Daily Living: The Classic Guide to Success and Fulfillment*). From 1978 through 1980, he was chairman of the psychiatry division of the U.S. Olympic Sports Medicine Committee. He worked with athletes in a variety of sports, helping them reach their goals and maximize their performance.

Using the techniques he honed in that practice, Kiev went on to run a series of public seminars (called the Life Strategy Workshops) designed to help people access their untapped potential and master their fears. His entrée to trading occurred when, in the early 1990s, Cohen approached him, telling Kiev the principles in the workshops would be relevant to traders. A partnership was born, and Kiev went on to work with Cohen and the traders at his firm.

The program Kiev developed for SAC became his first trading book, *Trading to Win.* Cohen credited Kiev's techniques with helping SAC grow from a $20-million hedge fund to one managing in excess of $500 million in 1998 (the firm now trades more than $2 billion). "If you want to learn how to be a super-trader, then closely examine the concepts in this book," Cohen stated in the book's foreword.

According to Kiev, both *Trading to Win* and his upcoming book detail his "experiences helping traders master the emotional roller-coaster ride of trading; to ride out their fear, anxiety and carry out the discipline of their trades—to stick with their discipline in the face of discomfort." Kiev's second trading book, *Trading in the Zone: Maximizing Performance with Focus and Discipline,* was recently published.

Kiev shared some of his insights about how traders must manage the stress of trading, and how they can improve their results by identifying and curbing bad habits.

ME: Does it take a particular kind of personality to succeed at trading?

AK: There's a wide range of personalities that trade and a wide range of trading disciplines, but there are certain fundamental things people have to learn how to do, irrespective of how they experience trading.

I think there are probably some characteristics like drive, ambition, competitiveness, willingness to take risk in a measured way, discipline. Those are things that are there but probably have to be developed over time.

ME: What separates successful and unsuccessful traders?

AK: I think the willingness to commit to a result is critical to both Olympic athletes who win gold medals and to traders who produce outsized returns. It's the willingness to set a target and then really ride out discomfort in order to reach it—to follow their discipline in the face of anxiety.

Successful traders are willing to deal with the uncertainty of trading and the markets, and are willing to self-examine and review their performance—correcting what they may have done wrong, or figuring out what they may have stopped doing that previously worked.

They're also willing to be objective about themselves and recognize how their emotions get in the way of what they're trying to do. Trading is a very intense, emotionally arousing activity; it produces euphoria and despair. The skillful trader really learns to ride those things and follow his discipline in the face of his own reactions.

ME: Can emotions ever work in your favor?

AK: They can, to the extent that you're able to use your emotions as an indicator of what the market may be doing. From your own responses to the market, you can extrapolate what other people are likely to be feeling and doing and, thus, have some sense of what's happening in the market. A skillful trader can then counterintuitively trade in the opposite direction.

ME: What are some of the reasons so many traders fail?

AK: Ego, complacency, relaxing your guard and getting away from your discipline, and fear. Traders can take too much pride—or too much self-criticism—out of their trading. And there's the vicious cycle of doing more and more stupid things to try to recover from a loss. So, you might hold on to a loser instead of admitting your mistake, getting out of it and moving on to the next trade.

Another problem is the inability to "be in the moment"—psyching yourself out of being in the game.

ME: How can traders identify their weaknesses and take steps to fix them?

AK: You have to review your trading experiences, kind of like an athlete looking at game film. You review what your options were, what you were experiencing at the time, why you decided to do what you did, what alternatives there might have been, what kept you from using them if you didn't.

I teach people to ride out their anxiety, visualize their objectives and develop skills to review various scenarios in advance, things they may be able to follow in the midst of trading to increase their flexibility.

ME: Are there kinds of thought patterns or behavioral characteristics useful in other areas of life that can be particularly harmful in trading?

AK: Being stoic, persevering, and putting up with a lot of pain may be good in dealing with some problems in your life, but it may not be that useful in a trade when it would be better to admit you're wrong and get out. Perseverance can lead to stubbornness, which can sometimes get in the way in trading, where you need to be a little more nimble.

ME: Have the successful traders you've worked with had similarities in terms of their basic trading philosophies or approaches?

AK: No. I think the most critical thing is that the best traders, regardless of their method, stick to it—in the face of tough markets, drawdowns. They're really able to tow the line.

On a short-term basis, the critical thing is to stick to the discipline. On a longer-term basis you want to review your trading statistics with an objective observer, make decisions about what can be improved and try to adhere them.

ME: Do you find that good trading is a matter of learning some rules, or is it an ongoing process?

AK: I think you have to keep doing it because the game keeps changing. You have to keep honing your skills to better read or adjust to the market.

There's always more to learn. The master traders are always increasing their efforts to keep up with things. And also, once they've succeeded at a certain level, part of it has to do with raising the bar so they're bringing more of their resources into play. They have a greater challenge and find it more interesting.

ME: Is good trading necessarily comfortable?

AK: It's not about being comfortable, it's about doing all the work and preparation and focusing to trade the best possible way given your methodology. It's not necessarily about feeling good. There are certain times when it all comes together, it works, and feels good, and so forth—and that's fine, but that can also lead to euphoria which may take you out of the game.

Say you have a multiple-choice question with five possible answers. The first three are absolutely wrong, and the fourth looks right—it's the sucker answer. When you're anxious, you'll pick that one and feel really good.

The fifth answer is the right one. Selecting it takes a little "body English"—it isn't exactly comfortable, but if you've studied, you know that the one that doesn't look quite right is the right answer.

After you start taking those answers, you start to feel like you're really in the zone, even though you're doing something that's a little bit uncomfortable.

Linda Bradford Raschke
the rituals of trading

Those who have been lucky enough to attend one of Linda Bradford Raschke's infrequent speaking engagements know she is a rare breed: a professional trader who can explain practical trading concepts in plain English. Her peers simply know her as one of the hardest working and most dedicated traders in the business.

Her trading career has encompassed the stock, options, and futures markets, both as a private trader and a money manager. She has been profiled in Jack Schwager's *The New Market Wizards,* CNBC anchor Sue Herera's *Women of the Street,* and any number of magazine and newspaper articles. She also is coauthor of *Street Smarts,* a popular book on short-term trading strategies.

Raschke started out as a floor trader in the early 1980s, spending six years trading options at the Pacific Stock Exchange and the Philadelphia Stock Exchange, before making a successful transition to "upstairs" trading—no mean feat, considering the high failure rate of floor traders who try making a living away from the pits. She began managing money in 1993, while continuing to aggressively trade her own account. She trades a variety of markets, but concentrates on short-term trading in the S&P futures.

Raschke still devotes long hours to analyzing the markets and preparing for each day, even though she's been trading professionally for 20 years. She is a strong believer in daily rituals and disciplines that keep her trading focused, even if they don't immediately impact her trading decisions. And she practices simplicity, bypassing complex indicators in favor of price-based techniques that identify (for example) pauses or pullbacks within trends.

ME: Would you categorize yourself as a systematic or discretionary trader?

LBR: Discretionary—I pretty much always have been. I came from the trading floor, and in that environment you learn to become a kind of tape reader, in a way. But I also spent years testing trading concepts, much of it with Steve Moore [of Moore Research Center]. We tested a million patterns and tendencies, and did a lot of modeling.

I've come up with some great systems, but I use them as indicators, with discretion, because I need to have that control (*laughing*). The systems have forecasting value—they give me an idea of the probabilities of the market continuing in a certain direction. That doesn't necessarily mean I get in where the system would, or manage the trade the way the system would. If a particular system is signaling a buy or a sell, I might look to scalp in the direction of that system's signal.

Also, sometimes a failed signal can have even greater forecasting value than the original signal. I'll give you a classic example. Let's use the Holy Grail pattern (*described in her book* Street Smarts)—buying a pullback to a moving average, looking for a move back up. I might think, "That's a normally high-probability trade; let me see if I can make a system for when that system fails."

ME: Do you routinely reverse positions?

LBR: I don't stop and reverse at all. But I will look for failed signals because very often they can result in strong moves in the opposite direction. They just don't happen as often, so your trade frequency is lower. But if you have something that works, say 70 to 80 percent of the time, there's a pretty darn good reason why it doesn't work those times it fails. You actually learn more from the signals that *don't* work.

So let's say I make a system based on a failed Holy Grail buy trade—one that fails to hold the moving average. First, if a grail buy trade fails, I know I'm not going to look to buy pullbacks in that market. Second, because there must be a good enough reason the system went short, perhaps it has forecasting value of a downside move of *x* number of bars or days. Therefore, I'm going to look to trade from the short side.

ME: Do you think your trading style is a natural outgrowth of your experience as a floor trader?

LBR: Well, understanding order flow is helpful, but it's probably more helpful to understand the type of environment you're trading in these days. In a high-volume market, in a trending market—for Pete's sake, use market orders. If you're in a sloppy, choppy environment where the volume is contracting as a seasonal function—people are exhausted after the first four months—you have to be careful about using market orders. In a trading range environment, your initial trade location is far more critical, so you have to price (*use limit*) orders.

If I'm trading in a good volume, trending market, I can take my time and sell at the market when I want to get out. But in a trading range market, I have to be working an offer ahead of time: If I buy the S&Ps at 1420, I need to have an offer out there at 1424. Because if it runs up and pops through 1425 and I try to sell at the market, I might be selling at 1422.

You know, there are so many misconceptions about short-term trading. Even as a floor trader, I could have a position with a directional bias lasting two to three months and I would continue to trade a stock or market leaning to one side.

What you do is supplement those longer-term positions with lots of scalping.

That's pretty much what I do now. I'll sit with positions much longer than people might think, but I can still scalp S&Ps for five minutes at a time.

A general rule of thumb is that the more volatility a market has, or the longer the length of the intraday line—the S&Ps are a good example—the shorter the time frame you can scalp on.

ME: What do you mean by the "intraday line"?

LBR: It's how much ground a market's intraday swings cover during the day. Say the S&Ps rally six points, sell off 10 points, then rally another four points. They're unchanged at the end of the day, but they've moved a total of 20 points when all is said and done.

For a short-term trading style, you really need that activity back and forth during the day, and there aren't that many that have it. Even the T-bonds don't have that much.

ME: How long is your average short-term trade?

LBR: In the S&Ps, my average holding time is around 10 minutes. But I position trade the Nasdaq futures. I've stayed with Nasdaq positions two weeks or so. They trend more than the S&Ps, but the bid-ask spread is very wide—around $1,000—and there's a lot of noise.

ME: Do you use limit or market orders for these trades?

LBR: I trade at the market on 90 percent of my trades.

ME: You once said that you believed in forecasting price direction but not magnitude. How do you manage your positions and take profits?

LBR: Let's say I go long and the market starts to show some upside impulse. First, you want to see some price and volume in that direction. I monitor everything by whether short-term continuation patterns set up.

If I'm in a long trade and it starts to break out to the upside, I want to see continuation patterns on an hourly chart—little bull flags, triangles, and so on. When a market breaks out and there's some momentum, there are usually three pushes up. On an hourly chart, those may develop over a two- or three-day period. The market should continue to hold its gains. The minute you see it give back more than it should, you get out on the first reaction or pause.

ME: Do you scale out of positions?

LBR: I usually do my trades in two pieces. I try to stay with a position as long as I can and take half off. I usually don't average into trades; I usually go in all at once. I try to find the best entry I can—somewhere I can easily manage risk. Once you see that spot, you might as well get in and put your whole position on.

If you put the entire position on at once, that's the closest you can get to your risk point. When you average a position, what happens is you'll always average the losers but you'll never put more on to your winning trades when they start to go up.

Averaging is a really bad habit unless you're in a very volatile market and you've already planned on putting the position on in two parts. But I've found averaging does more harm than good most of the time.

As far as getting out of trades, if the market reaches a price objective and you're really not sure if it's going to continue, you have to at least take half the position off.

ME: Is your trading based more on direct price action or on the indicators or systems you mentioned earlier?

LBR: Ninety percent of what I do is price-based. Indicators are just derivatives of price. So the actual price action is always going to be one step ahead of any indicator. The best things indicators do is tell you when there are either new momentum highs or lows, which signal continuation. It doesn't matter what you use—an oscillator, stochastics, an average true range function. I use pure rate of change—there are a million ways you can do it.

At least you can quantify indicators. It's difficult to back-test pure price patterns. So, for assessing market tendencies and modeling purposes, indicators are useful. But when I'm actually trading, I'm looking at price and thinking, "Okay, this market was down in the morning, now it's starting to make new highs on the day." Or, "We opened below yesterday's low, and now we've rallied back to unchanged." I do a lot more with price levels and pivots: Can we test the Globex high? Can we test the two-day high? Can we pull back to the moving average. That's what I do.

ME: What time frame charts do you watch during the day?

LBR: To watch the market intraday, I have 30-, 60-, and 120-minute for each market I'm watching. That gives a pretty good road map. If you can't see something with that, then there's really nothing going on. On one of those time frames, you'll always see either a retracement pattern, like a bear flag or a bull flag, or you'll see a test of a key support or resistance level. The market's either retracing or testing—that's about all there is to it.

ME: What else are you monitoring during the day for your shorter-term trades?

LBR: For intraday trades, I'm usually just watching the tape, so to speak. Sometimes I'll watch a one- or five-minute chart, but I'm usually watching the levels intraday, and the TICKs (*the difference between up-ticking NYSE stocks and down-ticking NYSE stocks*) and the TRIN (*an indicator that compares advancing issues/declining issues with the up volume/down volume ratio*).

ME: What specifically are you looking for?

LBR: I use the TICKs like a momentum oscillator: If the TICKs are making new highs, I'll look to buy the pullbacks. For example, recently there was a rally up in the S&Ps for about two weeks, followed by roughly a five-day correction. The TICKs hit −400, −500 yesterday and this morning (June 13, 2000), and it was the first time they corrected in a week and a half—that was a buy signal (see Figure 9.1). It's similar to when an

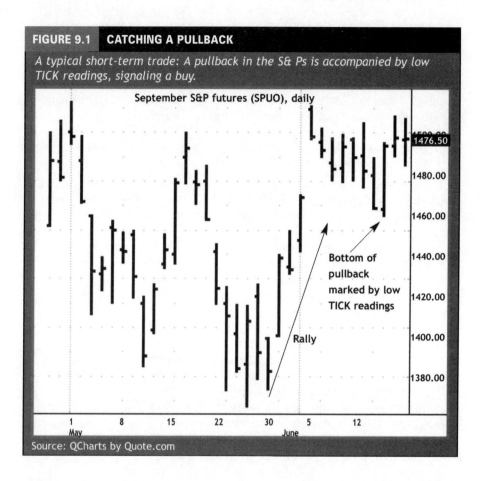

FIGURE 9.1   CATCHING A PULLBACK

A typical short-term trade: A pullback in the S& Ps is accompanied by low TICK readings, signaling a buy.

September S&P futures (SPUO), daily

Bottom of pullback marked by low TICK readings

Rally

Source: QCharts by Quote.com

oscillator rallies and becomes extremely overbought and pulls back a little bit. The TICKs behave almost exactly the same way. But I use them to confirm a trend as well. For example, this afternoon the ticks kept making new highs, which confirms the move to the upside.

The TICKs behave differently to the upside than they do to the downside. The bottoms of sell-offs will be accompanied by negative TICK extremes, like—1000, for example. Tops are characterized much more by complacency, with a lack of TICK readings. It's similar to the VIX (the Chicago Board Options Exchange volatility index) dropping down very low, reflecting low implied volatility levels. I watch the VIX, too.

ME: How many trades do you make a day?

LBR: Anywhere from two to six trades in the S&Ps and three trades in other markets.

ME: *Do you trade stocks as well as futures?*

LBR: Yes. Trading stocks keeps me fresh, but you can't trade with the same leverage you can in the index futures. With the futures, you can bang them out and you don't have to worry about the short side. Unfortunately, I can honestly say I've never bought a stock and had it rally 50 points—I've missed out on the Internet game (*laughs*).

ME: *How do you decide how much you'll risk on a trade or where you'll place your stops?*

LBR: You need to have some kind of initial risk point. In just about any market, except for coffee or S&Ps, I risk $500 per contract. That makes it really easy. That gives the positions (in the markets I trade) enough room to work or not work.

You have to think in terms of getting into a market and having a general window so if your timing is off a little, you still have some time to see how the trade should be managed. But you need that initial insurance or risk point. So even though I usually start out with $500, there are times when I don't want to risk that much.

After you've put on the position and established your initial risk, you manage the trade, which consists of getting out if it's not working or tightening the stop. In the S&Ps, if the trade is just a quick scalp where I'm trying to grab two to four points, I'll risk three points. For a longer position trade, I'll risk up to 10 points.

But it also depends on volatility. If the market is really swinging around, you have to give the trade a little room. I'll use a 100-point stop in the Nasdaq futures. That's big—$10,000 per contract, but I trade them on a longer time frame, so I don't mind doing that.

ME: *How long did it take you to develop your current trading style?*

LBR: I've always been price-sensitive and I've always been a tape reader. But in the 1980s, I was much more countertrend than I am now. When I started managing money in 1993, my trading style really changed.

First, I made it a policy to never average a trade, whereas in the 1980s, when I was just trading my own money, I used to scale into trades all the time. You have a lot of sleepless nights. My account had five times the volatility it has now.

I also started using much less leverage. And I started looking for more trades that constituted pullbacks within trends rather than trying to guess when a market had gone too far.

ME: *What are some of the basic principles you think traders should follow?*

LBR: I try to break trading down into four areas, each of which is important to your bottom line.

The first one, which is the one everyone wants to concentrate on, is the initial trade methodology—setups, indicators, patterns—that determine whether to buy or sell, at what level and when.

The second is execution. This is probably the most overlooked area of trading. Your execution skills account for at least 50 percent of your bottom line. When do you buy at the market? When do you work a bid? If you use a limit order, sometimes you'll miss a trade—it's a shame to price yourself out of a 10-point move because you're trying to get an extra quarter point. But on the other hand, you don't want to pay up at the market all the time, because you can give away too much, especially in a thin, trading-range environment.

Also, how do you exit your trades? How do you work your stops? Do you know how to bracket a trade? Say there's a position you want to get in—you work a bid underneath as well as a buy stop above the market, so you're at least guaranteed of getting in.

There's very little literature on this subject, but I see more money lost because of poor execution. People can lose money even when they're right on the market. For example, they're trying to exit a trade with a limit order and the market misses it by two ticks and then goes 10 points against them.

I could go on and on. It's one of those things you can give people tips and direction on, but it's only going to improve with practice. You have to get in there and make the trades and get a feel for how things work. That's where you get confidence, too. If you feel confident you're buying and selling in the right manner, you'll probably make three times as many trades.

There's no right or wrong. I probably trade with 90 percent market orders, but I have a friend who will never use a market order. It depends on the type of trade you're trying to execute and how good your general timing is.

The third element is money management. There are a lot of factors that fall into this category—it's so much more than how much you risk or where you place your stop. It's about how much leverage you use and when you use it. Do you have correlation in your portfolio? What are you going to do when your account draws down 10 percent? Do you step up your trading or do you cut back?

Finally, there's psychology. It's not about "Oh, I can't pull the trigger," or "I overtrade." It's about things like staying motivated and not burning out. Trading can be a wearing, stressful profession. Let's say you've been a trader for 15 years. How do you push yourself to get to the next level? How do challenge yourself? How do you keep yourself in a groove where you're not thinking about the markets too much?

Also, are you analyzing your tendencies? For example, many people tend to make money in the morning and give it back in the last hour of the day.

You could add a minor fifth category: Organization and structure. How do you structure your business and working environment. Do you keep worksheets? Do you log market numbers? Do you keep records of trades and analyze what you're doing?

ME: Are you talking about analyzing your trade performance?

LBR: Yes. But the record keeping is more of a ritual for me. I actually log lots of numbers—without ever really looking at them later. But the simple practice of writing them down somehow sends the information to somewhere in my brain where I can access it later.

I have a fax service I put out every night. The work I have to put into that is great preparation for the next trading day. I go over game plans in around 20 markets, even though I might only act on a couple of the scenarios. If I'm monitoring my account, my positions, and the prices I'm entering them at, I'll do twice as good as if I hadn't. The routine and ritual are wonderful tools for managing anxiety and stress.

ME: Do you actually experience much stress from trading?

LBR: I tend to feel the effects of stress at the end of the year, the end of the quarter, and the end of the month. So this year, I put in my business plan that I would close out all positions at the end of the quarter.

ME: Will you back away from trading on a bad day, or for a certain amount of time, if you've hit a certain drawdown level?

LBR: I never walk away when I'm down. Never. It's important for me to get that money back. It makes me angry that I lost that money in the first place. If I walked out of the office, I couldn't relax. I'm so involved in this I don't even like taking vacations. If I were on a beach on an island somewhere, I wouldn't know what to do with myself.

But I have my horses, so I can go out riding after the close. I spend time with the horses every day. It takes my mind completely off the markets. After that, I can do my analysis at night with a fresh eye. You have to have something that allows you to walk out of the office and leave trading completely behind. Other than that, the only time I really "walk away" is when I speak at trading conferences.

ME: What do you tell people who want to become better traders?

LBR: Get a good, basic foundation in technical analysis. By that I mean study basic chart patterns. Do yourself a favor and ignore all the oscillators and neural nets and the fancy little indicators and [instead] fully understand things like gap theory, trendlines, and continuation patterns. Murphy's book, Schabacker's book, and Edwards and Magee are good sources. Understand the definition of a trend and the principles of confirmation and non-confirmation Dow put forth. Learn chart patterns, Schabacker's and Wyckoff's books, to understand what goes on in distribution and accumulation areas, things like springs and upthrusts (discussed in Chapter 7), and volume tendencies.

These are really good principles that will hold up in any market, in any time frame. Understanding simple trendlines and chart patterns, and when to trade continuation patterns versus when you're in a trading range, testing environment is probably the best thing you can do.

It's interesting. These people wrote about the markets when there were no computers, so everything they wrote about was really price-based. And you also discover these people spent 80, 100 hours per week studying the markets. It makes you appreciate how much time it takes to really understand price behavior and the markets. For me, it's a lifelong journey. I've been doing this for 20 years, and I learned a lot this past year.

New traders seem to spend the first three years trying out different things and finding out they don't work. You have to test lots of different styles and markets until you find what works for you. And you might find out that you're a two-minute S&P trader, or that you like volatility break-outs, or something else. But you need patience, because it takes time to

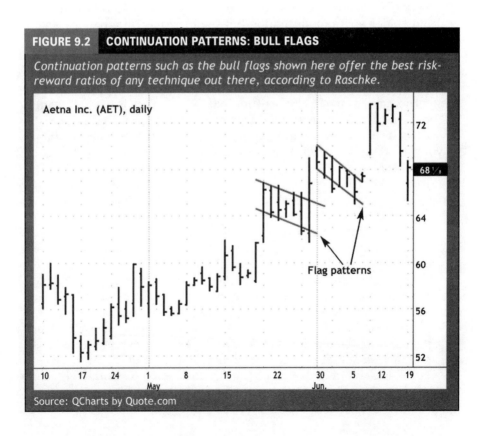

FIGURE 9.2   CONTINUATION PATTERNS: BULL FLAGS

Continuation patterns such as the bull flags shown here offer the best risk-reward ratios of any technique out there, according to Raschke.

Aetna Inc. (AET), daily

Flag patterns

Source: QCharts by Quote.com

find what fits your personality. And you'll learn something from everything you look at in that investigative process.

ME: *Given what you said about understanding basic chart analysis, do you think simpler trading ideas work better than complex ones?*

LBR: Oh, absolutely. Listen, all you need to do is understand bull or bear flags (see Figure 9.2). If you can recognize those on a chart and understand that those points have the best risk-reward ratios of any technique out there—where you can get the most bang for your buck in the least amount of time and use the most leverage—you don't need anything else.

John Saleeby
mastering the trading arcade

John Saleeby is certainly a model for trading in the digital age. Engulfed in a bank of computer screens in his downtown Chicago office, the 36-year-old trader splits his attention between the markets, the TV, and a video game, manipulating all of them with his high-tech joystick.

To Saleeby, trading is just a big electronic game that he enjoys as much as any kid in an arcade.

"I don't find trading stressful," the energetic Saleeby exclaims. "Since the day I started, my attitude has been, 'This is a video game, it's not money.' I look at it like that because my approach has been to never touch the money in my account. It's different if you have $20,000 in your account and you need to make $2,000 rent money. I'm sure that's stressful."

Ironically, while Saleeby has been a successful stock trader nearly his entire adult life, he never really considered trading as a full-time career until the past few years.

"I won trading competitions in high school and college, but I never looked at it as a way to make a living," he says. "I've just always traded stocks on the side. I always considered it an avocation."

Saleeby's original vocation was the law, and although he was making a good living, he knew he wanted out fairly early in his career. Not surprisingly, his dislike for the work helped push him closer to trading.

"I just didn't really enjoy law to be honest with you," he says. "I had four jobs in four-and-a-half years. I tried tax law, I tried corporate litigation, I tried assistant attorney general, and I hated it all."

"I really started actively trading because I was so bored," he continues. "I'd sit around my office and trade. The head partner even came by once and said, 'You know, we always hear you talking about stocks.' I told him, 'Well, I make more money trading my stocks than I do with the law.' With comments like that, needless to say, I wasn't going to spend my whole life in law."

When his stint with the bar had run its course in 1995, Saleeby started a home automation company, which proved to be a short-lived venture.

"I began trading to create cash flow to pay for the losses, which I was able to do," he says. "And then I realized if I just closed down the damn company, I'd be making a lot of money."

Two years later, Saleeby is still going strong. He bought a seat on the Chicago Mercantile Exchange, although he trades almost exclusively from his office, and in the last year he has added the S&P and E-Mini S&P futures to the stock trading that has been his bread and butter for years.

For his stock trading, Saleeby has always believed in blending technical and fundamental data, often combining trendline analysis with an understanding of the fundamentals of a particular stock and its industry. Not surprisingly, Saleeby collects and dissects copious amounts of market information, something he never skimps on.

"You can never pay too much for information," he explains. "I want to know everything that actually occurs in the entire market. I'm a strong believer in a confluence of all types of information. The more information you track, and the more information that meshes, the better everything is going to work for you."

He keeps an extensive trading diary, tracking every important development each day in a market calendar he maintains by hand, a process that helps him internalize the information.

Saleeby, who admits to being somewhat "obsessed" with the markets, spoke to us over three days, explaining various trades he had recently made and others he was making at the time.

on fundamental and technical trading approaches

ME: How do you combine technical and fundamental analysis?

JS: I want something that is fundamentally strong that also gives me a good chart point. In early December of 1999, for example, I was buying Advanced Micro Devices (AMD) between 26 and 28, and I loaded all the way up to 31, with a price target of 45.

I bought AMD for a number of reasons. The chip sector was red-hot—the fourth quarter is the strongest one for the sector. AMD had produced a high-end chip superior to Intel's for the first time and Intel was having execution and supply problems at the time. In terms of technicals, the stock was stuck in a trading range between 18 and 31.

Given the company, sector, and market were bullish, I thought AMD would break out of its range. It was moving toward the top of the range after forming a bottom pattern. Also, the stock had just made a "fractal breakout" of the long-term pattern within the range, which means it had broken out of a smaller range within the larger range (see Figure 9.3).

I projected a couple of different potential price targets—51 using a doubling of the range method and 48 using a Fibonacci projection. So I placed a conservative (exit) price of 45. When AMD's earnings came out (48 cents per share versus a projected 1 cent per share), the stock broke out of the larger trading range and I got filled.

I'm buying for a reason—a stock has met a chart point and I believe that charts are entry points to fundamentals. That is, fundamentals have to coincide with chart points. I won't buy on fundamentals alone. I won't buy on chart points alone.

I use several technical techniques. I have a system to project trend-lines and I also use ratios similar in concept to Fibonacci numbers.

Much of my trendline technique is based on John Murphy's book, *Technical Analysis of the Financial Markets*. I modify everything I use to suit my needs, but my trendline analysis is fairly straightforward. When anyone asks me about technical analysis, I always say the same thing: Read John Murphy's book. I basically draw trend channels of different magnitude and adjust them as the market moves.

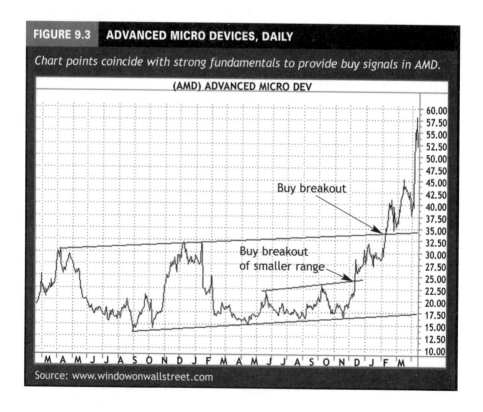

FIGURE 9.3   ADVANCED MICRO DEVICES, DAILY

Chart points coincide with strong fundamentals to provide buy signals in AMD.

Source: www.windowonwallstreet.com

ME: Do you have any purely technical systems—strictly price-based strategies—that don't use any fundamental inputs for short-term trading?

JS: I have technical systems, but I always keep the fundamentals in the back of my mind. You have to understand fundamentals, but if you trade solely on them, you're dead. You can make money trading technicals alone, but you can't make money trading fundamentals alone.

Also, I don't believe you can trade individual stocks, especially highly volatile ones, without having a feel for the market itself. I definitely watch the S&P futures as well as the Nasdaq futures before I execute a stock trade.

I calculate all kinds of intermarket spreads and ratios, and I also maintain an extensive historical diary and databases in which I record fundamental information—earnings, the price-to-book ratio, the dividend yield, and things of that nature. I look at the markets and each trade from a fundamental standpoint and a historical standpoint as well as a technical standpoint.

on short-term trading techniques

ME: What kind of trading approaches would you suggest for a short-term stock trader?

JS: Tick-trading stocks is impossible, as far as I'm concerned. I've never met anyone who does it profitably and I've never been able to do it profitably.

The strategy is mathematically unsound. If you're trying to capture a sixteenth, where's your stop loss? One-sixteenth on the other side of your entry? You can end up having to take three-tick losses to make one tick. That's the wrong ratio! And the ratio of commission costs to trading profits is prohibitive.

I did some calculations for a guy and discovered you'd have to be 80 percent correct just to break even. I don't want to trade in a way that I have to be a genius to make a little bit of money. A lot of people think technology has put them on the inside with the market makers and it really hasn't. The market makers still have superior execution techniques, superior information, and lower transaction costs.

However, I think it's possible to swing trade very profitably.

ME: How would you suggest finding the best stocks to trade and which approaches to use for that kind of trading?

JS: That has to do with your personality. If you have a low-risk personality and you don't like to see things move a lot, you should really work with big-cap, blue-chip stocks that have sold off. Wait until they sell off hard and buy them for a bounce—that's a pure swing trade. SBC Communications was a perfect swing trade (when it sold off sharply starting in late December 1999 and bounced in early March).

I know a trader who doesn't do anything but buy dips in these kinds of stocks, using a 2-to-1 profit-to-loss ratio, and he's one of the most successful short-term traders I know. He takes no more than 5 percent heat on the downside and gets out on a 10 percent move to the upside. I look for a 3-to-1 ratio myself.

ME: But do you think that kind of approach would work in a stagnant or bear market?

JS: A downtrending market is fine as long as you trade individual stocks and not the market. I believe in the adage "It's not a stock market, it's a market of stocks." Most importantly, you must have a predefined strategy for getting in and out of trades.

Here's another simple technique: IPO lock-ups and quiet periods. A really hot IPO generally tops early on and then comes right back down. Why? Because of the four-week quiet period when the syndicate can't tout it and the insiders can't talk about it. You won't hear another word about a hot IPO until four weeks have passed. At that point, the syndicate and the company will begin hyping the stock again, so it's smart to look for buying opportunities toward the end of the quiet period.

The lockup period is the opposite situation. Generally, I don't like to short stocks because most people are naturally buyers. But look for a selling opportunity in any stock that is up significantly—I've been using five times the IPO price as a benchmark recently. Check the chart pattern. It should start to go into a downtrend about two days before the end of the lockup period. But always wait until the chart pattern turns down coinciding with the lockup expiration.

The insiders are going to sell at least portions of their positions to take huge profits. Remember, the insiders have gotten in at pennies on the dollar, not at the IPO price. If you were an insider, what would you do when your stock comes off lockup, cash in some of your huge profit or buy more stock? I've yet to meet the person who would buy more stock.

But be careful. Generally companies will announce very bullish news and analysts will tout the stock the week before lockup ends so they can sell into the retail buying (see "Analysis In Action" on page 251; Commerce One [CMRC] announced a deal with GM and a 3-for-1 stock split, while an analyst set a $1,000 price target, right before lockup ended).

ME: You mentioned that you calculate a number of market ratios and spreads. How do you use them?

JS: I'll compare indexes like the S&P and Nasdaq, for example. That spread was very predictable until around last October, when the Nasdaq just kept going.

Spread ratios give you indications of certain market patterns. I look at the market bias implied by a spread and trade the side of the spread with the greater potential for movement—gamma, convexity, or whatever else you want to call it. I rarely trade both sides—buying one and selling the other. Pure spread trading is stepping across dollars to pick up pennies.

on trade execution

ME: What kind of brokerage do you use?

JS: I use several brokerages and direct access firms, and I use Globex to execute my trades in the E-mini S&P. But I don't really like direct access firms because the ECNs don't have the liquidity to move any size.

I'd rather give the order to a market maker at a brokerage, especially with larger orders because they'll often improve your execution because of their access to Instinet. I'll give these guys a sixteenth—what do I care? The other day I couldn't get an order off on an ECN—there was nothing there.

I also think it's really important to have backups for all your technology—hardware, software, communication—in case something goes down.

ME: Do you make very short-term trades that rely on your information and trade execution capabilities—playing on earnings announcements or things of that nature?

JS: Yes, and since I have the fastest information and the fastest execution, I know I can beat the world into that kind of trade. This is what I always say: I'd rather be wrong fast than right slow. Because if you are right slow, you'll miss the profit and you'll lose anyway. But if you're wrong fast, you're in and out so quickly that there's no pain to it. If you're slow and wrong, you're double bad.

So, if you're right fast, you make the most money. I want to be the first person to know what's happening, then I want to be the first person to execute and then I want the market to confirm my position. If that doesn't happen, I'm out.

One thing to keep in mind is that you never need to chase a trade. The market has plenty of opportunities. The money runs out before the opportunities do.

ME: Is there a typical holding period on the type of trade you're describing?

JS: Under ten minutes. What I'm trying to do is be the first in. Then the rest of the world comes in, does 60 to 80 percent of the move in the next five to ten minutes, and then I get the hell out.

on stops and risks control

ME: What kind of stops do you use?

JS: I like using patterns rather than percentages or arbitrary money amounts. I use support and resistance levels and my trendlines—they function as a trailing stop. But it's equal parts art and science.

The biggest mistake people probably make, in my opinion, is to trade their account. In fact, right now I'm training a trader who doesn't have a lot a money and I tell him, "If you trade your capital you'll never make it, because you're undercapitalized." But if you're going to take the risk, you better put it all on this and believe in it and put your stops in and hope you don't have three losing trades in a row for a while.

ME: But wouldn't it also be valid to say to this person, "Wait until you have more money before you try to trade?"

JS: Yes. I can't believe it would be to your benefit to not have enough money to do things right. But some people say the best thing that happened to them is they had to start small and conservative and had to be very careful with their capital.

ME: Do you do anything like adjust your position size in an open trade to manage risk?

JS: I have another rule: If a stock doubles for me really fast, I "play with the house's money." I take my 50 percent off the table and I leave 50 percent of it in there so I've got a free stock now.

advice for new traders

ME: What kind of advice would you give to someone starting out?

JS: Well, they couldn't do many of the things I'm currently doing. When you start out, you have to be more conservative in terms of risk because you don't really know what risk is until you've experienced a big loss. If you've never experienced a big drawdown in your account, then you don't understand why it would happen or how it could happen. I think you have to go through that at some point.

I was fairly successful from the start, but it took a couple of times of being wrong to appreciate how wrong I could be. And I think that is important in a trader's maturation. As a beginner, I could not trade the way I trade now. But now I know how to recognize risk and minimize the risk of the type of loss that could really hurt me.

I think one of the reasons I was successful, quite frankly, is I never—I mean never—used margin, in stocks or futures, for over the first year I was trading. If I didn't have the cash, I didn't make the trade. I was never forced out of a position that I didn't want to sell. Also, it's easier to quantify your gains and losses—what kind of risk you're carrying—when you're not on margin. If it goes down five percent, you know that's five percent if you have your whole bankroll on it.

Now, I use margin. But I think the fact that I didn't early on is why I'm still around.

ME: *What about different ways a beginner can approach trading and analysis?*

JS: One thing that I will say is that if you're starting out, you need to be a pure technician. Don't talk to me about fundamentals, because most people don't know what fundamentals are. There are so many ways you can value a company—cash flow, price-to-earnings, price-to-book—and they can give you different numbers.

SBC Communications (SBC) valued on cash-flow analysis is 32; valued on the sum of its parts, it's 65—that's double the other valuation. Which one's right? Who knows? Fundamental analysis is very valuable, and I use it—don't get me wrong. But people who don't understand finance will need years to be able to do fundamental analysis. Everyone looks at price-to-earnings (PE) ratios. Well, what about price-to-earnings-to-growth (PEG) ratios?

Look at Intel. Last year they generated $4.5 billion in free cash flow. How much would you pay for that free cash flow? Think of it this way: How much would you pay for a cash machine that gives you $4.5 per year?

At Intel's current market valuation, you're paying $400 for a machine that pays you $4 per year. Even factoring its growth rate, it is very overpriced by traditional methods of valuation.

You also have to think about the time frame you're going to trade on. I say the same thing to everyone: Your technical analysis has to coincide with the time frame you're trading. If you're looking at a trade that will last a week, use daily and weekly charts; if you're looking for a five-minute trade, use five-minute bars; if you're looking at tick trades, look at tick charts or maybe one-minute or five-minute charts.

ME: *What do you do when you're not trading?*

JS: I'm pretty much addicted to this. Sometimes I work as many as 100 hours a week. The whole time we've talked I've been trading. I've got nine screens in front of me so I can watch two channels of TV, three different market screens and play on the Internet. As long as I'm going to sit around and watch TV, I might as well make some money while I'm doing it.

analysis in action

Many of John Saleeby's technical trading concepts are built on a simple base of support and resistance concepts. "This stuff is not rocket science," he says. "Generally, the simpler the technique, the better it works."

Two of his frequently used techniques are retracement percentages (modified Fibonacci levels) and multiple trendlines he adjusts as price action unfolds. He projects trendlines and price moves forward in time to calculate price targets and uses them also to determine likely support and stop levels.

A series of trades (Figure 9.4) in Commerce One (CMRC) illustrate some of these techniques, as well as the way he integrates fundamental factors into his decision making.

"Companies tend to put out the most bullish news, including stock-split announcements, right before they go off lockup," Saleeby explains. "That's what happened with CMRC. They announced a 3-for-1 stock split and an analyst came out with a $1,000 price target—two days before the lockup ended.

"It's a game!" he exclaims. "They give you [bogus] news right before lockup ends so they can sell into retail buying.

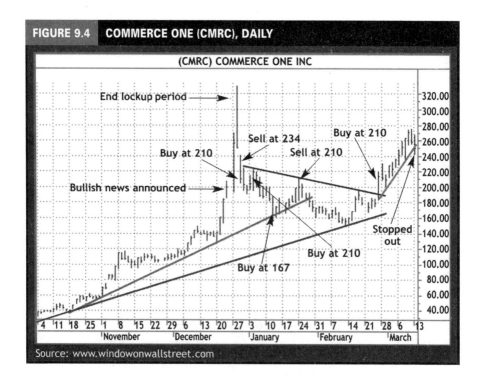

FIGURE 9.4   COMMERCE ONE (CMRC), DAILY

Source: www.windowonwallstreet.com

"The stock then went down to 210 and I went long, expecting a short-term bounce. The stock was very oversold at that point and it just bounced off its Fibonacci retracement level of 205 (approximately .618 of the high price of 331). I exited the trade the same day when the trend on the one-minute chart lost momentum and stalled between 230 and 234.

"When it went back down I bought again at 210, which was a mistake. I did it because I was able to buy there the first time—which is a bad reason. The stock continued to drop and I bought again at 167, at the resistance implied by a trendline. But it pierced that trendline and traded down to around 155, and I have to admit I was a little nervous. But fundamentally, I believed in the stock, so I was willing to take a little more heat. I got out of the entire position when it moved back up to 210.

"After that, the stock came back down and touched a longer-term trendline, forming a double bottom. So I waited and watched for another up move. I got in on a buy stop at 210 again. The stock has been in an uptrend, and I'll get out of most of the position on a downside penetration of the most recent up trendline, which functions as a trailing stop." (The trade was, in fact, stopped out around 245 on a penetration of this trendline.)

Courtney Smith
inside the trading lab

It's interesting. When asked about the keys to market success, top traders usually don't talk too much about what many people might anticipate hearing; namely, techniques for spotting high-probability trade entries.

Instead, conversation often revolves around techniques for limiting drawdowns, deciding how large a position to put on and the importance of sticking with a particular game plan. So it's only fitting that trader Courtney Smith focuses on discipline, objectivity, and risk control when talking about his lengthy run as a trader.

Smith, 48, started trading while still in high school in the 1960s and continued to trade his own account while working as a journalist and photojournalist through the early 1970s. Since then, he has compiled a long track record in the markets, ranging from individual futures trader to money manager, market commentator, and author.

Smith is indeed an active trader—in every sense. His businesses range from hedge funds to hotlines, from long-term investing to short-term trading, from stocks to futures. He is a regular commentator on CNBC, CNN, Bloomberg, and Fox News.

He is president and chief investment officer of Courtney Smith & Co. (http://courtneysmithco.com) and of Pinnacle Capital Strategies Inc., which manages hedge funds. The flagship Macro Fund has an average compound annual return of 23 percent over the past five years. Smith, who also manages individual accounts and is editor of Courtney Smith's Wall Street Winners (www.wallstreetwinners.net), an investment advisory service, as well as another site for very active short-term traders called Courtney Smith's Hot List (www.courtneyhotlist.com). Smith also is owner and editor-in-chief of *Commodity Traders Consumer Report* (CTCR), a tracking service for futures traders.

His past positions include stints as chief investment strategist of Orbitex Management Inc., which managed more than $6 billion in mutual funds and portfolios, and president and CEO of Quantum Financial Services Inc., a $100 million futures and stock brokerage firm.

When asked what initially attracted him to the markets, Smith gives an interesting response.

"To me, trading was very fascinating because it's applied psychology," he says. "I realized that when you look at the markets you're seeing a very clear, concrete indication of people's needs and desires. It's a true laboratory for human behavior."

Smith practiced in this "lab" as an individual trader until the mid-1970s, when he began his money-management career. His basic approach has remained fairly constant. For the most part, he uses an intermediate-term time horizon (for futures, approximately 3 weeks; for stocks, 6 to 12 months), "using a combination of fundamentals and technicals, which I find is superior to using one or the other exclusively."

Smith describes the approach used for the Hot List trades as "an extension of a fund I managed several years ago where we used very aggressive trading techniques. This is a far more active and far more technically driven product because we're now talking about a time horizon ranging from a few days to three weeks."

He described the roles fundamental and technical analysis play in his trading. On a certain level, there's a great deal of overlap between his short-term and long-term approaches because he uses the same underlying selection criteria for all his trades.

ME: *What approach do you use for the Hot List stocks?*

CS: First of all, I only buy stocks with bullish fundamentals. Then I use technicals to determine entry and exit points. But since we're looking at very short-term trades—under three weeks—the technical side is typically far more dominant than the fundamental side for the Hot List trades. Basically, I'm not going to look at valuations, because I'm not going to hold them long enough for that to matter. For the Hot List, I'll buy a stock that is skyrocketing, but is now overvalued in my opinion, because I may only be looking to hold it for a week.

ME: What are the "bullish fundamentals" you refer to?

CS: When you look at techniques that are proven to cause stocks to go up or outperform the market, you have to start out with earnings momentum and earnings surprises. We've seen a tremendous amount of clear evidence that companies with strong earnings momentum—accelerating earnings momentum—and earnings surprises will continue to have that in the future. And those stocks will continually outperform the market. So a very strong criterion for me is strong earnings momentum and surprises. Technically, I really look at the cash flow, but those numbers are more difficult to find and analyze, so earnings will generally be good enough.

We very rarely will buy a stock that is not outperforming consensus earnings estimates. My analysts come up with their own earnings projections, but we also rely on the commonly accepted sources like Value Line, as well as the Internet, to get consensus earnings. Sites like Yahoo Finance (http://finance. yahoo.com) show earnings surprises on a quarterly basis—that's very useful information. One thing I do not do is pay much attention to Wall Street analysts. I only pay attention to independent research and analysis.

ME: What is the technical side of your trading equation?

CS: I'm a breakout trader. For example, on the long side, if there's significant resistance at a particular point—say a stock has rallied to a particular point and faded several times—I'll look to buy that stock. Or I'll use a classic flag formation in a bull market.

The first thing I look for is that a stock must be in a bull market, and second, I want confirmation that the market is moving into a bull mode again—such as a breakout of a bull flag or a breakout from some kind of resistance level. (See Figure 9.5.)

It's relative strength. I want to buy those stocks that are leading the market, not lagging it. Even in a bear market, if I have stocks that are holding up well, they're going to be the leaders coming out of the bear market.

ME: Do you short stocks?

CS: Yes, I'll short stocks. I'm not doing much shorting right now, but in my hedge funds that's been a fairly common thing.

ME: What was your most difficult period as a trader?

CS: I've really only had one bad year, 1990, on the futures side. Other than that, I've been profitable. To me, the key to trading is self-discipline, and I've always been a pretty disciplined guy—except in 1990.

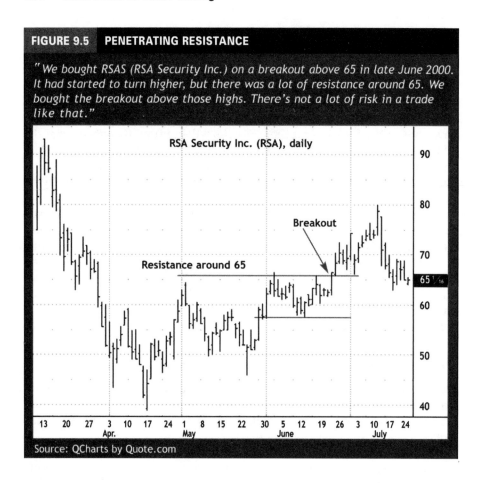

FIGURE 9.5 **PENETRATING RESISTANCE**

"We bought RSAS (RSA Security Inc.) on a breakout above 65 in late June 2000. It had started to turn higher, but there was a lot of resistance around 65. We bought the breakout above those highs. There's not a lot of risk in a trade like that."

RSA Security Inc. (RSA), daily

Breakout

Resistance around 65

Source: QCharts by Quote.com

ME: How does that discipline manifest itself in your trading?

CS: I've never cared about taking a loss; it's never bothered me. Well . . . every so often (*laughs*). Let's put it this way: There are smart mistakes and dumb mistakes. I'll feel bad if I lose money because of a dumb mistake, but if I lose money because of a smart mistake, that's okay—it's because I'm executing what I'm supposed to be executing. The more active you are as a trader, and the more short-term you trade, the more important discipline is. You can't wait for the market to bail you out of mistakes.

ME: What are the most common mistakes you see?

CS: The biggest thing is traders getting married to a position. They get emotionally involved in a trade and they think that it's important to be right. Ned Davis wrote a tremendous book called *Being Right or Making*

Money. The key to making money is to not care if you're wrong. Just take the loss—what difference does it make? Unfortunately, people think, "Well, if I sell it out, I'm taking a loss." But I can tell you right now there's no difference between a "paper" loss or profit and a "real" one. If you buy a stock at 50 and it's at 45, you've already lost the money.

I look at every position every day and ask myself, "Do I want to own this or not?" If I'm here to make money, I have to be willing to admit I'm wrong—a lot—and not care. The object is to make money, not to be right.

ME: Do you use trading systems to help you make those decisions?

CS: Right now my trading is discretionary, but I have a number of techniques I use very systematically, and I believe very strongly that systematic trading is a good idea. But right now, I'm using what I'd call "objective" subjective techniques, such as flag formations, that I can define objectively 95 percent of the time. (See Figure 9.6.)

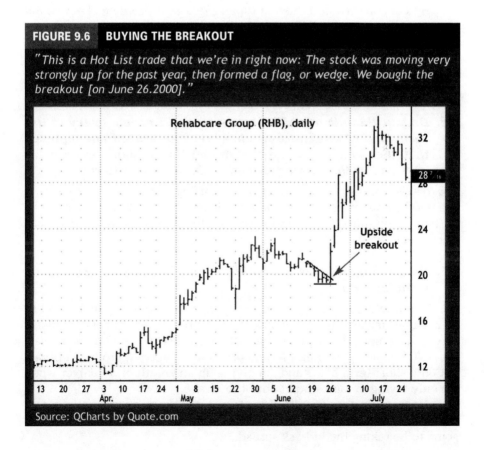

FIGURE 9.6   BUYING THE BREAKOUT

"This is a Hot List trade that we're in right now: The stock was moving very strongly up for the past year, then formed a flag, or wedge. We bought the breakout [on June 26.2000]."

Rehabcare Group (RHB), daily

Upside breakout

Source: QCharts by Quote.com

ME: What trading tools or techniques would you advise traders to use?

CS: I think the key is to look at breakouts, because if you use break-outs, by definition, the trend is your friend. For the most part, buying dips is a completely bogus concept, and it will only lead to failure, or underperformance.

As an active, short-term trader, you only want to be buying stocks that are breaking out to new highs, because that means you're making money right away. As a short-term trader, you have to have that edge all the time. If you're buying dips, you're immediately in a losing position 85 to 90 percent of the time, because you're not going to buy a bottom tick.

I know some people say, "Yeah, but if you buy on a breakout to the upside, you've got slippage . . ." I love slippage! Because it means I'm re-ally right. If I have a 50 stop and I'm filled at 55, my god, something incredibly bullish just happened. Slippage is not a problem as far as I'm concerned.

By contrast, traders buying dips have a real problem. They're im-mediately in a loss, which means they're psychologically beaten up right away.

My job as a trader is to make money every day if I can—not to be right. So if I buy a breakout, I'm making money right away. I'm getting positively rewarded by the market for doing the correct thing.

ME: Do you think it would be better for most people to try to use some kind of straight Donchian breakout system (an approach that goes long on an n-day high and flat or short on an n-day low), *rather than trying to analyze individual patterns?*

CS: Yes. We've done a lot of testing. Even using a straight four-week rule is a good thing, or using a Turtle modification and making it four weeks in, two weeks out. For a longer-term system, 40 days in, 20 days out works very well.

ME: Do these techniques work well on shorter time frames, say on intraday data?

CS: The problem there is that on a very short time frame, you do want to be a market maker—buying dips and selling rallies—because the bid-ask spread becomes a huge percentage of your potential profits. If the mar-ket is 40 bid and 40¼ offer, I have a problem if I'm trying to buy a break-out on a short-term basis and I'm giving up an eighth or a quarter when I'm only trying to take a point out of the trade.

Once you get into really short-term intraday trading, you definitely have to buy dips and sell rallies, because a lot of your profitability is going to be taking the bid-ask spread.

ME: But you don't think that's the case if you're swing trading?

CS: Once you go to a daily bar, you've got to be trading breakouts.

ME: What techniques do you use to control risk?

CS: I use stops extensively, both to enter and exit positions. I also prefer trading listed stocks simply because I can leave in resting stop orders. And I'll use contingency stops with my broker. For example, "Buy XYZ on a 50 stop; if filled, put in a protective stop at 40, good-till-canceled." It gives me the opportunity to spend a lot less time staring at a screen.

ME: How do you determine stop placement?

CS: Each trade is different. Very simplistically, I want to know at what point I'm wrong. Usually it's the previous swing low on a daily bar chart. That can be anywhere from 3 to 30 percent away from the entry point for stocks. Realistically, it's probably around 10 to 15 percent most of the time.

ME: How do you manage positions?

CS: I don't really use profit targets, per se, but typically I will have some short-term objective of where I think the market should move over the short run. When it does, I move the stop up. I want to raise the stop up to break even as soon as I can—I want to get to a no-risk position as soon as possible.

ME: How much of your equity do you risk on a trade?

CS: I keep it at one percent or less, because then I know I can live forever even with a lot of losers.

ME: In terms of the stocks you actively trade, do you pay much attention to correlation?

CS: Yes, but what generally happens is a particular sector is hot, and I'm going to be overweighted in that sector. So, I wouldn't own trucking companies right now, for instance. I want to buy the best stocks in the best sector in the market.

What that means is you might have five semiconductor capital equipment stocks, five semiconductor companies, and five other stocks in a portfolio of 15 stocks. That's a very high-risk thing to do, but that's why I put in stop-loss orders. I might lose 15 percent on my equity statement, but hopefully I've been making 30, 40, or 50 percent over the short-term before I lose that 15 percent.

ME: Do you have any kind of shutdown point?

CS: On the futures side I do. I won't risk more than 5 percent of my total equity in one day. On the equities side I don't do that because, in effect, everything is positively correlated. Offhand, gold stocks might be the only group that is negatively correlated with the broader market. So you can't quite diversify in the stock market as well as you can in the futures market.

ME: *Since you have experience in both the futures and stock sides of the business, what are the differences between the two markets? What do you think stock traders can learn from futures traders?*

CS: First of all, for futures traders, the bid-ask spread is not as big a problem because of lower transaction costs. That's a big advantage. Second, the best research and the brightest minds are in the futures side—they're light years ahead of the stock guys as far as their understanding of markets and their technical skills. You only have around 30 instruments to trade, so that means you can really concentrate on the futures side and get greater diversification.

But the problem with the futures side is that the futures markets are far more efficient—there's a lot of trading talent focused on a small group of markets. On the equity side you've got 12,000 stocks, of which there's only analyst coverage of the top 500 or 1,000. That means there's a lot of stocks out there that are incredibly inefficient and mispriced. With the exception of the S&P 100, maybe the S&P 500, most stocks are very inefficient. And then you have the benefit of secular drift of the market. So I think stocks are far easier to trade.

The main thing in trading is that you have to have discipline. You have to set a stop loss, you have to have a point where you can say "I'm wrong," and you have to be willing to admit you're wrong and have no problems with that.

I follow a saying: When in doubt, stay out. Because if you have a doubt about a position and you get out, now your mind is clear. You're not married to the position, and you can think about what you want to do.

The second important thing is money management. The least important thing is entry and exit techniques.

ME: *How do you convince people of that?*

CS: After they've lost money, they'll see.

ME: *So what did you do wrong in 1990?*

CS: I had just set up my new company and I wanted to go out and show the world that I was the King Kong of traders. So I basically abandoned the self-discipline that had gotten me to that point. Suddenly I was trying too hard.

I was down 30 to 35 percent after six months. I went back and I did an analysis of every trade I did, and I realized if I'd just followed my normal techniques, I'd have made money over that period.

Richard Saidenberg
sound views on trading

Whether you've just opened up your first margin account or are managing millions of dollars, the basic rules of trading are amazingly constant: Have a game plan, control risk, and strive for consistency rather than an overnight killing.

Witness trader Richard Saidenberg, president and chief trader of SoundView Capital Management, in Pleasantville, New York. With 20 years of experience in the markets under his belt and $10 million under management, he still attributes much of his success to a very simple fact.

"I haven't been anything close to a perfect trader," he says, "but I think one of the reasons I'm still here is that I've never allowed myself to get wiped out."

It doesn't get much simpler than that.

Saidenberg's method of eluding wipeouts has been to stick to mechanical trading approaches. While he may not think of himself as a perfect trader, he has done well enough to avoid having "a regular job" (as he puts it) for all but 10 months of the past 14 years, evolving from a somewhat fundamentally oriented stock-picker into a systematic S&P 500 stock index future, currency, and interest-rate trader.

Through SoundView, Saidenberg has posted compounded annual returns of 252 percent, 95.5 percent, 8.5 percent, 6.6 percent, and 23 percent for 1996 through 2000, respectively. The two trading systems he has sold to the public, R-Breaker and R-Levels, have been standouts on Futures Truth's list of top S&P 500 trading systems for years. (Futures Truth is an independent trading-system testing company.)

Saidenberg, 37, got started young in the markets, trading stocks while in high school and college, although his approach was a little more casual than the multiple-system one he uses today in the S&P 500, currency, and interest-rate markets.

"I just bought stocks that I knew," he explains. "I'd be long anywhere from five to fifteen stocks. I liked the Value Line Investment Survey—its summary page showing all the stocks that were rated No. 1 or 2 for timeliness and safety. It was a strong bull market from the time I started college at the end of 1981 to when I graduated in 1986. The market was up pretty big over that period, and if you were long stocks you were making money."

After graduating with a degree in economics from the University of Michigan, Saidenberg took a job as a specialist arbitrage clerk on the floor of the American Stock Exchange. The job lasted 10 months, but Saidenberg managed to squeeze some value out of it.

"One of my jobs was to make copies of different market letters and give them to the big guys in the company who liked to see them," he recalls. "One of the market letters I really liked and always made an extra copy of for myself was *Systems and Forecasts,* by Gerald Appel."

Saidenberg got a feel for both the equity options and futures markets during his tenure and decided to leave the floor and trade on his own. On the basis of *Systems and Forecasts,* Saidenberg further explored Appel's research and writings.

"I purchased a group of reports Appel wrote called the *Scientific Investment Research Group* reports, which were about technical analysis and systematic trading and showed historical back-testing results," he says. "That was my first exposure to trading systems.

"I also bought Time Trend II, Appel's stock index timing system. It was a trend-following system that used inputs like advances and declines, new highs and new lows, the closes of the NYSE and Value Line indexes and other calculations using the McClellan oscillator.

"The system was either long mutual funds or stocks, or out of the market and earning interest. But I traded NYSE stock index futures with it, either long or short the futures, so I was always in the market," Saidenberg explains. "That was a pretty heavy risk for one contract—the maximum drawdown might be somewhere around $25,000 per contract. But I didn't know that at the time."

Saidenberg was a full-time trader at this point, but he noticed a difference between his discretionary trading and the trading system he was following.

"I found the only thing that was making me money was the Time Trend system," he says. "I kept a position in that system consistently from late 1988 until 1995—that's a long time to follow a system. That systematic style was something that really stuck with me as the proper way to trade and make money. It was the actual experience of seeing something work that attracted me to systematic trading.

"Here I was, believing I could read the market by watching indicators and price action, but I was making many, many trades and not generating much in the way of profits from that process," Saidenberg says.

"With all the commissions I paid, I think I was, on balance, profitable—I had an account that went from $20,000 to $28,000 in approximately 2,000 trades. But at the same time I had this parallel account that I started with $15,000 and was trading one NYSE stock index futures contract that was at $45,000 in around five trades using a trading system."

In the early 1990s, Saidenberg had added another item to his trading resume, that helped further expand his understanding and appreciation for systematic trading approaches.

At a trading seminar, Saidenberg's computer proficiency (he helped out a speaker who was using a software program Saidenberg was familiar with) brought him to the attention of Alexander Elder, author of *Trading for a Living.* Elder invited Saidenberg to help out with computer duties at several other trading seminars. Besides exposing him to new trading ideas, it led to Saidenberg becoming something of a technical-analysis programming guru in the trading community.

"When somebody in the class would go up to Alex and say, 'Wow, this stuff is great. How do I set up my computer to do this on my own?' he would send them to me," Saidenberg says. "Most people didn't know much about computers at the time. So I started doing technical-analysis computer consulting for traders.

"I started doing this in late 1992, right when I started using Trade-Station (Omega Research's system testing program), and turned it into a business," he says. "I probably worked with over 1,000 traders. I was not necessarily as good at creating concepts as much as learning concepts and then being able to 'realize' them on the computer. Programming sort of matches my style of thinking. People would say, 'I'll share my wonderful system ideas with you if you'll do the programming.'"

Saidenberg continued to trade, consult for other traders, and design and test his own trading systems. In 1995, he began trading client capital, implementing his trading ideas on a large scale and managing accounts with a multisystem, multimarket approach.

One afternoon, promptly after the closing bell, he discussed his evolution as a trader and shared some insights on several trading ideas and about what works and what fails when put to the test of the markets.

ME: *When did you start designing your own trading systems?*

RS: I started experimenting with many different ideas while I was consulting with other traders. I was programming fairly complex systems three or four weeks after I started using TradeStation. I was still trading the Time Trend system at this point, but I put together my own half-hour-based S&P trading system that I followed religiously as well. It was one of the first complex things I programmed.

It was an always-in-the-market system based on 30-minute price bars and a nine-bar relative strength index (RSI) with overbought and oversold lines of 70 and 30. The rules for buys and sells were identical.

When the RSI moved below 30, I'd watch for the lowest value it reached after moving below that threshold. Then I waited for it to move back above 30. If it made a bottom by coming down and then turning up, and the new bottom was within 10 RSI points of the initial bottom below 30, that was a basic buy signal.

So, if the RSI made a bottom at 15, rallied above 30, then came down and made another bottom between 15 and 25, that was a buy. If the spread was more than 10 points, I wouldn't allow the buy—I'd wait for a subsequent bottom.

Sometimes I had two different bottoms working at the same time—the RSI would make a bottom at 5, move up above 30, then make another bottom at 25 and again move up above 30. So, now I could have a following bottom to get a buy that was either between 5 and 15, or between 25 and 35. If it went up from there and made a top above 70, I reversed the rules to generate sells.

Those are the basic buy and sell signals. There was also a breakout component that allowed you to get out of a trade if a basic signal in the opposite direction didn't trigger.

I tracked that system by hand even before I was using TradeStation. (*He searches through old records.*) I have charts for this system dating back from October 1990 to January 1992—319 signals.

ME: Did doing things by hand like that give you a better understanding of the strategy?

RS: Of course. It forces you to look at every trade very closely and makes you realize what all types of trades look like, good and bad. So when you experience all the different kinds of trades in real life, you are ready to take them and continue with your trading system; as opposed to someone who just looks at a performance table or equity curve and thinks, "Yeah, I can make that money," and then tries to trade it, not realizing there is a whole, long process to trading that can be difficult to endure.

ME: Did you have a preference toward a particular time frame?

RS: Trading very short-term—one-minute or five-minute time frames, for example—seemed like overkill. I might have eight trades in a month with a system triggering off 30-minute price data. But I could stand position trading, even though I preferred day trading.

But at the beginning I thought there was a big advantage to position-trading systems that were also sensitive to intraday movements and would adjust positions during the day. For example, my 30-minute RSI system was always in, long or short, with some positions lasting a few weeks even though I was tracking the market intraday with trading signals which were sensitive to intraday price movement.

One of the things I discovered was that I could use systems that didn't have overnight exposure, but were similar in style to the original 30-minute systems I was using. I turned my intraday position systems into day-trading systems. One of the biggest risks of trading in the S&Ps is overnight exposure—what can happen between the close and the next day's open.

I found that using intraday triggers for entry was a good concept. But to eliminate the risk of overnight positions, I turned my 30-minute position systems into day-trading systems. I'd have a lower overall return, but much lower drawdown.

ME: Was this a matter of adjusting the time frame of the bars you used, or did you put in an automatic exit rule on the systems?

RS: An exit-on-close rule. Also, I found that I moved away from indicators and toward complete price calculations just using highs, lows, and closes. I moved toward trading threshold levels and price breakouts: one level to first set up a trade and another level to enter the trade.

The levels are generally based on either the range of a certain period of a day, the entire day's range or the previous day's range. It really didn't matter which time frame chart I was using for those types of systems, because I was not using any indicator calculations that would require a specific number of minutes for the bars. Instead, I was using price action within a certain time interval. I found that by working with one-minute or five-minute charts I could be most accurate for system testing, even for a day-trading system which would trade only a few times per month.

ME: Do you still use any indicators?

RS: Yes. I still like to look at the stochastics and RSI on my charts. Also, I create custom indicators that are helpful in system development for making sure that when I'm writing a system it's doing what I expect. An indicator can help you track trades to make sure they're behaving correctly. I write all kinds of indicators that apply to certain systems.

ME: You're trading multiple markets, multiple systems, and multiple accounts. What kind of position sizing and money management techniques do you use?

RS: That's taken a long time to develop. I put together a group of trading systems I want to use, and call that my "trading plan." Since I trade different-sized accounts, I want to make sure the percentage drawdown is approximately the same in all of them. If an account is big enough to trade my complete trading plan, I will use six different S&P day-trading systems, six systems in each of the four major currencies and systems in the T-note futures.

I take the single-contract equity curves of the individual trading systems and I combine them to get a net combined equity curve. That gives me the performance of the group of systems as a unit.

Now, if I have an account of a certain size, say $100,000, and I want to make sure the maximum drawdown in an account is 30 percent—$30,000, peak to valley—I pick a specific combination of systems where the combined maximum drawdown is $30,000. That gives me the trading position size for that particular account. I trade one contract for each system that account uses, so the total number of contracts is based on the number of systems followed.

ME: Are your S&P systems literally day-trading systems—they're flat at the end of the day?

RS: Yes. I like S&Ps for day trading because of the large intraday price moves, but I like the currencies and the interest rates for trend-following or longer-term position trading because of the consistency of trends in those markets.

ME: *What kind of time frame do you use for these longer term systems?*

RS: One of the things I do, since I'm following, say, six different systems in the yen, is have them vary in time frame. The shortest term system will change positions on average about 20 times per year, and the longest term system will change positions around four times per year. If I'm going to use two systems, for example, they'll overlap so my position either is long, short, or flat.

ME: *How do your systems typically get in and out of the market?*

RS: A system is just something that tries to determine when and at what price to place your order. For triggers, regardless of time frame, I like to use stop orders for entry. I sell as the market goes down through my price level or I buy as the market goes up through my price level.

One style of day-trading system that I use is to take an average of the ranges of the previous days, maybe two to four days, then multiply that average by a factor, maybe a third, and now I have a volatility amount.

Then I'll use today's open, and add and subtract that volatility amount to the open to get buy and sell levels for the day. There are a couple of other things that go into this though, which I can summarize briefly: First, it pays to have those levels operate only at certain times during the day, as opposed to all day. Second, it also pays to have some days when the system is filtered out, so there would be no trades, either because the open doesn't satisfy certain conditions or a trend filter, or some other factor.

A really simple example of one of these conditions is to look at the gap between today's open and yesterday's close. Some people define gaps as the difference between today's open and yesterday's close; I also like the difference between today's open and yesterday's high or low. If that gap is, say, more than one-third the previous day's range or more than some other absolute amount, then, that day, that is acceptable to trade.

ME: *Does this kind of system use a stop to control losses?*

RS: All my systems control losses. Once I get a trade on, the simplest thing to do is have a money-management stop to know what my maximum loss is. I use stops anywhere from 400 to 1200 S&P points.

ME: *How do you determine exactly how big that stop is?*

RS: There are all sorts of things you can do. You can use an arbitrary fixed amount, you can have it be a percentage of the price level—half of one percent is a reasonable percentage.

Looking at an absolute dollar risk amount on a trade is not great for extensive historical testing because the S&P has gone from the 200s to over 1400. The actual stop amount is not crucial to long-term performance. You really want to look at the risk of the system as a whole, following the system through multiple trades.

There are some other commonly used stop techniques, like using a volatility factor to determine the stop, that I don't really like—there is something fundamentally wrong with having a volatility-based stop. If the recent volatility is very low, your stop will be smaller. But breakouts out of small volatility situations are often very good trades, and I don't want to have that trade get knocked out with a tight stop.

Also, when there's extremely high volatility, your stop will be very large. On those trades, the market often reacts violently against the position right away and if it does, I don't necessarily want to wait for a very large stop to get me out—I'd rather get out sooner. I prefer to have consistent, similarly sized stops, in a particular system.

ME: Do you use any kind of profit-taking or trailing stop techniques?

RS: Well, I've been working things like that for many, many years, trying to come up with better stuff. The most painful aspect of profit-target development is that the systems that give you the most total profit are the ones that let the trade (*in a day-trading system*) run all the way until the close or until the initial stop loss gets hit. So even if you're up a huge amount, you have to be willing to give back that profit and let it turn into a loss.

A system like that does give you the most total net profit in the long run, but it's not as easy to trade as a system that trails a stop, which sometimes will knock you out of a trade that could grow into a much larger profit. The way to get long-term, large, total net profits is to make sure you capture all of your really large trades. So, eliminating the trailing stop makes sure you don't ever get knocked out of a really large profit.

However, there is a degree of consistency you can get by using some kind of exit routine that gives you a higher percentage of winning trades and prevents large winners from turning into losers, so your equity growth is more consistent, even though the long-term total profit is less.

What I specifically don't like about trailing stops is that you generally end up getting stopped out of a long trade in a low price area. I would prefer to exit with a limit order as the position is moving in my favor. I have some complex routines where I place limit orders for exit, but I don't want to place a target exit when I first enter a trade because I want to allow that trade to grow very big if it happens to do so very fast.

I'll give you an example. Say I'm running a one-minute chart, and on it I have a 15-bar stochastic. If I go long on a breakout, the stochastic reading is going to be up pretty high. If this trade gets profitable—the market is rising—the stochastic is still going to be in its upper zone. But at some point in the trade there's going to be a consolidation and that stochastic is going to go down.

One of the things I might do is wait for the stochastic to drop below some value, say 30, and at that time I'll make some calculation of the price bars from when the stochastic was at its peak, to where it is now— the range of those bars—and add it to a certain value, perhaps the middle of the range of the bars. Now I have a target price.

I call this a "late in the game" target because the absolute profit is not known at the beginning of the trade, as it is with a typical profit target. This allows the trade to grow as big as it can initially, but then when the market settles down, there's a mechanism for placing a profit target at some high level so you're exiting a long trade as the market is going up and price is moving in your direction.

That routine also works pretty well for trades that don't work out well at first. When the stochastic ends up going below 30 relatively quickly, you may be at a loss during that period, but not quite at your stop-loss level, and you end up placing a profit target in this manner—a very small profit target.

I've found that kind of exit routine is certainly satisfying to watch when it works in real time, but again, it does cut into your total net profits because there are some trades that exit at the profit target when they might have turned into much bigger winners.

ME: Do you trade on the open?

RS: For day trading, I never trade on the open because the opening price is often going into the calculation of the rules of the system. If it's not, I still have some kind of time factor—10 or 10:30 A.M. EST—and I don't do anything until then.

For position trading, if the market opens through my stop level, either to exit a position or to enter a new position, then I execute the trade at the open.

ME: Would you characterize most of your trading ideas as breakout-based?

RS: (*Laughing*) I wouldn't characterize most of them that way, but I would characterize the ones that actually work that way.

By contrast, most of the things I've programmed for people are things I would say don't work. There's a tremendous desire for people to be able to buy low and sell high. I don't know how to make it profitable on a purely mechanical basis.

I have worked out systems when the market goes into an extended flat period. Say, the market has been going down for two weeks in a flat area—I would allow a buy stop to come in the lower section of that range, so if the market turns around in that low area and then goes up through the buy stop, the system goes long. If you look at a chart, you'd say, "Look, you bought a low area," but you're still using a buy stop for the entry. Movement in your direction at the time of entry is crucial to profitable systems.

ME: How rigid are you with your systems? Do you stick with them regardless of circumstances—are you on autopilot?

RS: Well, the process of becoming a systematic trader was not something that just happened overnight. But the biggest problems I have, and the most uncomfortable feelings I get, are when I'm not following the rules of my systems.

ME: So you do use discretion?

RS: Technically no, I'm not supposed to, but you can't be perfect. Right now, I'd say the reason I've been successful as a trader is because I've followed systematic rules; the problems have come when I've tried to override those rules.

appendix

the paper trader

Traders may live online, but the best trading information isn't necessarily a mouse-click away. Some of the most valuable trading resources you can get your hands on (and your mind around) are found in the pages of that tried-and-true medium, the book.

Trading is often described in terms of speed: how fast you and your communications setup have to be to get a trade off in a here-one-second-gone-the-next market. But the wise trader makes room for reflection and research. We informally polled professional traders and searched through our own libraries to come up with a short list of notable trading books from several genres.

Because we tried to stick to titles for shorter-term traders who might be active in different markets, you'll notice an emphasis on technical analysis over fundamental, although some of these books are excellent sources of information on market psychology and sentiment. We couldn't take into account every book ever written, and the list is skewed toward books that have been around a while. With these caveats in mind, here's a look at some of the titles that should have shelf space in any well-rounded trading library.

general market and trading psychology

Edwin Lefèvre, *Reminiscences of a Stock Operator* (New York: John Wiley, 1994). Recommended for market realists everywhere. Lefèvre's tale of trader Larry Livingston (a pseudonym for market legend Jesse Livermore) is a favorite of industry insiders and is required reading at some of the largest trading firms in the world. Penned in 1923, the narrative paints a vivid picture of the thought processes and market tactics of a shrewd speculator who started out in the bucket shops and went on to make and lose (and make and lose) millions in the stock and commodities markets. It shows how little has really changed since the days of the ticker tape:

> [The successful trader] cannot bet on the unreasonable or on the unexpected, however strong his personal convictions may be about man's unreasonableness or however certain he may feel that the unexpected happens very frequently. He must always bet on probabilities . . .

Charles Mackay, *Extraordinary Popular Delusions and the Madness of Crowds* (New York: John Wiley, 1996). If you think some of the recent stratospheric tech stock valuations were unprecedented, pick up a copy of *Extraordinary Popular Delusions and the Madness of Crowds,* a book (written in 1841) that argues convincingly that, when the day is done, greed and fear have always and will always run the show.

With analysis of financial mania dating back hundreds of years, Mackay shows how market/psychology bubbles build and burst. It makes you wonder if the phrase "new paradigm" was being tossed around back in Holland in the 17th century, when tulips became worth far more than their weight in gold. Consider the following excerpt:

> At first, as in all these gambling mania, confidence was at its height, and every body gained. The tulip-jobbers specialized in the rise and fall of the tulip stocks, and made large profits by buying when prices fell and selling out when they rose. Everyone imagined that the passion for tulips would last forever . . . At last, however, the more prudent began to see that this folly could not last forever . . . It was seen that somebody must lose fearfully in the end.

Jack Schwager, *Market Wizards* (Paramus, NJ: New York Institute of Finance, 1989) and Jack Schwager, *The New Market Wizards* (New York: John Wiley, 1992). Part of Schwager's initial motivation behind conducting interviews with top traders was to get answers to questions that had been puzzling him about trading. The result is two insightful and readable compendiums of conversations with exceptionally successful traders, including Jim Rogers, Richard Dennis, and Paul Tudor Jones. If you want to know what separates the big trading fish from the little ones, bury your nose in these books.

trading strategies

Linda Bradford Raschke and Larry Connors, *Street Smarts* (Malibu, CA: M. Gordon Publishing Group, 1995). Judging from her popular speaking appearances, what Raschke (profiled in Schwager's *New Market Wizards*) teaches works. In *Street Smarts,* she and coauthor Larry Connors give you an excellent chance to learn the tricks of the trade from two successful short-term traders. Each strategy is spelled out rule by rule.

Gary Smith, *How I Trade for a Living* (New York: John Wiley, 2000). Smith is well known in trading circles as an outspoken critic of trading industry hype and as a grassroots trader who has mastered the market from the ground up. After 19 years of unsuccessful trading, Smith finally turned the corner in the mid-1980s and hasn't looked back. This book provides straightforward explanations of the techniques he's used to take a $2,200 trading account to nearly $1 million. There's no magic here, no secret potion—just a lot of experience and common sense from someone who learned how to make money in the market the hard way.

technical analysis and trading systems

Tom DeMark, *The New Science of Technical Analysis* (New York: John Wiley, 1994). In this book you'll find iconoclastic trading approaches from the man who has designed trading systems for George Soros and Paul Tudor Jones, among others. DeMark has explored virtually every corner of the market analysis and trading landscape, developing novel trading techniques and putting his unique spin on old standards.

Alexander Elder, *Trading for a Living* (New York: John Wiley, 1993). For those just starting out, Alexander Elder has written a great book explaining the intricacies of technical analysis and indicator interpretation. Make sure you get the study guide as well; it will help take your trading skills to the next level.

Perry Kaufman, *Trading Systems and Methods* (New York: John Wiley, 1998). Kaufman's encyclopedic tome on technical indicators and trading systems explains everything from charting and seasonality to expert systems and neural networks. It's not for beginners (it can put off readers with a low tolerance for mathematics), but for those interested in exploring technical trading system concepts, it covers nearly all the bases. The third edition, published in 1998, added welcome programming code, new sections, and expanded discussions of old topics.

John Murphy, *Technical Analysis of the Financial Markets* (Paramus, NJ: New York Institute of Finance, 1999). Written by longtime analyst, market commentator, and CNBC technical analysis consultant John Murphy, this is one of the best references for technical analysis and indicators. You can make up your own mind about the veracity of this or that indicator, but if you're interested in understanding the concepts, formulas, and standard applications of various technical trading concepts, this trading resource is both comprehensive and comprehensible.

Jack Schwager, *Schwager on Futures: Technical Analysis* (New York: John Wiley, 1996). The focus is on futures, but the technical indicators and trading system concepts Schwager outlines in this book are straightforward, thorough, and applicable to any market. A must read for any trader and a reference material you will return to time and time again.

money management

Ralph Vince, *The Mathematics of Money Management* (New York: John Wiley, 1992). Trading is so much more than just identifying chart patterns and interpreting technical indicators. In this book, Vince explains techniques that demonstrate how to maximize the growth rate of any trading account. It's not the friendliest book around—there's a lot of complicated mathematics—but it's still a must-read for serious traders interested more in making the most of their accounts, than in just being able to tell which way the market is heading.

additional reading

The following books are referenced throughout this text by the various contributors and offer additional sources of research and insight for traders.

for beginning traders
Kassandra Bentley, *Getting Started in Online Day Trading* (New York: John Wiley, 2000).
John Cook and Jeanette Szwec, *Day Trade Part-Time* (New York: John Wiley, 2000).
Toni Turner, *A Beginner's Guide to Day Trading Online* (Holbrook, MA: Adams Media, 2000).

money management
Bruce Babcock, *The Four Cardinal Principles of Trading* (Homewood, IL: Irwin, 1996).
Nauzer J. Balsara, *Money Management Strategies for Futures Traders* (New York: John Wiley, 1992).
Peter L. Bernstein, *Against the Gods: The Remarkable Story of Risk* (New York: John Wiley, 1998).
Fred Gehm, *Quantitative Trading and Money Management: A Guide to Risk Analysis and Trading Survival* (Homewood, IL: Irwin, 1995).
Frank J. Jones and Richard Jack Teweles, *The Futures Game: Who Wins, Who Loses, Why?* (New York: McGraw-Hill, 1998).
Ralph Vince, *The New Money Management: A Framework for Asset Allocation* (New York: John Wiley, 1995).

Raschke's reading list
Robert D. Edwards and John Magee, *Technical Analysis of Stock Trends* (New York: AMACON, 1997).
H.M. Gartley, *Profits in the Stock Market* (Pomeroy, WA: Lambert Gann, 1935).

Linda Bradford Raschke, interviewed in Chapter 9, recommended the following books:

Richard Schabacker and Donald Mack, *Technical Analysis and Stock Market Profits* (Upper Saddle River, NJ: Financial Times Prentice Hall, 1998). According to Raschke, "He [Schabacker] was actually the true father of technical analysis as a science. He was the one who classified many of the chart patterns—rounding tops and head-and-shoulder patterns, rising wedge, different kinds of gaps. In fact, his nephew was Robert Edwards (coauthor of *Technical Analysis of Stock Trends*). So Edwards and Magee's material was really Schabaker's stuff, but drier. Schabacker's book included lots of interesting insights on trading and human nature."

Richard Smitten, *The Amazing Life of Jesse Livermore* (Clearwater, FL: Traders Press, 1999). "A good read for fun," according to Raschke.

Richard D. Wyckoff, *How I Trade and Invest in Stocks and Bonds* (Burlington, VT: Fraser, 1997).

references

William Blau, *Momentum, Direction, and Divergence* (New York: John Wiley, 1995).

Mark Boucher, *The Hedge Fund Edge* (New York: John Wiley, 1999).

Ned Davis, *Being Right or Making Money* (Venice, FL: Ned Davis Research, 2000).

Tom DeMark, *New Market Timing Techniques: Innovative Studies in Market Rhythm and Price Exhaustion* (New York: John Wiley, 1997).

Mark Friedfertig and George West, *The Electronic Day Trader* (New York: McGraw-Hill, 1998).

Sue Herera, *Women of the Street* (New York: John Wiley, 1998).

Ari Kiev, *A Strategy for Daily Living: The Classic Guide to Success and Fulfillment* (New York: Free Press, 1997).

Ari Kiev, *Trading in the Zone: Maximizing Performance with Focus and Discipline* (New York: John Wiley, 2001).

Ari Kiev, *Trading to Win* (New York: John Wiley, 1998).

Victor Niederhoffer, *The Education of a Speculator* (New York: John Wiley, 1998).

Alpesh Patel, *The Mind of a Trader* (Upper Saddle River, NJ: Financial Times Prentice Hall, 1998).

Robert Rotella, *The Elements of Successful Trading* (Upper Saddle River, NJ: Prentice Hall, 1992).

Larry Williams, *Long-Term Secrets to Short-Term Trading* (New York: John Wiley, 1999).

index